ADVANCE PRAISE FOR

A Students' Guide to African American Literature, 1760 to the Present

"*A Students' Guide to African American Literature, 1760 to the Present* is a timely and very necessary resource for developing a critical understanding of a major body of texts in our literary tradition. Lovalerie King's authoritative, precise, and thought-provoking discussions of contexts, themes, and texts can generate rich classroom discussions. The reading questions and topics for critical essays are catalysts for exploration and discovery in the writing process. Students and their teachers will find this guide to historically situated aesthetic and rhetorical dimensions of African American writing and culture to be rewarding."

Jerry W. Ward, Jr., Professor of English and African World Studies, Dillard University, Louisiana

"This book provides a concise yet richly textured introduction for newcomers to the field of African American literature. The landscape that emerges through Lovalerie King's expert and deft presentation is complex yet easy to absorb and encourages the student to read further; the bibliographies that accompany each chapter are invaluable to teacher and student. I would enthusiastically assign this book to undergraduate students to stimulate in them a deep appreciation for the many historical, social, and political forces that have shaped and continue to shape African American literature. Professor King's book is compelling for the historical and thematic connections it reveals among texts and authors and for the wealth of debates and discussions it highlights within the African American literary tradition."

Rajini Srikanth, Associate Professor of English, University of Massachusetts-Boston

"*A Students' Guide to African American Literature, 1760 to the Present* is a long-awaited answer to the prayers of teachers and students of African American literature at any post-secondary level. Lovalerie King's accessible narrative style and concise but thorough handling of the African American literary tradition in fiction make this text invaluable for students who need a framework for solid critical reading in this area. This guide picks up where the anthologies leave off, and it bridges the gap between the primary texts and the literary criticism that often assume a standard body of knowledge that many students simply do not have. I am confident that this book will enrich students' experiences of African American literature and help them become much more responsible critics of literature and culture in general. I can't wait to assign it to my classes and recommend it to my colleagues who have expressed the desire to teach African American fiction with more authority in their American literature classes."

Valerie Matthews Crawford, Assistant Professor of English, Georgia Perimeter College

A Students' Guide to African American Literature, 1760 to the Present

PETER LANG
New York • Washington, D.C./Baltimore • Bern
Frankfurt am Main • Berlin • Brussels • Vienna • Oxford

LOVALERIE KING

A Students' Guide to African American Literature, 1760 to the Present

FOREWORD BY

TRUDIER HARRIS-LOPEZ

PETER LANG
New York • Washington, D.C./Baltimore • Bern
Frankfurt am Main • Berlin • Brussels • Vienna • Oxford

Library of Congress Cataloging-in-Publication Data

King, Lovalerie.
A students' guide to African American literature,
1760 to the present / Lovalerie King.
p. cm.
Includes bibliographical references and index.
1. American literature—African American authors—History and
criticism—Handbooks, manuals, etc. 2. African Americans in
literature—Handbooks, manuals, etc. I. Title.
PS153.N5K474 810.9'896073—dc21 2001029564
ISBN 0-8204-5521-0 (alk. paper)

Die Deutsche Bibliothek-CIP-Einheitsaufnahme

King, Lovalerie:
A students' guide to African American literature,
1760 to the present / Lovalerie King.
–New York; Washington, D.C./Baltimore; Bern;
Frankfurt am Main; Berlin; Brussels; Vienna; Oxford: Lang.
ISBN 0-8204-5521-0

Cover design by Lisa Barfield

Peter Lang Publishing, Inc., New York
275 Seventh Avenue, 28th Floor, New York, NY 10001
www.peterlangusa.com

Dedicated with love to the memory of

Johnnie Eva (Dillard) King
and
Chris King, Sr.

TABLE OF CONTENTS

FOREWORD
"The Second Teacher in the Classroom"

One of the most striking classroom encounters I can remember occurred in the summer session preceding my first full year of employment in academia. I had just finished up at The Ohio State University and was taking advantage of the opportunity to earn a few dollars before leaving Columbus. My survey course on African American literature featured some of the usual writers, characters, and cultural phenomena. In the midst of a stage-setting lecture for the depiction of Charles Chesnutt's focus on interracial interactions in the south, an African American student raised her hand and asked, "Who was Jim Crow?" Before I could really focus on that question, a second African American student, entranced by the discussion of the shape of Chesnutt's stories having been influenced by Joel Chandler Harris and Uncle Remus and the folkloric legacy from which Uncle Remus was drawn, asked: "Who is Brer Rabbit?" The first question was startling enough, but the latter was cause for true cultural disconnect. I had grown up in Alabama with the erroneous assumption that everybody knew about racist Jim Crow strictures and everybody knew about Brer Rabbit. Well, they did not, and the teaching moments proceeded wonderfully well. I initially concluded that those students, one from Ohio and one from New York, were just imitation black folks, geographically dislocated, masquerading in a skin coloring that did not bring with it all the cultural saturation that I automatically assumed that black skin coloring brought. I obviously moved beyond those initial superficial judgments, and the students moved a few inches forward in their college educations.

I can not imagine how many similar encounters Lovalerie King has had, or how much more complicated those encounters would have become for her if the students asking the questions had not been African American. I do know that this volume is designed to enhance the learning experiences of students who come into African American literature classes with little or no background in reading the literature and little saturation in African American cultural experiences. Since we can not perform Dr. Spock's mind-meld procedures and provide them with all the information they need, a text such as this one is designed to fill some of the void. King has conceived of this volume with the intent of providing students enrolled in African American literature classes, especially those who are studying African American narrative, particularly fiction, with the opportunity to enrich their reading and learning experiences. In addition to what students can learn from their teachers, and what teachers can learn from their students, this text becomes the second teacher in the classroom, the one that can bridge the gaps between the other two.

A constant challenge to the teacher of any African American literature course is to bring students to the same level of knowledge. Frequently, there are great gaps among students as to who has had minimum exposure to African American literature, who has read several works, and who has had no exposure at all. While some students may be very familiar with Frederick Douglass's *Narrative of the Life of Frederick Douglass* (1845), others may only—or never—have heard his name. Those who are familiar with Douglass may not be aware of the connection of his narrative to the larger bodies of slave/freedom narratives that form the basis of postnineteenth-century African American literature. A text such as this one, which situates Douglass in the tradition of which his narrative is a part, even as it introduces concepts central to his volume as a singular work, will go a long way in bringing students to a level of commonality of knowledge that will allow for more enriched classroom exchanges.

Indeed, enrichment is a key concept in this volume. By providing background materials that are essential to a broader understanding of African American life and literary production, King enables students initially encountering African American literature as well as those who share some familiarity with it the opportunity to build upon where they start and thereby enrich their learning experiences. They can add to the story line of Harriet Jacobs's narrative an understanding of the roles of amanuenses in the construction of African American narrative; knowing that Jacobs and Douglass wrote their own narratives could then lead to focus on literacy and the acquisition of literacy for African American writers. A discussion of literacy in turn leads directly to engagement with questions of the roles African American writers, because of their literacy, were expected to play as advocates for the masses of African American people. These associative enrichments of subjects and topics in African American literary and cultural history illustrate how the second teacher in the classroom can broaden the range of knowledge for students engaged with African American fiction as well as deepen that knowledge.

In another consideration of how the second teacher can enhance student knowledge, consider the implications of the passage of the Fugitive Slave Law in 1850. Students will quickly come to realize why it was important that enslaved persons escape not just to the North but on to Canada and England, as in the case of Douglass. The interrelationships of politics, law, slavery, literacy, and individual human will thus come to play in students' understanding that African American freedom and the development of the African American literary tradition took place against an oppressive backdrop of many forces, not just slavery.

The freedom narrative tradition, as produced by Douglass, Jacobs, and numerous others, provided the roots for the literary development of the twentieth and twenty-first centuries. The ties begin with the first-person narrative or autobiographical component so integral to freedom narratives. An understanding of how the black subject, pitted against slavery, could define and articulate itself leads students naturally from Douglass and Jacobs into such works as Ralph Ellison's *Invisible Man* (1952) and the protagonist's plight in that novel. Ellison's narrator's encounters with systemic forces that could crush him differ only in degree from the system of slavery under which Jacobs and Douglass forged their identities. Certainly there are differences; the important thing is for students to understand that twentieth-century African American literary works are not heads without bodies. King's volume makes clear that the feet, legs, and trunks are in the earliest part of the tradition, and contemporary writers have not forgotten them. The creation of identity, the "I," against countless destructive forces is one of the defining features of the African American literary tradition, and that applies to the writers as well as to the works themselves. It is absolutely crucial to the concept of double-consciousness, as W. E. B. Du Bois articulated the dual burden of being "Negro" and "American," that has influenced African American literary development throughout its history.

For early writers, the formation of that "I" was also frequently tied to the color representations they assigned to their characters as well as to the specific hue with which they had been born. The idea of the "tragic mulatto" is one that pervades freedom narratives as well as works written after slavery. The politics surrounding that figure are rooted in a tradition of slavery in which white men in the South did not want to suffer legal or moral consequences for their rapes of black women. They therefore consigned children born to enslaved mothers to the same status as the mothers, which meant that no mixed-race child could make claims on his or her father's estate, and they certainly could not claim freedom. Writers during and after slavery depict the politics as well as the personal and social consequences of being born too dark to be classified as white and too light, well educated, and "well-bred" to be comfortable being black. Characters who are presented with making choices about this dilemma range from Clotel in William Wells Brown's novel of the same title (1853) to Frances Ellen Watkins Harper's *Iola Leroy* (1892) to Chesnutt's Rena Walden in *The House Behind the Cedars* (1900) to James Weldon Johnson's protagonist who decides to pass for white in *The Autobiography of an Ex-Coloured Man* (1912). As King makes clear, issues of color have pervaded African American communities and have had as much of an impact upon the shaping of the literature as they have had upon the creation of character.

If one has not grown up in an African American cultural context and has not been exposed to the nuances of African American cultural expressions, forms, and creations, then this second teacher can help in additional ways. Here students can learn the relationship between a cultural form such as call and response in the blues tradition and call and response in the narrative tradition as reflected in works such as *Invisible Man*. Students may be familiar with B. B. King naming his guitar "Lucille" and "talking" to "her" during his performances, or with black congregations shouting "Amen" in response to sermons, but they probably will not know that Ellison does the same thing with speakers and their audiences as well as with patterns of narration in his novel. King helps students to make those connections and to see the importance of a seemingly insignificant form to African American literary expression. If students understand the concept of call and response, then they will be better prepared to read Langston Hughes's Simple stories and imagine themselves as part of a potentially responsive audience that shares kinship with Boyd, Simple's textual audience; understand Zora Neale Hurston's implied audience in *Their Eyes Were Watching God* (1937); connect with Alice Walker's Celie in *The Color Purple* (1982) by inserting themselves in the spaces within and between her letters; and begin to get some understanding of the theoretical notion of readers being constructed in the process of an author creating his or her text. Literature depends upon the text calling out to an audience and the audience responding in some way. Students can thereby take the concept of call and response from the specific arena of African American church or blues performance, transfer it to the construction of African American literary texts, and expand it to theories of reading those texts. This enrichment or saturation is what this second teacher provides.

Call and response is one of the central features of African American folklore, which, as with freedom narratives, has played a large part in defining African American literature. An understanding of the strong ties between the two forms will enhance greatly students' understandings of African American fiction. Consider the character of the trickster. In

African American folklore, he is most often portrayed as Brer Rabbit, the crafty underdog who bests all of his opponents through use of his wits. What he lacks in size, strength, and direct confrontation, he makes up for in intelligence and indirection. That concept can be transferred easily to understand how Uncle Julius in Chesnutt's "The Goophered Grapevine" and other short stories gets the best of the white man from whom he exacts a living. That white man, John, might be better educated, and he certainly has more financial resources and power in the community, but Uncle Julius knows human nature, and that knowledge allows him to stay ahead of John at every turn. Understanding how tricksters operate will enrich how students experience the interactions of the various characters in a novel like Ellison's *Invisible Man*. Dr. Bledsoe, the college president, is as much a trickster as is Uncle Julius; the same is true with Brother Jack, one of the leaders of the Brotherhood that lures Ellison's protagonist into its clutches. Of course, students could read Chesnutt and Ellison without this added dimension, but King does a wonderful job of offering them as a basis for a superior learning experience in African American fiction.

The second teacher advocates associative processing of information, texturing and blending, layering upon layers, the ten-item casserole instead of the tomato soup. In other words, while students certainly have the opportunity to enjoy the soup (the text) alone, King constructs the second teacher to enrich the text by encouraging students to understand how the text came to be, who created it, under what circumstances, why and how, its relationship to texts contemporary with it as well as those that preceded it or came after it, and its overall importance in the development of the African American fictional tradition, which really means the development of the American fictional tradition. The second teacher is therefore a ready and welcome companion to the study of African American fiction.

While the materials King presents are much more expansive than this brief commentary would suggest, I hope it will serve to make clear that knowledge-enhancing, discussion/reference volumes of this nature are long overdue in African American literary studies. King's focus on fiction is an important start to what I hope will become a pattern in the teaching of African American literature, that is, giving students as much saturated baptism into the history and culture surrounding the creativity of these great writers as can reasonably be provided. I heartily await the second teachers in poetry and drama.

Trudier Harris-Lopez 19 June 2002
J. Carlyle Sitterson Professor of American Literature
The University of North Carolina at Chapel Hill

ACKNOWLEDGMENTS

First and foremost, I acknowledge my debt to my parents, Chris and Johnnie King, as well as to the countless ancestors whose spiritual resolve works through me in the present. To the mentor with the spirit and drive of an Amazon warrior, Trudier Harris-Lopez, I offer my most heartfelt appreciation. From the time I entered the first "hostile" graduate program, Trudier was there with the characteristic understanding of one who recognizes what I saw in so many of my students at UMass-Boston, the potential of the diamond in the rough. I am most grateful to Trudier for telling me that "yes" I could write this book, and, later, for critiquing it in her patented subtle and guiding way. Thanks to Lynn Scott and Larry Landrum of Michigan State University for their careful, thorough, and thoughtful readings of early chapter drafts, and more generally for being the kind of supportive friends I hope to keep for life. Grateful acknowledgment is hereby made to the following UMass-Boston students for permission to use the following essays:

Noel Tieszen, "On Slavery and Religion," 2001.

Mark Triffitt, "Douglass and Washington," 2001.

Tammy Ames, "The Ties That Bind? The Problem of Community in Gloria Naylor's *The Women of Brewster Place* and Randall Kenan's *A Visitation of Spirits*," 2000.

David Fernandez, "*Our Nig*: Fiction, History, or Both?," 2001.

Latia King, "Motherhood Equals No Mercy," 2001.

Kaitlin Kelsey, "The Passing of Clare Kendry?," 2001.

I am also grateful to UMass-Boston professor Lois Rudnick, a generous colleague who took the time to read and critique an early draft of my prospectus. Finally, I would like to express my appreciation to the two women at Peter Lang who helped me see this project through: Heidi Burns and Bernadette Shade.

INTRODUCTION

Why does James Weldon Johnson create a black antihero in *The Autobiography of an Ex-Coloured Man* (1912) when so many black characters in the literature of the previous decades seemed almost too good and *moral* to be true? Is it significant that neither Johnson's protagonist nor Ralph Ellison's protagonist in *Invisible Man* (1952) has a name? Why are oration and storytelling so prominently represented in Frederick Douglass's *The Heroic Slave* (1853) and Zora Neale Hurston's *Their Eyes Were Watching God* (1937)? Why is there so much literature about "passing" during a certain period, and what is a "tragic mulatta"? How are Toni Morrison's *Beloved* (1987), Octavia Butler's *Kindred* (1979), and Harriet Jacobs's *Incidents in the Life of a Slave Girl* (1861) related? What do Victor Séjour and Langston Hughes have in common in terms of literature? What do the terms "double-consciousness" and "black aesthetic" mean? What is a "cultural mulatto"?

Welcome to African American Literature 101. This textbook is designed for college students with little background knowledge of African American literature. The difference between this textbook and other resource material lies primarily in its limited scope. It offers no anthology of literature. It does not claim to provide you with everything there is to know about African American literature, and it is not designed to teach you about the literature in relationship to the larger body of American literature and/or World literature—though clearly important relationships do exist. I do not discourage students from comparative readings of African American literature and other literatures. However, I am aware that the typical college student is simply not as familiar with, for example, names such as Harper, James Weldon Johnson, Wright, West, Petry, Marshall, Major, Killens, Naylor, Wideman, and Butler, as they are with Homer, Chaucer, Shakespeare, Brontë, Dickens, Melville, Twain, Hemingway, Joyce, or Faulkner.

Because one can not teach every text, it is my intention here simply to offer you useful information about a number of texts that are almost routinely taught as representative texts in a variety of courses and particularly in African American literature courses where no major anthology is used. In other cases, I have simply tried to provide a solid introduction for at least five texts and authors in each of the six chapters. I have included information and tools that I would have found useful as an undergraduate encountering for the first time texts such as Toni

Morrison's *Beloved* (1987), Ralph Ellison's *Invisible Man* (1952), or even Zora Neale Hurston's *Their Eyes Were Watching God* (1937). For example, knowing that *blindness* is a major trope in Ralph Ellison's *Invisible Man* is key to experiencing the text as literature, but understanding the historical basis for the representative black subject's *blindness* provides a much more intimate and intense experience of the text. It also provides insight into Ellison's goal of *textualizing* black American consciousness. Understanding the text's connection to works by James Weldon Johnson, Richard Wright, Ishmael Reed, and Charles Johnson further illuminates its subtler complexities.

In my introductory African American Literature courses, I begin our consideration of each text with a preface that includes some background information about the author and information about the social, political, and cultural context out of which the author produced the text. I try to show how each new text is connected to previous works and how it advances or otherwise fits into the tradition. If the course is on the novel, for example, I am likely to include a broad overview of the literature from the late 1700s through the 1990s—with some attention to context and movements. I use the term *tradition* in this volume as a way of calling attention to the fact that black Americans have been writing and/or publishing since at least as early as 1746, and that some connections in terms of themes and recurring issues exist from the eighteenth century forward. My use of the term *tradition* is also part of a continuing response to the long-held conviction in some quarters that there is no such thing as African American literature.

I wrote this book in response to students who wanted an easily accessible, straightforward overview of the tradition—something similar to what I provided in my lectures. To simplify this project, I have focused on early autobiographical narratives and both short and long fiction. Each chapter begins with an overview of the period and the literature produced, followed by a brief discussion of several representative authors and their works. Sections titled "Contexts and Texts" and "Recurring Themes and Issues" follow. It goes without saying that different writers with different influences writing at different periods for different reasons have produced a body of literature that defies any easy reduction. Therefore, I think it is important to note that when I use the subheading "Recurring Themes and Issues," I use it not as a way of reducing, but as a way of highlighting common ground that I believe will enhance your engagement with, and experience of, the literature. For example, in chapter 5, I point out that all the featured texts grapple with the idea of the American Dream.

Each chapter also comes with a set of suggestions for paper topics and a set of study questions for each featured text. I use study questions to focus students' attention on significant critical issues in a given text as experts in the field have articulated them. As the information for each chapter comes from my reading and consideration of primary and secondary materials, I have also included a bibliography of works for each chapter. Chapter bibliographies include primary readings and secondary materials related to the primary readings and authors featured in each chapter. Students can use the bibliographies for further inquiry into issues raised in the primary readings. Sample papers (short response papers and formal essays) and a glossary are included in the back of the textbook. The sample papers are from introductory courses, and are meant to provide students with practical examples of ways to address critical and/or socio-philosophical issues raised in the primary works. Glossary terms are represented in bold letters throughout the text.

Perhaps first and foremost, this book is intended for naturally inquisitive students who want to make the most of their critical thinking skills as they explore the rich tradition of African American literature. I have capitalized the term "Blacks" where it is used interchangeably with "African Americans" to identify a specific group of Americans of African descent, though I am aware that the term is often used in a more diasporic sense, and that it is sometimes contested or simply avoided altogether. Regardless, I hope that you will find this text to be a solid introduction that serves you well as you advance through your undergraduate education and/or prepare for graduate study in the field.

Bibliography

Butler, Octavia. *Kindred.* 1979. Boston: Beacon P, 1988.

Douglass, Frederick. *The Heroic Slave.* 1853. *Three Classic African-American Novels*. Ed. William L. Andrews New York: Mentor/ Penguin, 1990.

Ellison, Ralph. *Invisible Man.* 1952. Introd. Ralph Ellison. 1981. New York: Random House, 1995.

Hurston, Zora Neale. *Their Eyes Were Watching God.* Philadelphia: J. B. Lippincott, 1937.

Jacobs, Harriet. *Incidents in the Life of a Slave Girl, Written by Herself.* 1861. Ed. Jean Fagan Yellin. Cambridge: Harvard UP, 1987.

—. *Incidents in the Life of a Slave Girl.* 1861. Ed. Frances Smith Foster and Nellie McKay. New York: Norton, 2001.

Johnson, James Weldon. *The Autobiography of an Ex-Coloured Man.*

1912. Introd. Henry Louis Gates, Jr. New York: Random House, 1989.
Morrison, Toni. *Beloved.* New York: Knopf, 1987.

CHAPTER I
Autobiographical Narratives 1760–1901

Autobiographical narratives form a major part of the African American literary tradition, serving a foundational role for much of African American fiction. As a mode of writing, **autobiography** allows an author to recollect, reorganize, and share with readers experiences and events that transformed her or his life. In this literary tradition, the earliest of these narratives are sometimes referred to as **slave narratives**, though not all narratives about slavery are autobiographical, and not all autobiographical narratives deal with slavery or with slavery exclusively. Recently, scholars in this field have come to refer to narratives about slavery as **freedom narratives**. In keeping with that trend, I will use the term ***neo- freedom narrative*** to refer to certain fictional narratives that are either set during slavery or that deal with slavery and its effects; such works have previously been dubbed *neoslave narratives*. (The earliest of the neofreedom narratives include William Wells Brown's *Clotel* [1853], and Harriet E. Wilson's *Our Nig* [1859].) Both are discussed in chapter 2.

The broadest definition of the term *slave narrative* would include hundreds of brief personal accounts from formerly enslaved persons taken down by interviewers during the 1920s and 1930s, as well as longer dictated narratives such as *The Narrative of Sojourner Truth: A Bondswoman of Olden Time* (1850). Truth, an itinerant preacher and political activist—who also demonstrated a feminist consciousness—was not literate in the conventional sense of that term; she dictated her story to **amanuensis** Olive Gilbert. "The Confessions of Nat Turner," taken down and published by white attorney William Gray in late 1831, became the most widely read African American narrative up to that date. Several scholars have raised questions surrounding the fact that Gray mediated Turner's narrative.

This chapter will introduce you to five representative autobiographical narratives: *The Interesting Narrative and Life of Olaudah Equiano, or Gustavus Vassa, the African, Written by Himself* (1789); *Narrative of the Life of Frederick Douglass, an American Slave, Written by Himself* (1845); Harriet Jacobs's *Incidents in the Life of a Slave Girl, Written by Herself* (1861); Elizabeth Keckley's *Behind the Scenes, or Thirty Years a Slave and Four Years in the White House* (1868); and Booker T. Washington's *Up from Slavery: An Autobio-*

graphy (1901). The first three narratives are set against a general background of slavery. Published in Great Britain, Equiano's eighteenth-century narrative came on the heels of the American Revolution and during the century that witnessed the Great Awakening and some lesser periods of religious evangelism. Douglass's and Jacobs's narratives were composed in the political period leading to the Civil War and following the Second Great Awakening. One notes the influence of **transcendentalism**—popular at the time—on both narratives. Both Keckley and Washington wrote narratives after the Civil War. Keckley's narrative was composed during **Reconstruction**, a time of false hope for many newly freed persons. The appearance of white supremacist groups, the official end of Reconstruction in 1877, repeal of certain sections of the 1875 Civil Rights Act, a sharp rise in lynchings, and the development of the system of segregation known as **Jim Crow** signaled a dramatic change in the social climate. Washington published *Up from Slavery* in the midst of this period that has been described by historian Rayford Logan and others as the **nadir** for African Americans.

Because of the general belief that only humans possess the capacity for reasoning and that the production of literature requires the capacity to reason, the mere existence of autobiographical works by formerly enslaved persons worked against the notion that they were a subhuman species. The information contained within narratives served as further testament to the enslaved person's humanity and at the same time attacked the dominant society's system of ethics and morality—a system that not only condoned and attempted to justify slavery, but also made specific legal provisions for it. Chattel slavery functioned as a legal system that reduced, or attempted to reduce, human beings to the subhuman status of property. Law and social custom often worked in tandem to support the process of dehumanization. For example, the most powerful and wide-reaching **fugitive slave law** was enacted as late as 1850 (only eleven years before the Civil War began). Fugitive slave laws made it possible for slaveholders and/or their agents to retrieve and return to servitude those who managed to escape from slavery. The basic provision was included in the Constitution (Article IV, Section 2). The Fugitive Slave Law of 1850 made it a punishable offense for any citizen—even those in states where slavery had been abolished—to assist an escapee.

Attacks on the social institutions that supported the continued enslavement of African-derived people were a routine part of autobiographical narratives published before the Civil War. **Antebellum** narrators took great pains to demonstrate how slavery affected individual, societal, and ultimately national character. In this way they served as representative descriptions of life under the institution of slavery and potent instruments in the struggle to end slavery. Directed primarily to northern readers, they appealed for an immediate end to slavery. Narratives published after the Civil War and the end of Reconstruction portrayed slavery in a very different light. William L. Andrews and other scholars note that Keckley and Washington, for example, were much less concerned in their narratives with what happened during slavery than they were with demonstrating that formerly enslaved persons were graduates of the **school of slavery**, and were thus prepared to become useful, productive citizens.

Regardless of the time period, however, autobiographical narratives served as the individual voices of previously silenced persons and as the collective voice for the many whose stories would never be told or read. *Narrative of the Life of Frederick Douglass, an American Slave, Written by Himself* is the autobiographical narrative by a formerly enslaved person most familiar to American students, but it was certainly not the *first* in chronological terms. As early as 1760, Britton Hammon published *A Narrative of the Uncommon Sufferings, and Surprizing Deliverance of Briton Hammon, a Negro Man* (1760). Hammon's narrative moves quickly from his life in slavery to sea travels that result in capture by Native American Indians off the coast of Florida; his story is less an autobiography of slavery (or even a spiritual autobiography) than it is a captivity narrative. American captivity narratives are first-person accounts of spiritual and physical endurance of, and deliverance from, Native American Indian captivity, and their tradition has been traced to Cotton Mather's *Humiliations Follow'd with Deliverance* (1697). Some fourteen pages in length, the bulk of Hammon's narrative actually concerns his treatment by the Florida Indians. Similarly, *A Narrative of the Lord's Wonderful Dealings with John Marrant, a Black, (Now Going to Preach the Gospel in Nova Scotia) Born in New York, in North America* (1785) describes Marrant's treatment while he was held captive by Native American Indians and his subsequent deliverance from captivity. Born free in New York, Marrant witnessed chattel slavery but was never personally subjected to it.

Narratives from the late eighteenth and early nineteenth centuries, which were likely to focus specifically on morality and sin as part of an inner quest that was spiritual in nature and an outer physical struggle against the evils of slavery, also preceded Douglass's 1845 narrative. Some examples include *The Life, History, and Unparalleled Sufferings of John Jea, the African Preacher* (c. 1811) and *A Narrative of the Most*

Remarkable Particulars in the Life of James Albert Ukasaw Gronniosaw, an African Prince (1870). Equiano's narrative is the best known eighteenth-century autobiographical narrative of slavery, usually considered the first major work of African American autobiography. A successful combination of Equiano's inner spiritual struggle and his protest against the evils of slavery, *The Interesting Narrative* appeared in Great Britain contemporaneously with the ratification of the United States Constitution.

Equiano's narrative and the other four autobiographical narratives of slavery mentioned above are part of a tradition of life writing—of writing the self. They bear affinities to spiritual autobiography, captivity narratives, and freedom narratives, and they are related to one another in formal, contextual, and intertextual ways. Remember that this genre of African American literature deals specifically with the authors' lives in slavery and freedom.

Basic Structure of the Narratives

For several reasons, autobiographical narratives, especially those written before the Civil War, usually included **authenticating documents**. Attached to the front and/or the back of a text, authenticating documents certified that the text was the *genuine article*, that it was written by the person claiming authorship, and was a true account of that person's experiences. There were several reasons for this. The fact that individuals indeed had been successful in escaping slavery did not mean that they possessed the ability to read and write. Law, custom, and/or circumstance more often than not precluded enslaved persons from learning to read and write. The controversy surrounding the discovery of *phony* narratives—fictional accounts of slavery penned by white **abolitionists**—was an additional factor; readers needed to be assured that the story was not a fabrication. In most cases, prominent white citizens provided authentication documents. For example, editor William Lloyd Garrison's preface and attorney Wendell Phillips's personal letter to Frederick Douglass authenticate *Narrative of the Life of Frederick Douglass, an American Slave, Written by Himself* (1845). Garrison and Phillips were both well-known figures in abolitionist circles. Though Harriet Jacobs's own preface to *Incidents in the Life of a Slave Girl, Written by Herself* (1861) is placed at the beginning of her narrative, three additional documents complete its authenticating machinery.

Autobiographical narratives almost always begin with some variation of the phrase "I was born." Typically, narrators will relate their place of birth, while making much of the fact that they do not know their date of birth. Often narrators relate the fact that they did not know their fathers, or that their fathers were either the white men who owned them or some white employee or relative of that owner. Slavery was a matrilineal institution, and children born of enslaved mothers took on the legal status of the mother. Next, a narrator recounts early life experiences, of being "innocent" until the startling realization of her or his status as chattel. A traumatic event (or a series of traumatic events) in the enslaved person's life serves as a catalyst for new awareness—an awakened consciousness of her or his position in the world. The concomitant desire for freedom sets the narrator on the quest for freedom, around which the entire narrative is built. The narrator takes the reading audience through a series of graphic events that illustrate the horrors of the system; she then describes an escape to freedom in varying detail, and ends the narrative with (or soon after) arrival in the North—a supposedly free space of hope and deliverance. Thus, the narrative moves *from slavery to freedom.*

Literacy plays a strong role in the narrator's developing consciousness, and thus, in the quest for freedom. Frederick Douglass represents two things as paramount to his ability to shed slavery's shackles: acquiring literacy and asserting his *manhood.* For Douglass and other narrators, the ability to add "Written by Himself" or "Written by Herself" to a narrative's title page was a badge of honor and a symbol of great accomplishment under adversity. While literacy included the ability to read and write, it also included the ability to make sense of (to comprehend) signs that were not necessarily written down on paper. Linda Brent, Harriet Jacobs's **pseudonymous narrator**, knew how to read and write. Careful readers note the important role that conventional literacy plays in the text—in the "dirty" notes passed to her by her master, and in the letters she writes from her hiding place in order to manipulate certain circumstances. However, the type of literacy that drove her quest for freedom is perhaps best characterized by her ability to comprehend her situation vis-à-vis various American institutions—especially the institution of slavery—and to map out and execute an appropriate strategy for transcendence. So, literacy can be broadened in this context to mean "heightened awareness or knowledge and the capacity and determination to act on that knowledge." The achievement of literacy was only one part of the formula for obtaining freedom—the ultimate goal of the antebellum narrator. Later in this chapter, I will demonstrate how authors, such as Douglass and Jacobs, combined literacy in its broadest sense with systematic challenges to the authority of the slaveholding society.

Post-Civil War narrators spend less time dealing with the evils of slavery and focus instead on how they were able to survive the crucible (or test) of slavery and become useful, even prosperous, citizens. They construct themselves as examples of what formerly enslaved persons can achieve. In *Behind the Scenes* (1868), Elizabeth Keckley devotes only the first three chapters—about one-eighth of the book—to her life in slavery. Though she suffers sexual exploitation, she chooses not to make it the focus of her narrative. Most of her narrative relates her many accomplishments as a modiste (designer/dressmaker) for Washington's elite, as well as her contributions to the newly freed black community. Postbellum narratives differ in structure in that they typically move quickly through that part of the author's life spent in slavery to amplify the narrator's successes in freedom. Both Elizabeth Keckley's *Behind the Scenes*, and Booker T. Washington's *Up from Slavery* exemplify this strategy. Born a few years before the Civil War began, Washington was not even ten years old when the war ended. He went on to found Tuskegee Institute (now Tuskegee University) and to become a major power broker in black America. Similarly to Keckley, he uses the bulk of his narrative to showcase both personal and professional accomplishments and contributions to "the race." Both these narratives bear affinities to the quintessential rags-to-riches story. In the larger scheme of American letters, such narratives resemble the type of self-made man (or for that matter, woman) story represented in Benjamin Franklin's autobiography.

Contexts and Texts

In the late eighteenth century, America's founding fathers were working to develop and ratify the Constitution. An important offshoot of this task involved defining who would be titled to property and citizenship rights. Increasingly, the idea of America and American identity had come to include the prerequisite of whiteness (or European ancestry); coincidentally, rights and privileges for nonwhites had gradually decreased. For tax assessment and political representation purposes, the Constitution counted each slave as three-fifths of a person; slavery and freedom were joined in a paradoxical marriage. (The ambiguities of this *marriage* are captured in Thomas Jefferson's writings from the period.)

Equiano's *The Interesting Narrative* has long been considered the first major work in this subgenre of African American literature, and one sees its influence on subsequent narratives. Though Equiano represents himself as a somewhat picaresque, at times awe-stricken (stranger-in-astrange-land) figure in the early part of his narrative, he eventually portrays himself as industrious and enterprising—even heroic. In the originally two-volume work, Equiano asserted morality and Christian faith along with an unprecedented first-person account of slavery and freedom. The Christian theme, as with that in the eighteenth-century narratives mentioned above, helped to establish a common bond of humanity between the formerly enslaved person and his free reading audience. The protest Equiano registered is more against the evil and immorality that slavery bred than it is against the institution itself. Whether we can attribute this stance to the fact that Equiano grew up in a household that included a number of enslaved persons, and/or the fact that he helped to establish and run a Virginia plantation in the mid-1770s, is a question for Equiano scholars. We do know from his narrative that he became so disenchanted with the inhumane practices he witnessed during his New World plantation duty that he left the States as soon as he was able to do so.

Equiano's narrative is unique in that it recalls not only his pre-enslavement life in his homeland but also the horror of the **Middle Passage**—the long voyage across the Atlantic in the ship's hold under the most inhumane conditions. Thus, Equiano is able to provide for his readers the contrasting experiences of African slavery and New World slavery. Before he was kidnapped (along with his sister) into African slavery at the age of eleven, Equiano had been part of a family that enslaved other humans. Eventually, Equiano was sold to European traders and transported from Africa to Barbados. From Barbados he was transported to Virginia and sold to a British Royal Navy captain.

Part of New World slavery involved replacing the African name with a name chosen by the slaveholder, and Equiano's owner gave him the name of a Swedish freedom fighter, Gustavus Vassa. Two sailor friends introduced him to literacy and religion, which were to form the basis of the quest for freedom he expressed in his autobiography. Equiano describes his service on various ships; eventually he purchased his freedom on July 10, 1766, and settled in Great Britain. He wrote *The Interesting Narrative* as part of that country's movement to abolish the Atlantic slave trade.

Abolishing the Atlantic slave trade—making it unlawful to import people from Africa to serve as slaves—was not the same as outlawing the institution (or the domestic practice) of slavery. The movement to end slavery as a domestic enterprise in the United States gained its momentum during the decades leading up to the Civil War—the antebellum period. Most American college students are familiar with

Harriet Beecher Stowe's *Uncle Tom's Cabin* (1852) and, perhaps to a lesser degree, with its impact on the **antislavery movement**. Antebellum narratives contributed to this effort as well. Published and circulated by antislavery societies in the United States and Great Britain, these narratives were usually written by persons who had escaped from slavery and were living as fugitives. *Narrative of the Life of Frederick Douglass, an American Slave, Written by Himself* and Harriet Jacobs's *Incidents in the Life of a Slave Girl, Written by Herself* are today the most familiar of the antebellum narratives.

Though Douglass actually published two subsequent full-length autobiographies, *Narrative* is the one most often encountered in undergraduate college courses. Following its authentication documents, the body of *Narrative* consists of eleven chapters and an appendix. In the first nine chapters, Douglass describes in some detail his life in slavery. The two remaining chapters tell of his experiences with notorious "nigger-breaker" Edward Covey. The narrative culminates in his successful escape from slavery, ending with Douglass's recollection of his first antislavery speech at Nantucket, Massachusetts, on August 11, 1841. An appendix to the narrative reinforces and encapsulates its antislavery message and clarifies Douglass's stance on religion.

Douglass begins with the sketchy details of his birth; he tells us that he was born on the Eastern Shore of Maryland and that he has no accurate knowledge of the date of his birth. He shares with us the rumor that his owner was probably also his father and explains that—while still an infant—he was separated from his mother. Douglass used the information that enslaved persons were routinely deprived of such basic information as their actual dates of birth to launch an attack on the institution of slavery and the way it functioned as a system of deprivation. (See Gates and Stepto, for example.) Throughout *Narrative*, Douglass expressed both a belief in his entitlement to certain basic rights and his outrage at being deprived of those rights. Time and again, he points to the enslaved person's wretched and impoverished existence in the midst of the prosperity and abundance that slaveholders and their families enjoyed.

When Douglass was about six years old, his owner sent him to Baltimore to serve the Auld family. Relatives of Douglass's owner, the Aulds later inherited the child in an estate settlement. While enslaved with the Aulds in Baltimore, Douglass acquired the magic of literacy that would enhance his developing consciousness about his situation in the world. He describes the beginning of his new awareness in a passage that is echoed a hundred years later in Richard Wright's autobiographical

Black Boy (1945). In both instances, an authority figure discourages the young boy's attraction to literature and literacy in an attempt to limit his access to knowledge. Both Douglass and Wright found a way to overcome the barriers to literacy and self-awareness; in each case, literacy became for a time a "double-edged sword"—making the newly literate person more aware of the injustice of his situation. Douglass returned to plantation life as a teenager, and his owner eventually sent him to Edward Covey to be turned into a willing slave. In a famous confrontation, Douglass asserted his *manhood* by resisting Covey. Later he was sent back to Baltimore where he learned the caulking trade before making his successful escape from slavery on September 3, 1838.

Douglass asserts essentially in *Narrative* that law and custom worked together to support white supremacy and to give sanction to slaveholder rights. Attempts by enslaved persons to penetrate the boundaries set up by law and custom resulted in charges of deviance. He recounts the ways that he challenged what he believed to be an unjust system: He stole covering for warmth, achieved literacy by any means necessary, fought for his *manhood*, and escaped to freedom where he spoke out against slavery. *Narrative* broaches issues related to black consciousness and **identity** that continue to be the focus of African American literature. Much of the ensuing male tradition in African American literature can be traced to issues raised in Douglass's 1845 narrative.

Harriet Jacobs's *Incidents* serves a similar role for black American women's literature. Jacobs began her life in slavery in North Carolina, but she is now a member of the North Carolina Literary Hall of Fame. Her narrative differs from Douglass's in several ways. Jacobs wrote her own preface to the narrative and used it to explain why she wrote pseudonymously. She borrowed conventions from the nineteenth-century women's domestic novel. In addition, while one notes strong similarities between Douglass's *Narrative* and Jacobs's *Incidents* in terms of how they treat literacy, manhood, religious hypocrisy, and sexual and reproductive exploitation, Jacobs's central and primary concern is the issue of female sexual and reproductive exploitation.

Incidents contains forty-one chapters whose titles range from "Childhood" to "Free at Last." Heroine Linda Brent was, of course, Harriet Ann Jacobs. Jacobs used the names Ellen and Benny to refer to her children, Louisa and Joseph. Her grandmother, also referred to as Aunt Marthy, was in reality Molly Horniblow. The brother called William in the text was actually Jacobs's brother John S. Jacobs (who also published an autobiographical account of his life); the uncle called Benjamin was Jacobs's uncle Joseph—son of Molly Horniblow. The

Flints were actually James Norcum and Mary Matilda Horniblow Norcum; Sands was Samuel Treadwell Sawyer, a United States congressman. The Bruces were Nathaniel Parker Willis (a well-known writer) and his first and second wives, Mary Stace Willis and Cornelia Grinnell Willis, respectively.

Incidents opens with Linda's memory of her happy youth in a loving home with her mother, father, and brother. The harsh reality of her situation in the slaveholding South became apparent when, at the age of six, she learned that she did not belong to her parents. Readers should note the strong affinity Jacobs had for her father as well as the impact of his death on her life. (Her father's feelings about slavery are made more explicit in John S. Jacobs's narrative.) After her parents died, Linda depended on her grandmother for spiritual and emotional support. As an adolescent, Linda was sent to live and work at the Flint home. Dr. Flint subsequently began making lewd advances toward her. He told her that she belonged to him and that she must submit and become his concubine; Jacobs deliberately makes ambiguous those passages relating to Flint's "success" in this regard. Aware that Flint is building a concubine's cottage for her, fifteen-year-old Linda decides that it is in her best interest to begin an affair with a single white neighbor—Sands. Sands fathers her two children, and it is motherhood finally that provides the catalyst, or impetus, for Linda's escape.

Social and literary convention dictated that Jacobs mute some of her discussion of sexual exploitation in *Incidents*. *Incidents* was published during an era when the *true woman* was expected to exhibit ideals of domesticity, piety, submissiveness, and chastity. Bondwomen under sexual assault could not aspire to such ideals. Thus, the desire for sexual chastity that Jacobs expresses in *Incidents* must be considered in light of contemporary awareness that sexual freedom for black women under slavery meant the freedom to be *less* sexual, rather than *more* sexual. For Linda Brent, a measure of freedom lies simply in the act of choosing one's sex partner (or partners), because the institution forced enslaved black women to be sexual in one way or the other. As Flint had already forced Linda to end her love relationship with a free black man, the affair with Sands was her attempt to assert some measure of control over her own sexuality. In the typical women's domestic novel, whose convention Jacobs followed to some degree, explicit and frank discussion of sex and sexuality was inappropriate. Thus, in order for Jacobs to achieve the objective of reaching out to women and mothers on either side of the color line who could identify with her sense of outrage, she had to walk a very fine line.

Where Douglass presents himself heroically as a Renaissance man of sorts, Jacobs draws Linda Brent as an outraged, and ultimately heroic, mother. As Joanne M. Braxton has noted, contemporary black women writers, such as Gayl Jones, Toni Morrison, and Alice Walker, have followed this precedent. Jacobs's appeal was largely to women and mothers in both the North and the South. Today, her narrative effectively serves as "a manual for reappropriation"; during the course of Linda Brent's story (which is Jacobs's own story), the heroine claims ownership of her physical self, her offspring, and her sexual and reproductive rights. Her somewhat melodramatic plea to readers to forgive her for having sex with one white man in order to avoid being forced to have sex with another is undermined by her statements in support of "theft" and reappropriation in other parts of the narrative. A comparative reading of *Narrative* and *Incidents* should reveal the ways that both narrators go about claiming what they believe to be theirs by right. It should also reveal the individual (Douglass) versus collective (Jacobs) escape from slavery as each author represents his or her story. Douglass reveals in a subsequent autobiography that he was aided in his escape, but in *Narrative* that information is muted for practical as well as literary reasons. Jacobs tells us that African Americans and whites of both genders aided Linda Brent in her escape.

Incidents appeared just months before the start of the Civil War, so its antislavery message soon became a moot point. Thus, it did not receive the immediate attention of Douglass's narrative and was later dismissed for years as a work of fiction whose authorship was attributed to abolitionist editor Lydia Maria Child, who was also known as a writer of abolitionist fiction. (William Wells Brown had incorporated much of Child's short story "The Quadroons" into *Clotel*, his 1853 novel about slavery.) Historian Jean Fagan Yellin's efforts to uncover the real story behind Jacobs's narrative have been paramount in making *Incidents* a staple of African American literary study. Several editions, including a Norton critical edition, are currently in print. Both during and immediately following the Civil War, Jacobs and her daughter Louisa would go on to work on behalf of formerly enslaved persons.

Jacobs and Douglass shared the primary task of using their individual stories as evidence that slavery was an evil and immoral institution that should end. Post-Civil War narrators used stories of trial and triumph as a way to advance the "myth of uplift" (see Stepto). In short, they wanted to demonstrate that given a chance African Americans were quite capable of becoming useful and productive members of American society, that slavery had not degraded them beyond repair. Elizabeth

Keckley, Booker T. Washington, and J. W. C. Pennington, among others, offered their own success stories as examples or models. Think of such narratives as motivational speeches, workshops, or seminars. They are often "rags-to-riches" stories that focus on the formerly enslaved person's endurance of slavery to emerge triumphant, successful, and capable of contributing toward the formation of strong black communities. Slavery was a proving ground that prepared the formerly enslaved person for progress after freedom. Booker T. Washington's *Up from Slavery* is probably the best known and most successful post-Civil War narrative. Long before Washington's story of personal triumph, however, Elizabeth Keckley's *Behind the Scenes* related the story of how one former bondwoman became the modiste (dress designer) for the wife of Abraham Lincoln. Keckley also became the founding and later reelected president of the Contraband Relief Society, and Director of Domestic Arts at Wilberforce University in Ohio.

Elizabeth Keckley was never a fugitive slave. She insisted on purchasing her and her son's freedom rather than escaping and living a life on the lookout for slavecatchers. Her attitude stands in stark contrast to that of Harriet Jacobs, who balked at the thought of purchasing herself from someone who had no right to claim ownership of her body in the first place. This essential difference underscores an important point about how each woman represented and related to the institution of slavery in her autobiographical work. Jacobs represented slavery as an inherently evil breeding ground for corruption that must be resisted by any means necessary. Jacobs had stated in her 1861 narrative that she was not bound to respect any laws made by white men, a sentiment that invokes and reverses the Supreme Court's decision in the famous *Dred Scott* case of 1857. Keckley portrays herself in *Behind the Scenes* (1868) as someone who was aware of her place as a slave, who adhered to the institution's laws and rules, and who fought to maintain a sense of personal dignity and humanity within the institution.

Part freedom narrative and part memoir, Keckley's own personal life story is almost eclipsed in *Behind the Scenes* by the appended letters from Mary Todd Lincoln. Though she writes her own preface to her text, Keckley uses that preface in part to apologize for slavery, but mainly to talk about her relationship with Mary Todd Lincoln. In the three chapters of *Behind the Scenes* that are actually devoted to Keckley's life in slavery, she sometimes characterizes her mistreatment as savage. She illustrates through example how she managed to preserve her humanity under dehumanizing treatment, which included beatings and sexual exploitation.

Keckley's story begins with the chapter "Where I Was Born"; she soon makes the reason for the heading apparent in her statement that she is unaware of the *exact date* of her birth, though she was born in 1818 in Dinwiddie Court-House, Virginia. Students should note that, unlike Douglass and Jacobs, Keckley does not raise the issue of her parentage for several pages. Born the property of Colonel A. Burwell, her given name was Anne. Her mother, Agnes, was married to George Pleasant, who was enslaved at another location. Agnes was the property of Burwell. Though scholars suggest otherwise, Keckley refers to George Pleasant as her father in the narrative (see Foster's *Written by Herself*, for example). Pleasant called young Anne his "Little Lizzie," hence the name Elizabeth, the same as that of the master's daughter. That George Pleasant held some significance for Keckley is evident in the fact that she became publicly known by his last name. Despite his infrequent presence during her childhood—and his complete absence during her adulthood—she mentions him several times with great fondness in the early pages of her narrative. She also makes the last letter Agnes Pleasant received from George Pleasant part of her story by incorporating it into her narrative. Finally, she names her only child George.

The first episode that Keckley chooses to relate involves her being assigned the responsibility of rocking the master's infant's cradle at age four, and receiving a beating when her overzealousness resulted in the child being thrown to the floor. She includes the troublesome circumstances of her mother's long-distance marriage to George Pleasant, and she relates the story of "Little Joe." Little Joe was a young child sold away from the mother who is subsequently beaten for weeping. She recalls being loaned to her master's oldest son, a minister, to serve as his family's only servant when she was about fourteen years old. When the family moved to North Carolina, she was carried along; there she suffered physical abuse at the hands of a schoolmaster acting on behalf of her temporary mistress, who felt Keckley had too much pride for a bondwoman. Keckley fought back, and the series of battles that ensued call to mind Frederick Douglass's battles with Covey, the notorious slave-breaker described in *Narrative*. It was also in North Carolina that Keckley bore her son George, fathered by a white man who remains unnamed in the narrative, but whom scholars attribute to the master she was serving at the time (see Foster's *Written by Herself*). She discreetly omits all but the briefest mention of the unwanted sexual attention that resulted in her pregnancy. In her own very efficient way, Keckley provides information about a number of scenarios involving sexual and reproductive exploitation, even as she seems to mute its importance.

After serving in North Carolina, Keckley returned to Virginia to serve Ann Burwell Garland and Ann's new husband. The Garlands eventually moved to St. Louis, Missouri, taking Keckley along. When the Garland family fell on hard times and proposed to hire the aging Agnes out to help support the family, Keckley suggested an alternative plan, which would ultimately result in her flourishing enterprise as a dressmaker. She supported her master and his family in this way. When James Keckley, whom she had known in Virginia, found her in St. Louis and proposed that they marry, Elizabeth began seriously to ponder freedom. She wanted no more children born into slavery. She also rationalized that because her son George was half white, he should be free. After extracting a purchase price from her master for herself and her son, she consented to marry James Keckley—thinking he was a free man. He was not. The marriage was apparently a disappointment for Keckley in a number of ways, but she demurs from including many details; the marriage ended eight years later when James Keckley died. Elizabeth Keckley persisted, nevertheless, in raising the funds to purchase her and her son's freedom by borrowing and eventually repaying money that white clients and associates collected on her behalf. The fact that Keckley had gained the respect and well-wishes of certain members of the white slaveholding community points to ambiguities and complexities in black/white relationships among people in her town.

The document granting Keckley's freedom in 1855 is included as part of her autobiography; it also helps to complete the explanation of how Anne Pleasant came to be called Elizabeth Keckley. Keckley moved to Washington, D.C., and subsequently served as the modiste for Mrs. Jefferson Davis and other prominent women in the area. Fortunately, she declined an invitation to accompany the Davises when they returned to the South on the eve of the Civil War. Instead, she continued her position as modiste to Washington's affluent women, and finally secured the position of modiste to First Lady Mary Todd Lincoln. She became one of Lincoln's confidantes, spending many hours in the White House. The bulk of her narrative deals with her affairs with the Lincolns, and is thus set against the historic backdrop of the Civil War and its immediate aftermath.

Keckley also describes the indigent state of newly freed persons streaming into the nation's capital following the war, and the efforts of the Contraband Relief Society, which she had founded. Generally speaking, Keckley portrays herself as a workhorse—someone able to accomplish extremely high levels of productivity. She also downplays her own victimization and presents a self that has not been embittered by her particular American experience. This attitude is exemplified in her devotion of several pages of her narrative to the declining health, eventual death, and memorial tribute to Lincoln's son; she mentions only in passing the death of her own son.

The production of Keckley's narrative had a profoundly negative effect on her relationship with Mary Todd Lincoln. The two women had become intimate friends, and Keckley had been a source of comfort to Lincoln following the assassination of President Lincoln. When Keckley shared some of Mrs. Lincoln's personal letters with her ghostwriter for *Behind the Scenes*, James Redpath, he published the letters wholesale, creating a scandal (subsequently called the "Old Dresses Scandal") that drove a permanent wedge between the two women. Mrs. Lincoln saw it as a betrayal. The careful image of herself as trustworthy and diligent, which Keckley had labored many years to establish, was dashed in one tragic fell swoop.

Similarly to Keckley, Booker T. Washington did not need to convince America to end slavery. In fact, Washington deliberately sets out to create the impression that his story differs from those antebellum predecessors who concentrated their antagonism on the South. Washington blamed slavery on the entire nation. Dealing with the circumstances of his birth at the beginning of *Up from Slavery*, Washington seems on the surface to downplay the significance of birthdates, but he actually belabors the point of his ignorance by raising it several times in the first paragraph. This repetition suggests that it was indeed an important issue, especially since we know the date of Washington's birth to be April 5, 1856, and Washington must have known it as well by the time he published *Up from Slavery*. Washington's seeming attempt to distance himself from Douglass and others on the subject of his date of birth actually ends up calling attention to the missing information, even as he, almost sarcastically, dismisses it as unimportant.

He gives much credit for his own positive attributes to his black mother, not his white father. Indeed, implicit in his praise for his mother is his father's lack of responsibility for the exemplary individual Washington ultimately portrays himself to be. He conveys his mother's frugality in a passage explaining how she sewed him a cap rather than incur debt by buying one. He depicts frugality as a most desirable quality throughout his narrative. He illustrates that like his mother, he is also frugal, and fiscal conservatives are desirable business partners. They can be trusted to handle money wisely. His mother, as Washington portrays her, is not only a model of frugality, but she is also a model of resourcefulness and resilience. He endows his mother with the highest qualities of a desirable businessperson, and, thus, it is highly significant that he also uses her to address a most pervasive stereotype from American slavery—the black chicken thief. He explains simply that his mother was acting under the extreme circumstances of slavery, and he did not consider her action to feed her children as stealing.

With the image of his mother clearly so central to his mission, Washington proceeds in his quest to convince white people that black people are faithful and trustworthy. He reminds white southerners of how their former slaves protected their buried treasures during the Civil War. He also tells his audience that enslaved people were not bitter with white southerners for fighting a war to prolong slavery. As evidence, he points out that they nursed family relatives wounded in the war and grieved when their masters were killed in the war. For southern white people reeling from the aftermath of the war and the "effrontery" of Reconstruction, Washington depicts African Americans as loyal and self-denying. He stresses the idea that they are capable of moving up and away from slavery—hence, the title of his autobiography.

Like Keckley before him, he represents himself in a way that appeals to potential business partners. Washington clearly associates freedom with knowledge in *Up from Slavery*, and he knows that African Americans are dependent upon wealthy white philanthropists for the schools they will need in order to gain that knowledge. To would-be philanthropists, Washington offers images of frugality and pristine business ethics, even to the point of discussing one example of the repayment of a debt no longer owed. Ultimately, these portrayals helped enhance his position as a black leader serving as mediator between wealthy whites and the black community. He demonstrates that black people are, in some instances, more capable of moving up from slavery than white people are. Washington's narrative ends with the portrait of a thriving Tuskegee Institute, and with Washington himself as the black leader that whites in power can trust to assist in solving the "negro problem."

Washington weaves a remarkable story of trial and triumph, portraying himself as representative of what African Americans are capable of accomplishing, and he manages to win the endorsement of politicians, philanthropists, and businessmen. He incorporates his infamous "cast down your buckets" speech, which he presented at the 1895 Atlanta Exposition, into the narrative. Finally, Washington did succeed in becoming a major power broker, while Jim Crow segregation solidified in certain regions, and the myth of equal opportunity seemed an ever-elusive dream. The big issue surrounding his tenure as leader remains one of whether his substantial and significant achievements came at too high a price in terms of social inequality.

Recurring Themes and Issues

The five texts discussed so far all address to varying degrees the material reality of authors who experienced New World slavery firsthand and lived to write about it. The central question driving any autobiographical narrative is one of identity—"Who am I?" Equiano, Douglass, Jacobs, Keckley, and Washington all grappled with this question as they dealt with the issue of slavery's effects on their self-identities. Of the five authors discussed above, Equiano is the only one who possessed any firsthand knowledge of Africa when his narrative was published. Equiano's unique situation and experiences made it possible for him to assert easily that he was both African *and* British—especially after he was no longer enslaved. Whereas Douglass and Jacobs clearly articulate feelings of entitlement to rights as Americans, prior to the Fourteenth and Fifteenth Amendments to the Constitution, they could not legally claim to be Americans. In terms of national identity, they existed in that liminal space between African and American. Recall that Douglass points out on the first page of his narrative the fact that he was deprived of certain knowledge about his date of birth and the identity of his father. In addition, he was separated from his mother as an infant. Later, he learned that the reason why enslaved persons were kept illiterate and "in the dark" was to make them more willing slaves. Clearly for Harriet Jacobs, motherhood is an essential element in the way she chooses to define herself. So, questions of identity in these narratives involve more than the legal right to identify as an American of African descent. They go to the core of identity formation—to the most basic and primary relationships between children and their parents.

Voice and/or **oration** in autobiographical narratives are tied to identity and also to literacy (discussed above). First of all, the written works serve as evidence that the voices of individual authors are no longer silenced by slavery. Secondly, the authors' works function in a more representative way—by speaking on behalf of an entire group. When Douglass and Jacobs hold forth on the subject of theft and reappropriation, they are speaking not only for themselves, but also for the silenced voices of others forced to exist under similar social conditions. They anticipated in a sense the persistence of negative stereotypes such as the "thieving negro" and the "lewd black woman" that continue to linger in American popular culture. Their narratives provide information that helps to counter these negative stereotypes. Douglass, for example, uses the appendix in *Narrative* to label all those who benefited from slavery as thieves and "manstealers," who had committed the worst possible kind of theft. Jacobs's ninth chapter deals explicitly with *Exodus* 20:15—the biblical commandment against theft. Throughout the tradition, authors from Equiano in the eighteenth century to science fiction writer Octavia Butler in the late twentieth century address these important issues. Finally, some narratives give voice and oration a particular prominence. For example, near the end of *Narrative*, Douglass describes how he felt when first asked to speak at an antislavery meeting. He hesitated because he had learned silence both as an enforced mode of deference and as a tool of survival during slavery. Most students know from their study of American history that Douglass *found his voice* and achieved great fame as an orator. Whether through the spoken word or the written word, freeing the formerly silenced voice equates to freeing the formerly enslaved person and asserting a strong sense of self.

All five of the narratives focus to varying degrees on the issue of freedom in a literal and figurative sense. Because enslaved persons were considered chattel (property), to take one's freedom by escaping from slavery was to commit grand larceny under the law. Douglass and Jacobs deal with this by discrediting the slaveholding society whose rights such laws protect. Freedom took on new meaning once physical freedom was obtained. For Douglass, it meant, among other things, being able to earn wages for his labor and being able to tell his story in his own way. For Harriet Jacobs, reuniting with her children and living away from the pressure associated with sexual exploitation represent important aspects of freedom. Booker T. Washington is the only one of the five authors discussed whose actual physical freedom did not need to be purchased or stolen. For Washington, real freedom for African Americans lay in education and property ownership.

Antebellum narrators Douglass and Jacobs offered harsh critiques of the so-called Christianity that slaveholders practiced. Along with Keckley, they pointed out that oftentimes the cruelest slaveholder was also the strongest professer of so-called Christianity. Douglass charges slaveholders with religious hypocrisy throughout his narrative and especially in the appendix. While Jacobs stresses the importance of faith, invokes many biblical passages, and makes her very conventionally religious grandmother a major aspect of her story, she also demonstrates how slaveholders attempted to use religious instruction to convince enslaved persons that they were born to be the slaves of whites. Jacobs manages to incorporate some references to African religious traditions into her narrative. Both Douglass and Jacobs level the charge of religious hypocrisy in support of a basic premise that slavery is an evil, un-Christian institution that must end. Some early narratives were closely related to spiritual autobiography and focused on Christian faith and spiritual deliverance. Equiano makes religion a major part of his life's story. He represents it as key to his physical and metaphysical development.

Another feature common to a number of narratives about slavery, and particularly *Narrative* and *Incidents*, is the question of *manhood.* In chapter 10, after detailing Covey's many abuses in attempting to turn Douglass into a willing slave, Douglass makes his infamous statement about the man that was made a slave being remade into a man. Following this expression, Douglass recounts the details leading up to a major physical confrontation with Covey that ended Covey's physical domination of him. The classic confrontation formed the core of Douglass's treatment of manhood in *Narrative*. In her chapter titled "The Slave Who Dared to Feel Like a Man," Harriet Jacobs describes a similar incident involving her brother, John (called William in the text), and one of his young masters. Both examples involve an enslaved black male besting his oppressor during a physical confrontation that has been initiated by the oppressor. However, the argument can be made that such a struggle is not the sole province of those seeking *manhood*, or perhaps *manhood* is not the proper descriptive term, for Elizabeth Keckley (and Harriet Wilson in the autobiographical novel *Our Nig*) represent women who also resist physical assaults. The struggle is ultimately for a measure of personal dignity and autonomy under a system that functions best by denying those things to some.

Harriet Jacobs made sexual and reproductive exploitation a dominant theme in *Incidents in the Life of a Slave Girl* (1861), and though somewhat muted, it is also a significant issue in *Behind the Scenes* (1868). Douglass makes the issue implicit in *Narrative* with his personal story of being denied a childhood at his mother's side. He tackles the issue more overtly with his description of Edward Covey's forced breeding of Caroline with an enslaved married man from a neighboring plantation. A poor man, Covey was beside himself with pleasure when Caroline delivered twins as the result of this forced cohabitation. The twins became part of Covey's property.

Such arrangements also speak to the radical disruption of black family life under slavery, a well-represented theme in the first four narratives. Equiano describes being separated from his family and, eventually, removed from the continent of his homeland as a young boy. Douglass uses his family's disruption as part of his overall rhetoric of deprivation. Not only was he separated from his mother at a very young age, but he was also sent alone to Baltimore as a young boy to serve his master's relatives. The story about Caroline and the married man from a neighboring plantation also implies family disruption at several levels. Both Keckley and Jacobs devote substantial energies to the theme of family disruption. Keckley tells us that her mother and the man she called her father lived on different plantations. She also relates the story of Little Joe, and later her own separation from her mother when she is sent to North Carolina. Jacobs makes her quest for a return to what she remembers as ideal family relations second only to her quest for freedom. Booker T. Washington discusses very early in his narrative the difficulty his mother faced in caring properly for her children. He had neither intimate knowledge of, nor a relationship with, his white father. Still, Washington lived as a slave for a comparatively small period, having been born five years before the Civil War began. The minstrel show inherent in *Up from Slavery* included some strong descriptions of disrupted white family life during and following the Civil War.

Questions of morality are also central to each of the five narratives discussed above. Equiano, particularly in the fifth and sixth chapters of his narrative, describes numerous situations in which the morality and ethics of the ruling class are brought into question. In a number of cases, Equiano describes how enslaved persons were defrauded of property and generally precluded from accumulating resources. Indeed, issues surrounding the access to resources and/or the accumulation of private property are prominent in all of the narratives. The socioeconomic conditions slavery fostered mandated the creation of alternative possibilities for action, for measuring moral behavior, and for asserting the **subjectivity** that slavery and racism denied them. With very limited *legal* access to the very resources their labor produced, enslaved persons often engaged in the practice they defined as "taking" from whites. Whites called it "stealing" (see Blassingame, Genovese, or Stampp). Under American chattel slavery, the term *thief* became "racialized," suggesting an automatic correlation between blackness and acts defined legally as theft, burglary, robbery, or larceny. Each of the five authors discussed above seems all too aware of this tendency in law and custom to paint African Americans as naturally inclined toward certain immoral practices. They include important information that, taken collectively, offers us a different version of that particular American story.

Bibliography

Andrews, William L. *African-American Autobiography: A Collection of Critical Essays*. Englewood Cliffs: Prentice-Hall, 1993.

—. "The Changing Moral Discourse of Nineteenth-Century African American Women's Autobiography: Harriet Jacobs and Elizabeth Keckley." *De/Colonizing the Subject: The Politics of Gender in Women's Autobiography*. Ed. Sidonie Smith and Julia Watson. Minneapolis: U of Minnesota P, 1992.

—. *To Tell a Free Story: The First Century of Afro-American Autobiography, 1760–1865*. Urbana and Chicago: U of Illinois P, 1988. [Volume contains an excellent annotated bibliography of autobiography and biography before 1865.]

Andrews, William L., Frances Smith Foster, and Trudier Harris, eds. *The Oxford Companion to African American Literature*. New York: Oxford UP, 1997.

Andrews, William L., and Henry L. Gates, Jr., eds. *The Civitas Anthology of African American Slave Narratives*. Washington, D.C.: Civitas/Counterpoint, 1999.

Aptheker, Herbert. *American Negro Slave Revolts*. New York: Columbia UP, 1943.

Baker, Houston. *Long Black Song: Essays in African American literature and Culture*. Charlottesville: UP of Virginia, 1972.

Berlin, Ira. *Many Thousands Gone: The First Two Centuries of Slavery in North America*. Cambridge: Harvard UP, 1998.

Berlin, Ira, Marc Favreau, and Steven F. Miller. *Remembering Slavery: African Americans Talk about Their Personal Experiences in Slavery and Emancipation*. New York: The New P, 1998.

Blassingame, John W. *The Slave Community: Plantation Life in the Antebellum South*. New York and Oxford: Oxford UP, 1979.

Blassingame, John W., ed. *Slave Testimony: Two Centuries of Letters, Speeches, Interviews, and Autobiographies*. Baton Rouge: Louisiana State UP, 1977.

Bontemps, Arna, ed. *Great Slave Narratives*. Boston: Beacon P, 1968.

Braxton, Joanne. *Black Women Writing Autobiography: A Tradition within a Tradition*. Philadelphia: Temple UP, 1989.

—. "Ancestral Presence: The Outraged Mother Figure in Contemporary Afra-American Writing." *Wild Women in the Whirlwind*. Eds.

Braxton and Andrée Nicola McLaughlin. New Brunswick: Rutgers, 1990. 299–315.

Brown, William Wells. *Clotel, or The President's Daughter*. 1853. Bedford Cultural Edition. Ed. Robert S. Levine. New York: Bedford/St. Martin's, 2000.

Butterfield, Stephen. *Black Autobiography in America*. Amherst: U of Massachusetts P, 1974.

Carby, Hazel. *Reconstructing Womanhood*. New York: Oxford UP, 1987.

Child, Lydia Maria. "The Quadroons." 1842. *The Other Woman: Stories of Two Women and a Man*. Ed. Susan Koppelman. New York: Feminist P, 1984. 1–12.

Davis, Charles T., and Henry L. Gates, Jr., eds. *The Slave's Narrative*. New York: Oxford UP, 1985.

Douglass, Frederick. *Narrative of the Life of Frederick Douglass, an American Slave, Written by Himself*. 1845. Norton Critical Edition. Ed. William L. Andrews and William S. McFeely. New York: Norton,1997.

—. *My Bondage and My Freedom*. New York and Auburn: Miller, Orton, Mulligan, 1855.

Dudley, David. *Intergenerational Conflict in African American Men's Autobiography*. Philadelphia: U of Pennsylvania P, 1991.

Ernest, John, ed. *Shadowing Slavery: Five African American Autobiographical Narratives*. Acton: Copley, 2002.

Equiano, Olaudah. *The Interesting Narrative of the Life of Olaudah Equiano, or Gustavus Vassa, the African, Written by Himself*. 1789. The Interesting Narrative and Other Writings. Ed. Vincent Carretta. New York: Penguin, 1996.

Fabre, Geneviève, and Robert O'Meally, eds. *History and Memory in African-American Culture*. New York: Oxford UP, 1994.

Fishel, Leslie H., and Benjamin Quarles. "The Dred Scott Decision." *The Black American: A Documentary History*. New York: Scott Foresman, 1967, 1970. 203–7.

Fleischner, Jennifer. *Mastering Slavery: Memory, Family, and Identity in Women's Slave Narratives*. New York and London: New York UP, 1996.

Foster, Frances Smith. *Witnessing Slavery: The Development of Ante-Bellum Slave Narratives*. 2nd ed. Madison: Wisconsin UP, 1994.

—. *Written by Herself: Literary Production by African American Women, 1746–1892*. Bloomington: Indiana UP, 1993.

Franklin, John Hope. *From Slavery to Freedom*. New York: Knopf, 1979.

Franklin, V. P. *Living Our Stories, Telling Our Truths: Autobiography and the Making of the African American Intellectual Tradition*. New York: Scribners, 1995.

Garfield, Deborah M., and Rafia Zafar, eds. *Harriet Jacobs and Incidents in the Life of a Slave Girl: New Critical Essays*. New York and Cambridge: Cambridge UP, 1996.

Gates, Jr., Henry Louis. *Figures in Black: Words, Signs, and the "Racial Self."* New York and Oxford: Oxford UP, 1987.

Gates, Jr., Henry Louis, ed. *Bearing Witness: Selections from African-American Autobiography in the Twentieth Century*. New York: Pantheon, 1991.

Gates, Jr., Henry Louis, and William L. Andrews, eds. *Pioneers of the Black Atlantic: Five Slave Narratives from the Enlightenment*. Washington, D.C.: Civitas/Counterpoint, 1998.

—. *The Classic Slave Narratives*. New York: New American Library, 1987.

Genovese, Eugene. *Roll Jordan Roll: The World the Slaves Made*. 1972. New York: Random House, 1976.

Goble, Myron. *Down in the Delta*. Burbank: Miramax Films, 1998.

Greene, J. Lee. *Blacks in Eden: The African American Novel's First Century*. Charlottesville: U of Virginia P, 1996.

Gronniosaw, James Albert Ukasaw. *A Narrative of the Most Remarkable Particulars in the Life of James Albert Ukasaw Gronniosaw, An African Prince*. Ed. W. Shirley. 1770. *Pioneers of the Black Atlantic: Five Slave Narratives from the Enlightenment 1772–1815*. Ed. Henry Louis Gates, Jr. and William L. Andrews. Washington, D.C.: Civitas, 1998. 29–59.

Hammon, Briton. *A Narrative of the Uncommon Sufferings, and Surprizing Deliverance of Briton Hammon, A Negro Man....* Boston: Green and Russell, 1760.

Hawkins, Hugh, ed. *Booker T. Washington and His Critics: Black Leadership in Crisis*. 2nd ed. Lexington: D.C. Heath and Company, 1974.

Jacobs, Harriet. *Incidents in the Life of a Slave Girl, Written by Herself.* 1861. Ed. Jean Fagan Yellin. Cambridge: Harvard UP, 1987.

—. *Incidents in the Life of a Slave Girl.* 1861. Ed. Frances Smith Foster and Nellie McKay. New York: Norton, 2001.

Jea, John. *The Life, History, and Unparalleled Sufferings of John Jea, the African Preacher*. 1811. *Pioneers of the Black Atlantic: Five Slave*

Narratives from the Enlightenment 1772–1815. Ed. Henry Louis Gates, Jr. and William L. Andrews. Washington, D.C.: Civitas, 1998. 366–439.

Jordan, Winthrop. *White over Black: American Attitudes toward the Negro 1550–1812*. Baltimore: Penguin/Pelican, 1969.

Keckley, Elizabeth. *Behind the Scenes, or Thirty Years a Slave and Four Years in the White House*. 1868. Introd. James Olney. New York: Oxford UP, 1988.

Marrant, John. *A Narrative of the Lord's Wonderful Dealings with John Marrant, a Black....* 1785. *Pioneers of the Black Atlantic: Five Slave Narratives from the Enlightenment 1772–1815*. Ed. Henry Louis Gates, Jr. and William L. Andrews. Washington, D.C.: Civitas, 1998. 60–80.

Mattison, H. *Louisa Picquet, the Octoroon: Or Inside Views of Southern Domestic Life*. 1861. *Collected Black Women's Narratives*. Introd. Anthony G. Bartholemy. New York: Oxford UP, 1988.

McBride, Dwight A. *Impossible Witnesses: Truth, Abolitionism, and Slave Testimony*. New York: New York UP, 2001.

McDowell, Deborah E., and Arnold Rampersad, eds. *Slavery and the American Literary Imagination*. Baltimore and London: Johns Hopkins UP, 1989.

McFeely, William S. *Frederick Douglass*. New York: Norton, 1991.

Nelson, Emmanuel S. Ed. *African American Autobiographers: A Sourcebook*. Westport, Conn.: Greenwood P, 2002.

Nichols, Charles H., ed. *Black Men in Chains*. New York: Lawrence Hill, 1972.

Osofsky, Gilbert. *Puttin' on Ole Massa*. New York: Harper Torchbooks, 1969.

Painter, Nell Irvin. *Sojourner Truth: A Life, a Symbol*. New York: Norton, 1996.

Patterson, Orlando. *Freedom*. Volume I: *Freedom in the Making of Western Culture*. New York: HarperCollins, 1991.

—. *Slavery and Social Death*. Cambridge: Harvard UP, 1982.

Peterson, Carla L. *"Doers of the Word": African-American Women Speakers & Writers in the North (1830–1880)*. 1995. New Brunswick, N.J.: Rutgers UP, 1998.

Preston, Dickson J. *Young Frederick Douglass: The Maryland Years*. Baltimore: Johns Hopkins UP, 1980.

Rawick, George P., gen. ed. *The American Slave: A Composite Autobiography*. 41 vols. Westport, Conn.: Greenwood P, 1972–1979.

——. *From Sunup to Sundown: The Making of the Black Community.* Westport, Conn.: Greenwood P, 1972.

Rushdy, Ashraf. *Neo-Slave Narratives: Studies in the Social Logic of a Literary Form.* New York: Oxford UP, 1999.

Sekora, John, and Darwin T. Turner, eds. *The Art of the Slave Narrative: Original Essays in Criticism and Theory.* Macomb: Western Illinois UP, 1982.

Smith, Sidonie. *Where I'm Bound: Patterns of Slavery and Freedom in Black American Autobiography.* Westport, Conn.: Greenwood P, 1974.

Smith, Valerie. *Self-Discovery and Authority in Afro-American Narrative.* Cambridge: Harvard UP, 1987.

Stampp, Kenneth. *The Peculiar Institution: Slavery in the Ante-Bellum South.* New York: Knopf, 1956.

Starling, Marion Wilson. *The Slave Narrative: Its Place in American History.* 1981. Washington: Howard UP, 1988.

Stepto, Robert. *From Behind the Veil: A Study of Afro-American Narrative.* 1979. 2nd ed. Chicago: U of Illinois P, 1991.

Sterling, Dorothy. *We Are Your Sisters: Black Women in the Nineteenth Century.* New York: Norton, 1984.

Tackach, James, ed. *Slave Narratives: The Greenhaven Press Companion to Literary Movements and Genres.* San Diego: Greenhaven P, 2001.

Truth, Sojourner. *Narrative of Sojourner Truth* (as dictated to Olive Gilbert). 1850. Ed. Margaret Washington. New York: Vintage Classics, 1993.

Washington, Booker T. *Up from Slavery.* 1901. Ed. William L. Andrews. New York: Norton, 1996.

White, Deborah Gray. *Ar'n't I a Woman? Female Slaves in the Plantation South.* New York: Norton, 1985.

Wideman, John Edgar. *My Soul Has Grown Deep: Classics of Early African American Literature.* Philadelphia: Running P, 2001.

Williams, Roland Leander. *African American Autobiography and the Quest for Freedom.* Westport, Conn.: Greenwood P, 2000.

Williamson, Joel. *The Crucible of Race.* New York: Oxford UP, 1984.

Wilson, Harriet. *Our Nig; Or, Sketches from the Life of a Free Black.* 1859. Ed. Henry L. Gates, Jr. New York: Vintage/Random House, 1983.

Wright, Richard. *Black Boy.* 1945. New York: Harper Perennial, 1993.

Suggested Topics for Writing Critical Essays

1. Conduct a comparative analysis of the two authenticating documents in Douglass's *Narrative* or the authenticating documents affixed to Douglass's *Narrative* and Jacobs's *Incidents*.
2. Examine the significance of missing information in a given narrator's quest for identity.
3. Explore the theme of sexual and reproductive exploitation of black women in one or more of the narratives.
4. Explore possible reasons for the contrasting depictions of slavery in antebellum narratives and those narratives written after slavery had ended.
5. Examine the importance and use of literacy in Douglass's and/or Jacobs's narrative.
6. Trace the running discourse on religion and morality in Douglass's and/or Jacobs's narrative.
7. Undertake a comparative reading of any theme represented in Douglass's first two autobiographies.
8. Explore the theme of religious and moral hypocrisy in *Narrative* and *Incidents*.
9. Contrast Harriet Jacobs's engagement with the theme of sexual and reproductive exploitation to Elizabeth Keckley's engagement with the same theme.
10. Note similarities and parallels in Equiano's, Douglass's, and Washington's narratives.

Questions to Guide Your Reading

The Interesting Narrative of Olaudah Equiano

1. Is it significant that Equiano grew up in an African household that included enslaved persons? How does he describe the slavery he experienced in Africa as compared to the type of slavery he experienced in the New World? How did Equiano end up in Great Britain?
2. How does Equiano depict the Middle Passage? Have you read any other freedom narratives in which you received firsthand information about the Middle Passage?
3. What role do religion and literacy play in Equiano's life-transforming experiences? Ultimately, how does Equiano define and represent himself?
4. How does Equiano gain his freedom? Does Equiano believe that slavery is inherently wrong?

5. When is Equiano's narrative published, and what other important document was presented that same year? Why might this coincidence be considered significant?

Narrative of the Life of Frederick Douglass

1. Slavery and freedom are quite literally defined in narratives of this sort. In describing the state of enslavement, Douglass advances a "rhetoric of deprivation." That is, beginning on the first page of the narrative, he starts a running discussion of all the ways that slavery deprives enslaved persons of resources. Try to remember to underline these as you go along. What is the first deprivation of which he speaks? Under what name was Frederick Douglass born?
2. How does Douglass point out how slavery affects black family stability? Note specific passages.
3. When and where does Douglass learn to read? How does he complete the process acquiring the magic of literacy? How important is it to him? How does it affect his life in the long run? What other major event does Douglass represent as having a significant impact on his resolve to be free? Hint: It occurs at Covey's farm.
4. Scholars generally agree that antebellum freedom narratives follow a basic structure: First, they begin with a description of the narrator's birth and early life in slavery; second, they continue with the narrator's growing awareness of his/her reality of slavery and the horror associated with it—usually depicted as entering the doorway to Hell; third, they point out how much moral hypocrisy is a part of the system, while listing further cruelties of the system and expressing a burgeoning desire to be free and planning toward that eventuality; fourth, they describe the escape and joy upon arrival at the North, followed by a resolve to serve in the effort to end the evil institution. See if you can correctly identify these four aspects of Douglass's narrative. There will, of course, be overlap in places.
5. How does Douglass depict women in his story? What roles do women play in Douglass's life, or in what we know of it from this text? What are some of the basic differences among the various slaveholders Douglass represents? How, finally, does Douglass represent himself in *Narrative*?

Incidents in the Life of a Slave Girl

1. Who is Linda Brent? Who is Dr. Flint? Profile each character. What seems to be the most important aspect of Brent's self-identity—of how she identifies herself and her place in the world? Flint's? Elaborate. What is Linda Brent's most pressing need? How important is it for her to be able to claim ownership of her sexuality, of her children, of herself? How, finally, does Harriet Jacobs represent herself? What kind of person is she?
2. Discuss the other characters in this story in terms of their importance to the protagonist (Linda's grandmother, her brother, her children, her parents, Sands, Flint's wife, and so forth). Who or what is Jacobs's touchstone for "evil," for "moral authority"? What do you suppose is the purpose of the story about Luke, about Mr. Litch (chapter 9)?
3. Consider the various ways that Jacobs uses Christianity, the Bible, and biblical references in her narrative. What non-Christian religious references do you encounter?
4. Who are the real-life persons represented by the following characters: Linda, William, Ellen, Aunt Marthy, Flint, Sands?
5. What does Linda Brent say about her sexual compromise (choosing to have sex with Sands to avoid becoming Flint's concubine)? Are there other references to moral/ethical compromise in the text? Elaborate. Upon whom or what does Brent (Jacobs) place the blame for her "corruption"?

Behind the Scenes

1. How did Anne Pleasant become Elizabeth Keckley? Trace the evolution of her naming process. Who was Anne/Elizabeth's biological father?
2. Only a small part of Keckley's narrative deals with her years in slavery. Why is this?
3. Aside from her own personal history, what other historical information and historic events are part of Keckley's narrative?
4. Does Keckley's narrative contain authenticating documents? Of what significance are the documents contained in the appendix?
5. What are the implications of Keckley's apologetic tone in part of her narrative? Speculate as to why she refused to escape from slavery and chose instead to raise the money to purchase herself and her son.

6. Ultimately, how does Keckley represent herself? What three adjectives would you use to describe the person that emerges from the information she provides in *Behind the Scenes*?

Up from Slavery

1. Washington represents slavery as a school. How does he characterize the type of preparation the school of slavery provides? Does he depict it as useful preparation, and if so, in what sense?
2. On the first page of *Up from Slavery*, Washington tries to downplay the fact that he does not know the date of his birth, and scholars point out that he is trying to distance himself from Douglass who made much of this missing information. Does Washington's strategy work, or does it simply call attention to the missing information?
3. How does Washington represent his mother? Was she an important figure in his life?
4. What two adjectives would you use to describe her based on the information Washington provides?
5. Why is Washington's story characterized as a "rags-to-riches" story? In the end, is he a realistic representation of what the typical black person can accomplish at that particular moment in history? Explain.
6. What documents does Washington incorporate *into* his story, and what is the effect of those documents being included? What authenticating documents are attached to Washington's text? Analyze the tone and content of those documents.

CHAPTER II
Fiction Before 1865

Black Americans published very few works of fiction before 1865; such a dearth is due in large part to the political and material realities of colonial and antebellum America. Though the practice of importing Africans to serve as slaves had been outlawed by 1808, and most states outside the American South had made slavery illegal, the slave population in the South actually expanded from 700,000 to 2,000,000 between 1790 and 1830. As the South generally placed greater restrictions on enslaved persons between 1830 and the time of the Civil War, free African Americans invested much of their energy in the abolitionist effort and in the fight against discrimination. Much of the literature they produced and published in this period dealt with slavery and discrimination. It often took the form of the freedom narratives discussed in the previous chapter or other works of nonfiction, such as David Walker's *Appeal* (1829), Henry Highland Garnett's "An Address to the Slaves of the United States of America" (1843), Martin R. Delany's *The Condition, Elevation, Emigration, and Destiny of the Colored People of the United States, Politically Considered* (1852), and Maria Stewart's essays and speeches between 1831 and 1833. Frances Ellen Watkins Harper was also active as a speaker during the antebellum period, and some of those speeches were subsequently published. Ann Plato's *Essays: Including Biographies and Miscellaneous Pieces of Prose and Poetry* (1841) provides one notable exception to the typical fare authors produced during this time. Harper is also believed to have published a volume of prose and poetry, *Forest Leaves* (or *Autumn Leaves*), around 1851, but no actual copy of that title has surfaced. Short pieces from various authors appeared in newspapers such as *Freedom's Journal*.

The list of available published works of fiction from this period includes the following texts: Victor Séjour's short story, "The Mulatto" (published as *Le Mulâtre* in France in 1837); Frederick Douglass's novella, *The Heroic Slave* (1853); William Wells Brown's novel (and neo-freedom narrative), *Clotel* (published in Great Britain in 1853); Frank J. Webb's novel *The Garies and Their Friends* (1857); Frances Ellen Watkins Harper's short stories, "The Two Offers" (1859) and "The Triumph of Freedom—A Dream" (1860); Harriet E. Wilson's autobiographical novel (also called a neofreedom narrative), *Our Nig*

(1859); and Martin R. Delany's *Blake* (1862). As with the previous chapter, we will focus here on five texts: "The Mulatto," *The Heroic Slave*, *Clotel*, "The Two Offers," and *Our Nig*.

Though they often share common concerns, themes, and literary conventions, each of these works reflects something of the unique experience and perspective of its author. Séjour, Harper, and Wilson were all free-born, but the conditions of their everyday lives differed substantially. Séjour, whose full name was Juan Victor Séjour Marcou et Ferrand, was born a free Creole of color in New Orleans in 1817; his parents were Juan François Louis Séjour, a mulatto from Hispaniola, and Eloisa Phillippe Ferrand, born in New Orleans. They were able to accumulate means sufficient to send Victor abroad to continue his formal education. In Paris, he became a well known and highly successful dramatist, though his fortunes would eventually decline. His short story, "The Mulatto," is set in prerevolution Haiti, or Saint Domingue, which shares the island of Hispaniola with the Dominican Republic. Many of the Africans that ended up enslaved in Saint Domingue were taken from Senegal. Thus, "The Mulatto" centers on the fate of Georges, the mulatto son of Laïsa, a beautiful Senegalese maiden, and Alfred, a haughty, unsympathetic French plantation owner.

Frances Ellen Watkins was born free in the slave state of Maryland in 1825. Her mother's name has not come down through the information available from that period, and Harper scholars speculate that the mother was probably unmarried and the father was probably white. Orphaned at an early age, Watkins was reared in the home of her uncle, William Watkins, who instilled in her a solid sense of discipline and devotion to racial uplift. She attended the William Watkins Academy for Negro Youth in Baltimore until she was around thirteen. Thereafter, she found work as a housekeeper, and she was fortunate to obtain a position with a family that allowed her access to books. Through her own initiative, she developed her natural literary talents, eventually directing her substantial gift of writing and public speaking toward the cause of racial uplift before *and* after the Civil War. She married Fenton Harper in 1860, but she was widowed four years later. To date, four Harper novels have been found, three of these in the last two decades of the twentieth century. Harper's best known novel is *Iola Leroy* (1892), considered for most of the twentieth century (before the discovery of the Wilson novel discussed below) to be the first novel published by a black American woman. Harper also wrote regular newspaper columns and served as role model and mentor for younger black women activists; she earned a good living writing and speaking. Her short story, "The Two Offers," focuses on the destinies of two free black women—one who accepts one of two offers of marriage and the other who directs her intellectual and literary abilities toward racial uplift and antislavery activities.

The other woman writer for this period is Harriet E. Wilson. Details about her exact year of birth are sketchy. Wilson scholars locate her birthdate between 1825 and 1828 in Milford, New Hampshire. Born free and mulatto as Harriet E. Adams, she was (like the heroine of her novel) abandoned as a child. Primarily through letters appended to the novel and subsequently unearthed information, we learn that she suffered a fate similar to that of her novel's protagonist. The experience, serving as an indentured servant until the age of eighteen, left her health permanently impaired. She later married Thomas Wilson and bore him a son, George Mason Wilson; Thomas Wilson abandoned the family. Wilson notes in her preface to *Our Nig* that she wrote the novel as a way of earning money to support herself and her child. Her son died only months after the novel was published, and Wilson eventually died in extreme poverty. Thus, the story of Alfrado in *Our Nig* strongly resembles what scholars have been able to piece together of Wilson's life. *Our Nig* has been described as an allegorical representation of a slave/freedom narrative.

Next, we consider the work of Frederick Douglass. Douglass and William Wells Brown are the only two authors we will consider in this chapter who were actually born in slavery. Indeed, they were born only a few years apart—Brown in 1814 in Kentucky, and Douglass in 1818 on the Eastern Shore of Maryland—and both were born of a white man and an enslaved black woman. Both escaped from slavery around the age of twenty—Brown in 1834 from St. Louis, Missouri, and Douglass in 1838 from Baltimore, Maryland. Each subsequently changed his surname, became active in the antislavery movement, and published both fiction and nonfiction that focused attention on the material realities of American chattel slavery. Though each man holds a place of prominence in African American history and literature, Douglass's fame greatly surpasses Brown's in the larger realm of American history and culture.

Douglass's novella, *The Heroic Slave*, is a fictional treatment of an actual historic event—the successful slave revolt aboard the domestic slaver *Creole* in 1841. In the story, Douglass dramatizes the inherent right of African Americans to be free (as he had argued in his 1845 *Narrative*) and provides a portrait of black manhood and heroism in the central character, Madison Washington. Scholars recognize Douglass's novella as the earliest extant work of long fiction published in the United States by an American of African descent.

Similar to *The Heroic Slave*, William Wells Brown's *Clotel* offered a story not likely to be encountered in more mainstream publications. Published in Great Britain the same year as *The Heroic Slave*, *Clotel* is the earliest extant novel published by a black American of either gender. The story is based in part on rumors of a sexual relationship between the third president of the United States, Thomas Jefferson, and Sally Hemings, a black woman enslaved at Monticello (the Jefferson homestead) near Charlottesville, Virginia. The novel explores several generations of sexual exploitation and family disruption in one family primarily through the lives of Currer, her daughters, and granddaughters.

Because so few other works of long fiction from the antebellum period are extant, it seems worthwhile here to take note of them. Frank Webb's *The Garies and Their Friends* chronicles the lives and varying economic destinies of three families from the South—one white family, one light-skinned, mixed-race black family, and one dark-skinned black family. The novel foreshadows some of the economic issues that would surface with the coming Industrial Age and deals with the issue of color and caste. Martin R. Delany's *Blake* centers on the life of a nationalist-minded black hero named Henry who travels all over the south (on an odyssey of sorts) looking for the wife that has been sold away to Cuba. Along the way, he engages in a number of adventures with one major aim: freedom from bondage.

Contexts and Texts

During the last decade of the eighteenth century and the early years of the nineteenth century, African-descended persons living in the French colony of Saint Domingue fought for their independence, eventually renaming their new nation Haiti. Historians cite this event as an underlying reason that the United States was able to acquire the Louisiana Territory from France in 1803 at a substantial bargain. The purchase doubled the size of the new nation and increased the demand for slave labor. The enslaved population grew substantially between 1790 and 1830. Slave codes were enacted in order to control and restrict the growing black population. A 1793 Fugitive Slave Law gave legal sanction to the practice of entering free territory for the purpose of returning to slavery those who had managed to escape. Indeed, while America shaped its new identity within the confines of the paradoxical marriage of slavery and freedom, Thomas Jefferson captured his ambivalence about slavery on paper, particularly in his *Notes on the State of Virginia*. Jefferson thought slavery was wrong, but he also believed Africans to be inferior. Regardless, he owned many human beings and is even believed to have fathered several children by one of the women enslaved at Monticello, the aforementioned Sally Hemings.

In 1829 a free man named David Walker published and began distributing his *Appeal*, which called for African Americans to take militant action to end their oppression. Forced to leave the South because of what was considered a very radical position at the time, Walker died in 1831 under mysterious circumstances. Some believe he was poisoned. That same year the Nat Turner-led Southhampton County Virginia insurrection against slavery struck terror in the hearts of southern slaveholders. Other events surrounding this period of African American literary production include the following: the Missouri Compromise of 1820, which limited the expansion of slavery into new territories; the "new and improved" Fugitive Slave Act of 1850, which effectively made whites in free states *responsible* for returning suspected fugitives to slavery, and generally increased the capacity of slaveholders to seek out and recapture persons who had managed to escape from slavery; the Kansas-Nebraska Act of 1854 repealing significant sections of the Missouri Compromise, thus extending slavery into new territories; the *Dred Scott* decision of 1857, which declared that black people had no rights under the law; and John Brown's doomed raid on Harper's Ferry in 1859. The period also saw the development and evolution of transcendentalist thought, especially in figures such as Ralph Waldo Emerson, Henry David Thoreau, and Theodore Parker. Harriet Beecher Stowe's *Uncle Tom's Cabin* appeared in 1852, and in 1855 Herman Melville published *Benito Cereno*, a fact-based novella about a slave revolt on board a domestic slaver. Melville's novella is often paired with Douglass's *The Heroic Slave*.

With this general context for the literature produced during the period before 1865, we focus first on Séjour's "The Mulatto," whose action is set in prerevolutionary Haiti—or Saint Domingue. Some attention to Haitian history adds richness to Séjour's story and helps to explain why the protagonist initially identified more readily with Alfred, his white master, than with **maroons**. Haiti has been referred to as the first black nation in the New World—though others would give that distinction to Palmares in Brazil, formed at least a century earlier but later destroyed by colonial forces. It is important to note the significance of the French Revolution and, especially, the American Revolution, as major historic events leading up to and surrounding the revolution in Saint Domingue. African-derived people from Saint Domingue served among the French troops who came to America's aid during the Revolutionary War with

Britain. The irony of fighting for American freedom while living under French colonial rule was not lost on them.

According to historians, revolution in Saint Domingue was actually precipitated by a free colored population responding to laws and practices aimed at reversing progress in terms of their legal rights and protections. During the latter part of the eighteenth century in Saint Domingue, people of color outnumbered the French 15 to 1; in order to maintain colonial rule, it was necessary to impose the rule of European superiority while fomenting a caste system and its resultant antagonisms among mixed-race persons. The colored elite (mulattos, quadroons, and octoroons) that had descended from intermarriage and other intimate arrangements with European colonizers had by the late 1700s acquired sizable property interests. They also owned many slaves. The system of laws that had previously protected the interests of mixed-race persons based on the degree of their "whiteness" or European ancestry now sought gradually to divest this same group of the rights and privileges they had enjoyed for generations. In addition, large groups of maroons existed in Saint Domingue. Members of these groups often raided plantations for supplies, women, and other resources. Thus, not long after America's successful revolution ended and the United States Constitution was ratified, persons of African descent joined forces in Saint Domingue to transform it from a French colony to the independent nation of Haiti—established officially in 1804.

Published only thirty-three years after the official establishment of Haiti, "The Mulatto" revisits recent Haitian history and conjures up images of caste divisions. Antoine, the narrator, tells us that Georges almost lost his life trying to protect Alfred from a maroon raiding party. Georges's later decision to take his young son and join the maroons after the plea for his wife's life falls on deaf ears reveals his evolving black consciousness. The argument might be made that the story's central conflict between the mulatto Georges and his European master/father is an allegorical representation of the conflict that united people of color in their successful battle against European colonial rule.

"The Mulatto" opens with a first-person white narrator and soon gives way to the third-person narrative voice of Antoine, an elderly black man. The two converse, and the first-person narrator (who remains unnamed except for the title "Master") asks Antoine to tell him the story of his friend Georges. Though the present moment of "The Mulatto" is set in postrevolution Haiti, over 90 percent of the story is rendered through Antoine's memory of Georges and the recent colonial past. Antoine describes Alfred's purchase of Laïsa, who had been kidnapped from

Senegal and sold into slavery. He describes her subsequent sexual exploitation (tantamount to rape) and the birth of her son Georges. As Georges grows up, he longs to know who his father is, but Laïsa keeps the man's identity secret. On her deathbed, she gives Georges a pouch containing a portrait of his father, but she makes the young man swear that he will not look at it until he turns 25.

Georges grows up to be a loyal slave. When he hears maroons plotting against Alfred, he goes to warn his master, and almost loses his own life trying to save Alfred's life. Touched by the gesture, Alfred provides Georges with medical care. Unfortunately, he also gets a good look at Georges's wife, Zelia, and decides that he must have her. Zelia is unwilling, and in the ensuing struggle, Alfred is slightly injured. He bleeds, and as punishment Zelia is sentenced to be hanged; no amount of pleading on Georges's part will make Alfred speak the words that would save her life. In trying to reason with Alfred, Georges crosses the line between master and slave (and between who is in charge of defining "truth") by suggesting that Zelia was only trying to avoid being raped.

Because slavery as a system functions by denying rights and protections to the enslaved, and because sexual exploitation of enslaved women was a routine part of the system, the defense of "rape" was not likely to hold up in a colonial court, even where the defendant was afforded a trial and allowed to speak on her or his behalf. Though Georges does not live long enough to appreciate the full irony of his charge—because he owed his existence to Alfred's rape of his mother—he demonstrates the depth of his commitment to his wife by broaching the taboo subject. For someone who has demonstrated Georges's degree of loyalty, this behavior is highly significant.

Under threat from Alfred, Georges leaves, vowing revenge; Zelia is hanged. Prior to the actual hanging, two young French children gleefully discuss the coming event with some anticipation, and Antoine includes a description of the carnival-like atmosphere of the actual event in his retelling of the story. Meanwhile, Georges and his young son escape and join a maroon camp. Georges waits three years—until the day that Alfred's adored new wife bears Alfred a long-awaited and treasured son. He then slips back to the plantation and succeeds in killing Alfred and his wife; however, just as he drops the ax on Alfred's neck, Alfred reveals that he is Georges's father. Too late, Georges checks the pouch his mother had given him and realizes that he, too, is doomed, for he has just killed his own father; he dies moments later of a gunshot wound. Students should not miss this tragic story's similarities to the story of Oedipus.

Though the end of "The Mulatto" will seem very contrived to contemporary readers, Séjour succeeds in the tight space of the short story to portray slavery at its most inhumane while introducing a number of themes and issues that continued to appear in the literature well into the twentieth century. In addition, the first-person white narrator prompting a story from an elderly black man is a technique that Charles Chesnutt would use in his short stories over half a century later. The act and prominence of storytelling as a built-in aspect of the story itself figures in the work of a number of American and black American authors, and it is especially prominent in Douglass's *The Heroic Slave*.

The Heroic Slave is set in pre-Civil War Virginia and Ohio; the hero/protagonist travels back and forth between slavery and freedom. In Part I, the setting is Virginia—a natural, somewhat idyllic location in the woods. Narration is from the third-person point of view. The narrator tells us that he will relate the story of a great statesman who has been left out of Virginia's historical records. Several pages later, we learn that the great statesman was once enslaved, and that his name is Madison Washington. Venturing into the woods one day, and thinking himself alone, the enslaved Washington expressed aloud a profound desire for freedom and his resolve to escape from slavery. A northern traveler, appropriately named Listwell ("listen well"), overheard the speech, was deeply moved, and resolved to become an abolitionist. In addition to bringing Listwell and Washington together, Douglass uses this first part of the story to describe Madison Washington as manly and heroic, and to stress those qualities that make him so. Oration, the expression of the voice that announces subjectivity in this context, is an important aspect of Madison's assertion of *manhood* as Douglass represents that quality.

In Part II, the setting is Ohio, and five years have passed since the initial "meeting" between Washington and Listwell in 1835. Madison Washington had indeed escaped from slavery and had come, by chance, upon the Listwell home in Ohio—a free space just across the Ohio River from the slave state of Kentucky. The Listwells *listened well* to Madison's story of escape, fed him, and offered him a nice, clean bed in their home. Douglass reinforces in this section Madison's manliness and his heroic nature—stressing the synthesis of intelligence and mercy, militancy and physical strength. Listwell assists Madison, who makes it to Canada West (the area around Toronto, Ontario) and freedom. The bond between the two men is set.

In Part III, the setting is again Virginia, but this part of the story begins in a tavern that has lost something of its previous splendor. It contrasts nicely with the idyllic setting of Part I. Listwell, stopping there for the night, learned of a slave auction scheduled the following day in Richmond; the next day, he was horrified to see Madison Washington among the men in chains. Washington explained to him that he had been re-enslaved while trying to rescue his wife from slavery, that he could not bear the thought of her remaining in slavery. The information further underscores Madison's heroic nature, and Listwell again assists Madison by slipping him some metal files. The section ends with Madison aboard the domestic slaver *Creole* bound for the southern markets.

Part IV begins with an expression of outrage at the hypocrisy of outlawing the transatlantic slave trade while allowing the domestic practice to continue. Tom Grant, who had been the first mate on the *Creole*, tells the story of the successful Madison Washington-led revolt after the vessel left Virginia. At a coffeehouse in Virginia, Grant converses with Jack Williams, who suggests that it was only through gross mismanagement that a bunch of cowardly slaves got the best of the *Creole*'s crew. In response, Grant explains how the successful revolt occurred, expressing as he does his newfound respect for persons of African descent. He describes Madison Washington in heroic terms, again underscoring Douglass's definition of manliness and heroism as involving a balance of militancy and physical strength, coupled with mercy and intelligence. Thus, the novella's final irony is that Tom Grant, who began the sea journey believing Africans (and African-derived persons) to be inherently inferior, tells the story of Madison Washington's heroism.

The Heroic Slave is Douglass's blueprint for whites interested in aiding the antislavery effort. Published shortly after the harsh new Fugitive Slave Law of 1850 and coming on the heels of the popularity of *Uncle Tom's Cabin*, Douglass's 1853 novella offered white Americans a rationale for continuing to assist fugitives from slavery while providing an example of black manhood that was sorely missing from texts such as *Uncle Tom's Cabin*. The novella also offers a discourse on the "nature of the negro" at a time when even liberal whites wondered whether African Americans had—through scores of generations—been so degraded by slavery that they would only become liabilities in freedom.

Published in Great Britain the same year as *The Heroic Slave*, William Wells Brown's *Clotel* is the earliest extant novel published by a black American. Three subsequent versions of the novel were published in the United States: *Miralda, or The Beautiful Quadroon: A Romance of American Slavery Founded on Fact* (serialized 1860–61); *Clotelle: A Tale of the Southern States* (1864); and *Clotelle, or The Colored Heroine: a Tale of the Southern States* (1867). Brown revised them to make them more palatable to American audiences. The original version of *Clotel* chronicles the lives of three generations of enslaved women who are the descendants of an American president. The story is based in part on rumors surrounding the relationship between Thomas Jefferson and Sally Hemings. DNA testing has lent a certain amount of credibility to rumors that descendants of Sally Hemings are indeed related biologically to descendants of Thomas Jefferson.

The story of Clotel and her disrupted family is preceded by a short biographical piece on Brown, which Brown renders in the third person. *Clotel* is divided into twenty-nine chapters, most of which begin with a verse of poetry. Like Laïsa's story in "The Mulatto," Clotel's story begins at the auction block. Currer, a mulatto woman, and her two quadroon daughters, sixteen-year-old Clotel and fourteen-year-old Althesa, have been put up for sale following the death of their owner. Currer had previously been the slave and concubine of Thomas Jefferson, who purportedly fathered Clotel before he moved on to Washington, D.C. The real Sally Hemings actually remained the property of Jefferson until his death, so students should be warned not to draw direct parallels between Currer and Hemings. In his novel, Brown imagines what might have happened to someone like Sally Hemings. The story is typical of nineteenth-century sentimental literature in that it includes some strong coincidences and moments of high **melodrama**.

On the auction block, Clotel, a beautiful quadroon, is in great demand as a concubine by Richmond's white male elite. Horatio Green purchases her; she becomes his concubine and bears him a daughter/slave named Mary. Clotel becomes emotionally attached to Horatio, but Horatio eventually marries a white woman named Gertrude; being no fool, Gertrude banishes Clotel, but holds on to Clotel's daughter Mary. Mary suffers much abuse at the wife's hands. Sent to Vicksburg, Mississippi, Clotel eventually escapes by disguising herself as an ailing white man traveling with a servant. Here, Brown borrows from the true-life story of William and Ellen Craft, described in William Craft's narrative *Running a Thousand Miles for Freedom* (1860). The Crafts escaped from slavery in Georgia to freedom in Boston in 1848, and their story was known among antislavery activists. Indeed, Brown borrows liberally from several sources, including Lydia Maria Child's "The Quadroons," in crafting this story. Ultimately, slavecatchers track Clotel to Virginia, where she ends up leaping into the Potomac in sight of the house where her father, the president of the United States, resides. In another story line, Currer ends up in Natchez, Mississippi, as the property of a Reverend Peck. She dies there without ever reuniting with her daughters.

Reverend Peck believes that African Americans are subhuman and were meant to serve white Americans. He represents the type of religious hypocrisy that autobiographical narrators such as Frederick Douglass, Harriet Jacobs, and Elizabeth Keckley described in their freedom narratives.

Currer's other daughter, Althesa, had been purchased by a man named Henry Morton. They marry, and she gives birth to Ellen and Jane. When Henry and Althesa die, the children become property to be disposed of on the auction block. Jane ends up dying of a broken heart, and Ellen commits suicide rather than submit to a life of sexual abuse from her new master. Meanwhile, Clotel's daughter Mary helps a fellow enslaved person named George to escape and is sold south for her efforts. She ends up in New Orleans where she meets a Frenchman who helps her escape to France; they marry and he conveniently dies, leaving her available for a liaison with George, whom she encounters (in a very melodramatic moment) quite by chance. The novel closes with their marriage.

Like *Clotel*, Harper's short story, "The Two Offers," tracks the lives of nineteenth-century black women. The women in Harper's story are free, however, and Harper's story is unabashedly didactic. In this story she tackles a topic that recurs in her fiction, poetry, and nonfiction: a woman's need for intellectual development that will lead to self-actualization and ultimately the capacity for a heightened and enlightened level of community service. The story surrounds the options available to two cousins, Laura and Janette. Laura's parents have always overindulged her, and the suggestion is that she expects that things will always work out well for her. The story opens with her considering two simultaneous marriage proposals; hence, the "two offers." Janette, who has grown up comparatively poor but in a nevertheless nurturing environment, is contemplative and self-reflexive. Depicted as the epitome of level headedness, she is accustomed to hardship and hard work. She chooses to develop her intellect, which—as Laura notes—makes her less attractive to men.

Laura follows convention and sets her sights on marriage as the road to personal fulfillment. Janette warns Laura that because she gives serious consideration to both offers of marriage, neither man can really be her soul mate, her true love. Laura, in turn, chides Janette for being too smart to be marriageable. Laura marries the man she considers the better of the two, and Janette leads a single but worthy life as an intellectual and activist in the fight against slavery and other forms of oppression. Janette is self-actualized and has found a way to be an asset to the larger community. (Though Harper was married for four years, and Janette does not marry in the story, one recognizes aspects of Harper's own life in Janette and other characters in her stories and novels.) In the end, Laura dies hoping that her spouse, who has proven to be errant and indifferent, will come and pay his last respects. Laura is a variation of the staple ruined woman character of nineteenth-century domestic fiction. In this case, her ruin is related to the fact that she did not marry for true love, and the suggestion is that her husband turns out to be a philanderer and an abuser of alcohol. In her speeches and essays, Harper was a strong advocate for temperance; she identified intemperance as a major problem confronting the race.

Though she clearly means to engage with **true womanhood** ideology prevalent at the time, she also extends her message that for the race to succeed, it needs exemplary women *and* men. The story is a straightforward discourse on the need for upstanding men as well as upstanding women who will work together for the benefit (uplift) of the entire black community. In the larger society, true women were supposed to exhibit the qualities of piety, submissiveness, domesticity, and chastity. Harper's true women found a way to self-actualize while being of service to racial progress. Though Laura would seem (on the surface) to be a prime candidate for true womanhood in the larger society, both she and her husband are useless in Harper's scheme for racial progress. Thus, the meaning of the story's title changes from Laura's two offers of marriage to a woman's choices for self-actualization. Harper suggests through Janette that there is more than one way to be a true woman. Janette does not close off the possibility for marriage. Rather, Harper suggests with this character that such *overlooked* women might possibly make better partners in the long run. By including the fact of two offers of marriage for Laura, versus none for Janette, she underscores a tendency among men to pass over the Janettes of the world to get to the Lauras.

The protagonist of Harriet Wilson's 1859 *Our Nig* was too preoccupied with basic survival and too isolated from the black community to be concerned with its uplift. One understands from reading the novel that Alfrado had no ready access to a supportive black community (or at least no awareness of such access), and it was *she* who needed *the community* for her own uplift. The novel, whose full title is *Our Nig; or, Sketches from the Life of a Free Black, In a Two-Story White House, North. Showing that Slavery's Shadow Falls Even There,* centers on the life of Alfrado, who as a child of six is abandoned by her mother and stepfather. She spends the next twelve years as an indentured servant in the home of the Bellmont family. A mulatto, whose biological father is described in the story as African, Alfrado is the archetypal abandoned, and subsequently abused, child. Numerous examples of such children exist in literature from this period.

With the exception of the final chapter, Alfrado's story proceeds from the third-person perspective, though some chapter headings, such as "A New Home for Me" and "My Father's Death," suggest a first-person point of view. Scholars have noted that the novel bears a strong resemblance to narratives about slavery (freedom narratives), at least in terms of structure and certain elements of plot and theme (as discussed in chapter 1). For example, a period of youthful innocence comes to an abrupt halt, as the child becomes aware of his or her status as an enslaved or indentured person. The initiation into the hellish nightmare of slavery precedes a recounting of cruelties witnessed and suffered. Evil characters are juxtaposed against good ones. Scholars point out that the evil Bellmonts (Mrs. Bellmont and her daughter Mary) represent the South, and the kinder Bellmonts (Mr. Bellmont, Aunt Abby, and Mary's siblings) personify the well-meaning but generally ineffectual North. Alfrado embodies, of course, the enslaved person whose exploited labor benefits both groups either directly or indirectly. Alfrado is assigned substandard living quarters away from the main dwelling.

Epigraphs announce and summarize the themes of the novel's twelve chapters. The opening chapter tells a condensed tale of Mag Smith, Alfrado's mother, who was seduced and then abandoned—left to bear the shame of out-of-wedlock pregnancy alone. The child dies, but the experience and her subsequent impoverished condition so "lower" Mag's status in the white community that she marries a black man, Jim, out of economic necessity. Proud of his prize, Jim literally works himself to death trying to care for the family. After his death, Mag takes another lover, Seth, and they decide that they are better off without so many mouths to feed; by the beginning of the novel's third chapter, they have abandoned Alfrado to her fate at the Bellmont home. Alfrado endures years of cruel misuse and abuse at the hands of Mrs. Bellmont and her daughter Mary. Mr. Bellmont is sympathetic to Alfrado's plight, but, more often than not, he turns a deaf ear to Alfrado's maltreatment in order to get along with his wife. Mary's siblings, Jack, Jane, and especially James, are portrayed as genuinely kind and concerned, but they, too, are ineffectual. Aunt Abby, Mr. Bellmont's sister, does what she feels she can do to assist Alfrado without jeopardizing her own precarious situation. She manages to direct Alfrado toward church and Bible study. Indeed, while she is with the Bellmonts, Alfrado's only source of empowerment comes through her embrace of Christianity in the white church, where God is represented as white and male, and heaven is for whites only. Nevertheless, Alfrado finds through her faith a means by which to develop a measure of personal dignity and self-esteem, which she calls upon to resist Mrs. Bellmont's physical abuse.

Wilson depicts the young Alfrado as a delightfully devious child, who survives life at the Bellmonts by becoming resourceful and resilient. In a moment reminiscent of the battle between Frederick Douglass and the cruel Edward Covey in *Narrative* (1845), and which, in a literary sense, precedes Elizabeth Keckley's ongoing battles with an abusive school master and a Pentecostal minister in *Behind the Scenes* (1868), Alfrado finally stands up to Mrs. Bellmont. At the age of eighteen, her period of servitude ends, but by that time, her health has been permanently damaged by all the years of abuse and overwork. She finds a job with a woman described as truly Christian, but she is soon swept off her feet by a man described as a bogus ex-slave orator named Samuel. She accepts his offer of marriage, becomes pregnant, and is subsequently abandoned. She and her child end up in the poorhouse. Samuel returns and rescues them for a brief period, but he leaves again. At story's end Alfrado is busy trying to earn money for her family's support. The story offers a discourse on such topics as gender roles, miscegenation, indentured servitude, racial prejudice, religious hypocrisy, the color and gender of God, and motherhood.

Interestingly and ironically, the letters appended to the novel certify the authenticity of a story represented as fiction and point to the fact that Alfrado's story is indeed Harriet Wilson's story. Thus, Wilson's novel blurs the line between autobiography and fiction even as Alfrado's story blurs the line between slavery and freedom. Wilson's novelization of much of her own life story offers a view of what it meant to be a poor, black single mother in the middle of the nineteenth century. The novel received scant critical attention when it first appeared and all but disappeared into obscurity but for several references to it by other writers. Scholars suggest that the poor showing can be attributed to several factors; among them are problematic portrayals of black characters, the depiction of a black man marrying a white woman and fathering her children, the unflattering depiction of northern whites, and the use of the derogatory "Nig" in the title. Even during the period of the late 1960s through the 1970s, when black studies departments began to appear and created the academic space for the search and recovery of African American texts, Wilson's novel remained effectively buried; it was recovered through diligent scholarly research and subsequently reissued in 1982.

Recurring Themes and Issues

The most subtle theme in Séjour's short story has to do with the question of identity, represented in Georges's lack of self-knowledge, in his lifelong desire to know his father, and in his final identification with the group that exists as a physical manifestation of resistance to slavery. While it seems critically irresponsible to read into Georges's initial misplaced loyalty to Alfred some inherent or subliminal filial connection, authors from Douglass forward have addressed the issue of a multifaceted American identity that takes into account the fact of mixed African and European heritage (see, for example, Patricia Williams). In Octavia Butler's science fiction novel, *Kindred* (1979), the protagonist—a contemporary black woman—travels back in time and is confronted with the requirement of saving the life of the cruel slavemaster ancestor from whom she descended in order to guarantee her own continued existence. Thus, themes related to identity formation often examine the most basic and primary relationships between children and their parents.

Such questions and explorations concerning parentage and identity are prominent also in *Clotel* and *Our Nig*. Interestingly, and coincidentally, these two texts along with Séjour's short story focus on the lives of mixed-race characters. Séjour, himself the son of a mulatto from Hispaniola and an octoroon from New Orleans, certainly must have known something of implications of miscegenation and the intricate web of skin color and caste. His protagonist in "The Mulatto" learns only a moment before his death the identity of his father, whom he has just killed; prior to that event he has joined forces with other Blacks in a statement of black nationalism. William Wells Brown also explores the theme of miscegenation in representing Clotel as the offspring of a United States president and the black woman who serves as his concubine; Alfrado is the daughter of a white woman and an African man.

The use of the tragic mulatto in African American literature has often received criticism for seeming to suggest that mulattos, being part European, are more deserving of sympathy and/or humane treatment than full-blooded Africans. One possible explanation for the use of the character type is that it illustrates the degree to which slavery corrupts white men, who exploit sexually those over whom they have power and who subsequently enslave their own children. Another possible explanation is that whites in the position to help end the institution would identify more readily with enslaved persons who looked white. Scholars point out as well that the mulatto character in African American literature well into the twentieth century signifies the reality of ongoing sexual relations between African Americans and white Americans even during the years of Jim Crow segregation. In the late nineteenth and early twentieth centuries, the mulatto character gained prominence in novels of passing.

Voice and oration are important aspects of the literature discussed above. Students should pay particular attention to the significance of storytelling in "The Mulatto" and *The Heroic Slave*. In "The Mulatto," Antoine must give voice to Georges's story and to the allegorical tale of pre-revolutionary Haiti. In *The Heroic Slave*, Madison's overheard "soliloquy" about his desire for freedom helps pave the way for his successful escape to Canada and eventually to his second successful escape. Tom Grant gives voice to Madison Washington's heroism and manhood, and Douglass's retelling of Washington's story and the story of the *Creole* kept it visible and accessible to subsequent generations. Frances Ellen Watkins Harper's storyteller relates the story of Janette who was able to use her literary eloquence in the antislavery effort. William Wells Brown tries to give voice and visibility to the historical memory of Sally Hemings, who quietly bore black property for an American president's heirs. Harriet Wilson's voice provides testimony about the experience of a black woman who served as an indentured servant in the North during the nineteenth century. In *Our Nig*, Alfrado uses her voice to call a halt to Mrs. Bellmont's brutal physical assaults.

Four of the texts in this section deal directly with New World slavery and/or involuntary servitude. The fifth, "The Two Offers," deals indirectly with the topic. All focus attention on the idea of "freedom" in a literal and/or figurative sense of that concept. Examining this concept through black American fiction published before 1865 should help students toward an understanding of the preoccupation with freedom and liberation (even when that means liberation from a narrative form or other prescriptive tendencies) that drives black American literary production into the twenty-first century.

Séjour's short story set a number of precedents in terms of themes and issues that would be broached in future works of African American literature. Eight years after Séjour published "The Mulatto" in France, Frederick Douglass's 1845 narrative appeared. Douglass, whose father is believed to have been his master, Aaron Anthony, began his narrative by addressing the issue of parentage—of white slaveowners who were both father and master to their offspring. Harriet Jacobs makes the subjects of family disruption and the sexual and reproductive exploitation of enslaved women central to *Incidents in the Life of a Slave Girl* (1861). Elizabeth Keckley raises the issue briefly in *Behind the Scenes* (1868), and the theme continued to surface in black American women's literature throughout the twentieth century. Its most notable recent manifestations are found in Toni Morrison's neofreedom narrative *Beloved* (1987) and Alice Randall's *The Wind Done Gone* (2001). Closely related to the subject of sexual exploitation is the lack of legal protection, or rather how law and custom worked in tandem to give sanction to slavery and its inhumane practices. Séjour's short story indicates that despite the fact that Alfred meant to force Zelia to have sex with him, it was Zelia who ended up being executed. Students can find a real-life counterpart to Zelia's story in the story of a Missouri bondwoman named Celia as it is reconstructed in Melton A. McLaurin's *Celia, a Slave* (1991).

Students should note in particular the following recurring themes and issues for the texts discussed in this chapter: moral and/or religious hypocrisy, perversions of Christianity, the importance of literacy, the quest for manhood, sexual and reproductive exploitation, motherhood (the outraged mother figure), the definition of black womanhood, miscegenation, color and caste, black nationalism, family disruption, and the combined effect of race, class, and gender discrimination on the lives of black women. For example, in *Our Nig*, Christianity and hypocrisy receive substantial attention. When Alfrado is attracted to Christianity, Mrs. Bellmont, an ardent professer of religion, reveals her hypocritical nature by trying to dissuade the child from her Bible studies and conversion. She also discourages Alfrado from reading. Wilson connects Alfrado's ability to resist her most strident oppressor to her growing spirituality and literacy, her ability to perceive. Literacy and perception are also highlighted in Douglass's *The Heroic Slave*; however, Madison Washington's manhood and heroic nature are much more apparent concerns in Douglass's work.

Bibliography

Andrews, William L. "The 1850s: The First Afro-American Literary Renaissance." *Literary Romanticism in America*. Ed. Andrews. Baton Rouge: Louisiana State UP, 1981. 38–60.

—. "The Novelization of Voice in Early African American Narrative." *PMLA* 105 (1990): 23–34.

Andrews, William L., Frances Smith Foster, and Trudier Harris, eds. *The Oxford Companion to African American Literature*. New York: Oxford UP, 1997.

Barksdale, Richard, and Keneth Kinnamon, eds. *Black Writers of America: A Comprehensive Anthology*. Upper Saddle River, NJ: Prentice Hall, 1972.

Brown, William Wells. *Clotel, or The President's Daughter*. 1853. Bedford Cultural Edition. Ed. Robert S. Levine. New York: Bedford/St. Martin's, 2000.

Butler, Octavia. *Kindred*. 1979. Boston: Beacon P, 1988.

Carby, Hazel. *Reconstructing Womanhood: The Emergence of the Afro-American Woman Novelist*. New York: Oxford UP, 1987.

Delany, Martin R. *Blake; or, The Huts of America*. 1862. Introd. Floyd J. Miller. Boston: Beacon, 1970.

—. *The Condition, Elevation, Emigration, and Destiny of the Colored People of the United States*. 1852. Baltimore: Black Classic Press, 1993.

Douglass, Frederick. *The Heroic Slave*. 1853. *Three Classic African-American Novels*. Ed. William L. Andrews. New York: Mentor/ Penguin, 1990.

duCille, Ann. *The Coupling Convention: Sex, Text, and Tradition in Black Women's Fiction*. New York: Oxford UP, 1993.

Ellison, Curtis W. *William Wells Brown and Martin R. Delany: A Reference Guide*. Boston: G. K. Hall, 1976.

Ernest, John. *Resistance and Reformation in Nineteenth-Century African-American Literature*. Jackson: UP of Mississippi, 1995.

Farrison, William Edward. *William Wells Brown: Author and Reformer*. Chicago: U of Chicago P, 1969.

Foster, Frances Smith, ed. *A Brighter Coming Day: A Frances Ellen Watkins Harper Reader*. New York: The Feminist P, 1990.

Garnet, Henry Highland. *An Address to the Slaves of the United States of America*. 1848. *Call and Response: The Riverside Anthology of the African American Literary Tradition*. Ed. Patricia Liggins Hill et al. Boston: Houghton-Mifflin, 1998.

Gates, Jr., Henry Louis. *Figures in Black: Words, Signs, and the "Racial Self."* New York and Oxford: Oxford UP, 1987.

Gloster, Hugh M. *Negro Voices in American Fiction*. Chapel Hill: U of North Carolina P, 1948.

Harper, Frances Ellen Watkins. *Iola Leroy*. 1892. *Three Classic African-American Novels*. Ed. Henry Louis Gates, Jr. New York: Vintage, 1990.

—. "The Triumph of Freedom—A Dream." 1860. *A Brighter Coming Day: A Frances Ellen Watkins Harper Reader*. Ed. Frances Smith Foster. New York: The Feminist P, 1990. 114–17.

——. "The Two Offers." 1859. *A Brighter Coming Day: A Frances Ellen Watkins Harper Reader*. Ed. Frances Smith Foster. New York: The Feminist P, 1990. 105–14.

Jackson, Blyden. *A History of Afro-American Literature. Vol. 1. The Long Beginning, 1746–1895*. Baton Rouge: Louisiana State UP, 1989.

Levine, Lawrence W. *Black Culture and Black Consciousness: Afro-American Folk Thought from Slavery to Freedom*. New York: Oxford UP, 1977.

Loggins, Vernon. *The Negro Author in America: His Development to 1900*. New York: Columbia UP, 1931.

McDowell, Deborah E., and Arnold Rampersad, eds. *Slavery and the American Literary Imagination*. Baltimore and London: Johns Hopkins UP, 1989.

Moses, Wilson Jeremiah. *Black Messiahs and Uncle Toms: Social and Literary Manipulations of a Religious Myth*. University Park: Pennsylvania State UP, 1993.

Nelson, Dana. *The Word in Black and White: Reading "Race" in American Literature, 1638–1867*. New York: Oxford UP, 1992.

Peterson, Carla L. *"Doers of the Word": African-American Women Speakers & Writers in the North (1830–1880)*. 1995. New Brunswick: Rutgers UP, 1998.

Plato, Ann. *Essays; Including Biographies and Miscellaneous Pieces, in Prose and Poetry*. 1841. Introd. Kenny J. Williams. New York: Oxford UP, 1988.

Redding, J. Saunders. *To Make a Poet Black*. Chapel Hill: U of North Carolina P, 1939.

Séjour, Victor. "The Mulatto." 1837. *Norton Anthology of African American Literature*. Ed. Henry L. Gates, Jr., et al. New York: Norton. 1997.

Smith, Valerie. *Self-Discovery and Authority in Afro-American Narrative*. Cambridge: Harvard UP, 1987.

Stepto, Robert B. "Storytelling in Early Afro-American Fiction: Frederick Douglass's 'The Heroic Slave.'" *Black Literature and Literary Theory*. Ed. Henry Louis Gates, Jr. New York: Methuen, 1984. 175–86.

Sterling, Dorothy. *We Are Your Sisters: Black Women in the Nineteenth Century*. New York: Norton, 1984.

Stewart, Maria W. *Maria W. Stewart: America's First Black Woman Political Writer, Essays and Speeches*. Ed. Marilyn Richardson. Bloomington: Indiana UP, 1987.

Sundquist, Eric J., ed. *Frederick Douglass: New Literary and Historical Essays*. New York: Cambridge UP, 1990.

Webb, Frank J. *The Garies and Their Friends*. 1857. Introd. Robert Reid-Pharr. Baltimore: Johns Hopkins UP, 1997.

Williams, Patricia J. "On Being the Object of Property." *The Alchemy of Race and Rights: Diary of a Law Professor*. Cambridge: Harvard UP, 1991. 216–36.

Wilson, Harriet. *Our Nig; or, Sketches from the Life of a Free Black*. 1859. Ed. Henry L. Gates, Jr. New York: Vintage/Random House, 1983.

Yellin, Jean Fagan. *The Intricate Knot: Black Figures in American Literature*, 1776–1863. New York: New York UP, 1972.

Zafar, Rafia. *We Wear the Mask: African Americans Write American Literature, 1760–1870*. New York: Columbia UP, 1997.

Zanger, Jules. "The 'Tragic Octoroon' in Pre-Civil War Fiction." *Amerycan Quarterly* 18 (1966): 63–70.

Suggested Topics for Writing Critical Essays

1. Explore the use of the mulatto figure in two or more texts.
2. Explore the theme of sexual and reproductive exploitation of black women under slavery, or explore the theme by comparing and contrasting its treatment in a work of fiction from this chapter and an autobiographical work from the previous chapter.
3. Identify and analyze expressions of black nationalism.
4. Identify the most important aspects of the identity quest in a given text. How are "slavery" and "freedom" defined?
5. Examine one or more texts in terms of how they function as allegorical slave (freedom) narratives or as neoslave (freedom) narratives.
6. Explore the importance of voice and oration as these relate to subjectivity in one or more works.
7. Conduct a comparative analysis of the treatment of "manhood" and "heroism" in two texts.
8. Discuss the use of nineteenth-century literary conventions in one or more of the texts, or compare two texts in terms of common literary devices and/or narrative strategies.
9. Identify types and archetypes in several of the works and note differences and similarities in how they function in each.
10. Compare and contrast the lives of the free black women represented in Harper's story with those in Wilson's story, or

conduct a comparative analysis of Séjour's short story and the Langston Hughes play of the same title written a century later.

Questions to Guide Your Reading

"The Mulatto"

1. Describe the story's narration and the effect of that narration on the story being provided.
2. Consider the following issues in terms of the historical information that is implied in "The Mulatto": French colonization, the transatlantic slave trade, legally sanctioned treatment of enslaved men and women, and resistance to slavery.
3. Upon realizing that the man he has just killed is not only his master but also his father, Georges exclaims that he is doomed. Does this story sound familiar to you? Where have you heard it before, and is there a relationship to be drawn between the two stories? Why does Georges not learn of his father's identity before this moment?
4. During the course of this story, Georges undergoes a major transformation. Trace his personal evolution from loyal servant to rebel.
5. What events in the story suggest that Georges undergoes a *crisis of identity*?

The Heroic Slave

1. Note the significance of Virginia in the opening page of Douglass's story. How many times is it mentioned and why? With whom and what does Douglass wish to associate Madison Washington? Does all the action take place in Virginia? Note the various settings for significant events: Listwell overhearing Madison, Madison and Listwell's subsequent first meeting, Madison and Listwell's second meeting, the shipboard revolt, the retelling of the revolt.
2. Who is Listwell and why is he significant to the story? What happens to Listwell after he overhears Madison Washington's "soliloquy" on freedom near the beginning of the story?
3. How does Douglass define "heroism" in *The Heroic Slave*? What qualities does Douglass stress in his portrayal of Madison Washington, and where are they emphasized in the story?
4. How is perception (seeing, feeling, hearing [listening well/Listwell]) related to Madison Washington's capacity to

resist the oppressive conditions in his life? How is "manhood" represented?

5. The role of the storyteller is significant in this story. Describe scenarios in which witnessed events are passed along to others through storytelling.

Clotel

1. Describe some of the types and archetypes Brown makes use of in delivering this story.
2. Look closely at the more melodramatic moments in the story. What happens during each? What happens immediately preceding and following each? Which characters are involved?
3. What is the basic difference between Georgiana Peck and her father?
4. What happens to each of the women Brown represents as being the descendants of Thomas Jefferson?
5. Why do you suppose Brown removed references to Thomas Jefferson in subsequent editions of the novel that were published in America?

"The Two Offers"

1. What is the basic difference between Laura and Janette?
2. How does this story address the nineteenth-century ideology of true womanhood? What four qualities have been identified as central to the true woman? How does Harper revise or modify the definition of true womanhood?
3. How does Harper make use of certain types and/or archetypes from nineteenth-century literary convention? Conduct a compurgative analysis of Harper's story and another short story from the period.
4. How does Harper define "true manhood"?
5. What, finally, are the "two offers" implied by the story's title? In what ways can you see the notion of "two offers" expanded beyond the surface level of the text?

Our Nig

1. Is Alfrado free or enslaved? Is this a freedom narrative or a novel? Explain. What purpose is served by the documents in the appendix?

2. Do you agree that this story is an allegorical freedom narrative? Explain why you agree or disagree. Is Alfrado a tragic mulatto? Why?
3. Which chapter epigraphs do you find particularly effective, and why? What point of view does the narrator take? How do some chapter titles work against this perspective?
4. What types or archetypes do you find in this story? In what other works of nineteenth-century literature have you encountered villains like Mrs. Bellmont? What other examples of motherhood are depicted in *Our Nig?*
5. Why doesn't Alfrado simply leave the Bellmonts? Other than Alfrado, whom does Wilson portray as the most sympathetic character among the Bellmont household? Explain.

CHAPTER III
Fiction 1865–1911

The purpose and character of African American literature for the period between 1865 and 1911 is captured in two important nineteenth-century observations. Negative portrayals of African Americans abounded in white American literature of this and subsequent periods, and all too often they served as the basis upon which African Americans were judged. In the midst of the Civil War, William Wells Brown stated in *The Black Man, His Genius and His Achievements* (1863) that, through his writing, he hoped to provide evidence that would vindicate the Negro's much maligned character. Some thirty-two years later, when African Americans were being lynched at record levels, Victoria Earle Matthews wrote in *The Value of Race Literature* (1895) that black people must use their writing to counteract the effects of racism and racist representations in American culture. Brown, Matthews, and others like them understood the power of literature and the value of literary representation. Speaking partly in response to this phenomenon, author Pauline Hopkins wrote in the preface to *Contending Forces* (1900) that, "I am not actuated by a desire for notoriety or for profit, but to do all that I can in an humble way to raise the stigma of degradation from my race."

Faced with a rising campaign of black demonization, brutal lynchings, and social and economic apartheid that characterized the half century following the Civil War, black writers saw it as their imperative duty to represent black Americans in the most positive light. Much of the fiction black Americans produced during this unique period sought either to demonstrate that the black community possessed the requisite character and ability to take on the reins of American citizenship, and/or it protested the unequal and increasingly brutal treatment of African Americans under America's brand of democracy. To a lesser degree, the writers also tried to illustrate the psychological impact of race-based discrimination on whites. Stories, with some exceptions, were often rendered in the form of the sentimental romance, a popular form of writing in the nineteenth century. Through exemplary black characters and enlightened white characters, authors offered moral guidance and instruction on how to assist in overcoming the effects of slavery and racism. Oftentimes, the purpose for writing—to aid in the cause of uplifting the race—was made explicit and included in the preface.

Fiction writers of this period included William Wells Brown (1814–1884), Charles Waddell Chesnutt (1858–1932), W. E. B. Du Bois (1868–1963), Paul Laurence Dunbar (1872–1906), Sutton Elbert Griggs (1872–1933), Frances Ellen Watkins Harper (1825–1911), Pauline Hopkins (1859–1930), James H. W. Howard (?–?), Amelia E. Johnson (1858–1922), Emma Dunham Kelley-Hawkins (?–?), Alice Moore Dunbar-Nelson (1875–1935), and a few others. Before moving to the fiction of this and subsequent periods, students should read W. E. B. Du Bois's *The Souls of Black Folk* (1903), particularly the chapter titled "Of Our Spiritual Strivings" in which Du Bois provides the definition for the term ***double-consciousness***.

Significantly, all the works to be considered in this chapter were published after 1890. American literary production in general before the Civil War was small compared to what came after the war. The increasing popularity of the novel, cheaper modes of production, and a growing reading public all contributed to increased literary production after 1865. In the decades following the Civil War, some white American writers were able actually to earn a living from their writing. For a variety of reasons, this achievement was more difficult for black American writers, especially those who chose to write about America's race problem. William Wells Brown's 1867 version of *Clotel* (originally published in 1853—discussed in chapter 2) was long believed to be the only black American novel published during Reconstruction. (James Howard published *Bond and Free* in 1886.) Only in the last decade of the twentieth century did two "new" Frances Harper novels from the Reconstruction period—and one since then—come to light. Scholar Frances Smith Foster *excavated* the three novels and published them in a single volume. *Minnie's Sacrifice* (1869), *Sowing and Reaping* (1876–77), and *Trial and Triumph* (1888–89) first appeared in serialized form in the *Christian Recorder*, a periodical published by the African Methodist Episcopal Church. Like *Iola Leroy* (1892, previously believed to have been Harper's only novel), these three works reflect Harper's steadfast devotion to the cause of racial uplift. *Minnie's Sacrifice* centers on miscegenation and the life of a mulatta who chooses to devote her life in service to "the race" rather than enjoy the benefits of passing for white. (Other writers of this period would echo the "loyalty to race" theme in their fiction and nonfiction.) Harper's *Sowing and Reaping*, subtitled *A Temperance Story*, is about the evils of alcohol consumption and its potential for destruction at the individual, family, and community levels. Harper, like other writers in the racial uplift vein, was a strong advocate for temperance (as Harper called intemperance one of the three great evils facing the black community at the time); thus, the need for temperance is a recurring sentiment in the fiction from this period. The third newly excavated Harper novel, *Trial and Triumph*, is perhaps the most autobiographical of her novels. The protagonist is an orphan (as Harper was), and the strongest, most upstanding members of the black community must assist in her transformation from a mischievous, morally ambiguous child to a morally upright and self-actualized young woman (a teacher/poet) who, like Harper, becomes a valuable asset to her community. *Iola Leroy* is, however, the Harper novel most likely to be encountered in a college classroom and the one upon which we will focus in the next section. For most of the twentieth century, it was considered the first novel published in the United States by a black woman. (Harriet Wilson's *Our Nig*, published in 1859, now bears that distinction.)

As they were writing during one of the most regressive periods in terms of race relations, the five authors discussed below were forced either to compromise their voices and visions, to find subversive means of getting their messages across, and/or to rely on alternatives to mainstream publishing to get their stories into print. In this chapter we will consider the following representative works of fiction: Harper's *Iola Leroy* (1892); Chesnutt's "The Goophered Grapevine" (from *The Conjure Woman*, 1899), and "The Wife of His Youth" (from *The Wife of His Youth and Other Stories of the Color Line*, 1900); Dunbar-Nelson's "Sister Josepha" (from *The Goodness of St. Rocque and Other Stories*, 1899); Hopkins's *Contending Forces* (1900); and Dunbar's *The Sport of the Gods* (1902). All five authors were born of free parents (though Dunbar's parents had previously lived in slavery), and each wrote and published in more than one genre. A brief sketch of Harper's life is included in chapter 2 with the discussion of her short story, "The Two Offers."

The next author for consideration is Charles Chesnutt, who was born to free parents—Andrew Jackson and Anne Maria Sampson Chesnutt—on June 20, 1858, in Cleveland, Ohio. His paternal grandfather, Waddell Cade, was a wealthy white North Carolina tobacco merchant who carried on a sexual relationship with Chesnutt's grandmother, Ann Chesnutt. Committed to racial justice, Chesnutt's parents migrated from Fayetteville, North Carolina, to Cleveland before he was born. After the Civil War, they moved back to Fayetteville where they ran a grocery business. Chesnutt actually attended a school founded by the Freedman's Bureau. Like his mother (who had secretly taught black schoolchildren before the war), he became a schoolteacher, and subsequently continued his own education; in 1878 he married fellow teacher Susan Perry. He eventually served as principal at the North Carolina normal school he had attended before leaving the South (moving first to New York and then to Cleveland) to pursue a career in writing. (He had published his first short stories as early as 1872 while he was still living in the South.) Having studied stenography and law, Chesnutt passed the Ohio bar and joined a law firm. He also wrote and worked as a court reporter before his literary career flourished and again after it began to wane. Contemporary scholars credit Chesnutt with having made a significant contribution toward charting a new direction in African American literature—for the creation of literature that is distinctly and uniquely grounded in black life and experience.

With the publication of "The Goophered Grapevine" by *Atlantic Monthly* in 1887, Chesnutt gained entry into the realm of mainstream publishing. He managed in this and subsequent short stories to veil his political attitudes about race while, on the surface, continuing in the **plantation tradition** popularized by established white authors of the day. In 1899 and 1900, Houghton-Mifflin published *The Conjure Woman* and *The Wife of His Youth and Other Stories of the Color Line*, respectively. Chesnutt's short stories had enormous crossover appeal, but his novels were less well received because in them he grappled more overtly with the very real problems African Americans faced in a brutally hostile racial climate. Extant novels published during his lifetime include the following: *The House Behind the Cedars* (1900)—made into a film by Oscar Micheaux in 1921—a story about the tragic life of Rena Walden, a light-skinned black woman who chooses to pass for white (rather than devote herself to black racial uplift); *The Marrow of Tradition* (1901), based on the events surrounding the 1898 election and the subsequent massacre of African Americans in the Wilmington, North Carolina, riots; and *The Colonel's Dream* (1905), which focuses on the efforts of a southern white man to "do the right thing" by working against prejudice in his community, and the tragic repercussions that ensue. Several other efforts in the novel form—including *The Rainbow Chasers*, *Evelyn's Husband*, *Mrs. Darcy's Daughter*, *Paul Marchand, F.M.C.*, and *The Quarry*—were deemed unpublishable during Chesnutt's life, but very recently *Mandy Oxendine* (which some believe to be Chesnutt's first novel), *Paul Marchand, F.M.C.*, and *The Quarry* have been published. In this last work, which Chesnutt submitted unsuccessfully for publication in the 1920s, the author turns the notion of African Americans passing for white on its head by portraying an enlightened white character who chooses to pass for black ("Negro" in that context) in order to experience firsthand what it meant to live behind the veil of double-consciousness. We are reminded of Frederick Douglass's Mr. Listwell from *The Heroic Slave*, who, upon overhearing the enslaved Madison Washington's soliloquy on freedom, is transformed from observer to activist (see chapter 2). Politically active during the New Negro Movement, Chesnutt would come to identify with the "Old Guard" which, echoing the refrain of William Wells Brown, Victoria Earle Matthews, and Pauline Hopkins, called for literature that would continue to counter negative depictions of African Americans by casting them in the best possible light. Some residual effects of this mandate continued to affect African American literary production and criticism throughout the second half of the twentieth century.

Following Chesnutt is Alice Ruth Moore Dunbar-Nelson, who published short stories, poetry, essays, and plays. Once married to the much better known Paul Laurence Dunbar, Dunbar-Nelson has only recently begun to receive attention for her contributions to black American letters in the late nineteenth and early twentieth centuries. When contemporary feminist scholar Akasha Gloria Hull published Dunbar-Nelson's diary in 1984, she reintroduced the writer as a bisexual woman with a strong feminist spirit. Dunbar-Nelson was the younger of two daughters of a New Orleans Creole couple, Joseph (a seaman) and Patricia Wright Moore (a seamstress). As Alice Ruth Moore, she took advantage of the educational opportunities available to her; entering college at the age of fifteen, she completed a two-year teacher training program, and studied courses in law, nursing, printing, and stenography. Her teaching career spanned several decades, having begun when she was only seventeen. She acquired additional formal schooling at Cornell and Columbia, living for a time with aforementioned journalist Victoria Earle Matthews in New York City. It was also in New York that she first met Paul Laurence Dunbar in February of 1897. As the story goes, he proposed to her on their first meeting (he had seen a photo of her in *Boston Monthly Review*), and the couple were secretly married the following March. The marriage, reportedly plagued with a plethora of problems—including intraracial prejudice and charges of spousal abuse—was short-lived.

Dunbar-Nelson was politically active, having served as Executive Secretary for the American Friends Interracial Peace Committee between 1928 and 1931. She published two individual collections of her work, and during her lifetime a number of her essays, poems, and stories appeared in periodicals such as *Crisis* and *Opportunity*, two major venues for poetry and short fiction by budding black artists of the day.

She also edited two anthologies, wrote newspaper columns for the *Pittsburgh Courier*, and finished two novels—*Confessions of a Lazy Woman* and *This Lofty Oak*—neither of which was published during her lifetime. The story we will consider in this chapter, "Sister Josepha," is chosen from her best work in short fiction, the short story collection titled *The Goodness of St. Roque and Other Stories* (1899). Like the other stories in *St. Rocque*, "Sister Josepha" is set in New Orleans; it centers on the plight of a young woman, a beautiful bastard, who has come of age in a Catholic Church-run orphanage and who "chooses" to remain there as the lesser of two extremely limited options (virgin or whore). The author reveals in the piece her sensitivity to issues surrounding gender and caste in New Orleans Creole culture.

We move next to author Pauline Hopkins, who was born in Portland, Maine, to Northrup and Sarah Allen Hopkins. Her father had migrated from Virginia; her mother, a native New Englander, was related to poet James M. Whitfield and the famous Paul family that founded Baptist churches in the Boston area. Hopkins attended public school in Boston where, at the age of fifteen, she won ten dollars in a writing contest. Her paper was titled "Evils of Intemperance and Their Remedy." Hopkins graduated from Boston's Girls High School. She penned two plays—*Colored Aristocracy* in 1877, and *Slaves' Escape: Or the Underground Railroad* (later changed to *Peculiar Sam, or the Underground Railroad*) in 1879. The second play was produced and performed at Boston's Oakland Garden in 1880 by the Colored Troubadours, a group composed of Hopkins and several family members. Deeply influenced by writer/activist William Wells Brown (who had presented the prize money for the contest she won at fifteen), by the turn of the century Hopkins was publishing serialized novels and short stories in the *Colored American Magazine* (*CAM*). The magazine was published by The Colored Cooper-active Publishing Company of Boston, which also published Hopkins's best known work, *Contending Forces*. Hopkins served for a time as editor of *CAM*, but she lost the post in 1904, purportedly after repeatedly voicing her objections to the policies of Booker T. Washington, who was in the position to have her displaced by another editor. In line with other more radical thinkers, Hopkins felt (and stated openly) that Washington's accommodationist policies were not in the long-term best interests of African Americans.

After her exit from *CAM*, she opened her own publishing company in 1905; in 1916 she cofounded *New Era* magazine. That same year she published *Topsy Templeton*, a novella. In addition to publishing, she worked for the Massachusetts Bureau of Statistics and later for MIT.

Like other black women writers and activists of the day, Hopkins was concerned about racial matters in general, and gender matters in particular. Following in the vein of Frances Ellen Watkins Harper and, perhaps less obviously, Harriet Jacobs, Hopkins uses *Contending Forces* to confront the ideology of true womanhood and charges in the popular press that black women lacked virtue. Her goal was to provide positive images of black womanhood, and also to join in Harper's call for true men as well as true women to serve the interests of moving "the race" forward.

The next writer of this group is perhaps the best known—Paul Laurence Dunbar. Dunbar's parents Joshua and Matilda Murphy Dunbar had lived in slavery, though his father actually escaped from slavery and later served with the Union army during the Civil War. Dunbar attended the public schools of Dayton, Ohio, but it was his mother who taught him to read; from his parents he heard many stories about slavery that would form the substance of much of his own writing in later years. Best known for his dialect poetry (which some have criticized as his concession to a racist publishing industry and white reading audience), Dunbar also wrote novels, essays, and songs. His early childhood experience of the oral storytelling via his parents' recollections of plantation life prepared him well for the role he would later play in turning the black American folk experience into literature.

As the only black student at Dayton's Central High School, Dunbar distinguished himself by becoming an outstanding scholar, eventually editing the school paper and serving as class poet and Literary Society president. Two years after graduation, the Church of the Brethren Press published his first volume of poetry, *Oak and Ivy*. Dunbar also met and became associated with Frederick Douglass and other black leaders of the period. His professional work (like Chesnutt's) ultimately found its way into mainstream journals, including *Atlantic Monthly* and the *Saturday Evening Post*. White readers generally preferred his dialect poetry, particularly when it seemed to depict slavery in a positive light. Dunbar was merely capturing the spirit of the "good times" enslaved persons managed to create for themselves despite, and in spite of, the very real impact of slavery on their lives in general. Dunbar, of course, wrote equally well in Standard English. Eventually, he published eleven volumes of poetry and several volumes of short and long fiction, including *The Uncalled* (1898), *Folks from Dixie* (1898), *The Strength of Gideon and Other Stories* (1900), *The Fanatics* (1901), and *The Sport of the Gods* (1902). This last work, which we will explore further below, tackles a number of important issues. Its story line examines the implications of black demonization in the popular imagination. It responds to the questions: What happens when theft (or morality in general) is racialized? What are the social implications of adopting the mindset that African Americans are natural-born thieves, or inherently corrupt and deviant? What is the psychological impact of racism on the racist, of bigotry on the bigot?

Finally, we need to consider briefly the presence of author Sutton Griggs at this historic moment. Though we will not look at his work here—because it is highly unlikely that it would be encountered in an undergraduate curriculum—students should be aware of Griggs's uniqueness among the writers of this period. Largely self-published, Griggs was an early advocate for a "New Negro" who was revolutionary rather than reactionary. Born in Chatfield, Texas, in 1872 to a Baptist minister and his wife, he later became a Baptist minister and served at churches in Tennessee, Texas, and Virginia. He published his early work with Orion Publishers, a company he ran. Later works were published by a social uplift organization, the National Public Welfare League, which Griggs founded in Memphis. He published five novels: *Imperium in Imperio* (1899), *Overshadowed* (1901), *Unfettered* (1902), *The Hindered Hand; or, The Reign of the Repressionist* (1905), and *Pointing the Way* (1908). His work gives voice to a militant perspective seldom if ever found in the work of other black writers of the period. In *Imperium in Imperio*, Griggs envisions an underground organization of educated, militant black Americans who would fight to eradicate injustice or, failing that, to establish an autonomous state in Texas. The Imperium, or governing arm of the organization is revolutionary rather than reactionary. The novel ends, however, with the organization perched on the edge of destruction because of political infighting among would-be leaders. When Griggs died in Denison, Texas, in 1933, much of his work had already been forgotten.

Contexts and Texts

By the end of 1865, fugitive slave laws had been repealed, slavery had been outlawed by the Thirteenth Amendment, the Freedman's Bureau had been established, and General Sherman had ordered that black families receive up to forty acres of land each (though this order would later be reversed by Andrew Johnson). Elizabeth Keckley, who had purchased her freedom in 1855, described in *Behind the Scenes* the destitute condition of many of the newly freed people streaming into Washington, where she lived and worked during and after the Civil War. In response to what she witnessed, Keckley founded the Contraband

Relief Society to aid in their transition from slavery to freedom. Harriet Jacobs and her daughter Louisa would join other volunteers assisting in the monumental task of transition by going south to establish refugee centers, schools, hospitals, and other kinds of service centers. Time and again, Frances Ellen Watkins Harper in her fiction, poetry, speeches, and essays would remind the black community of its need to function as a cooperative.

Adult black males in the rebel states had been granted the franchise with the 1867 Reconstruction Act, and the Fifteenth Amendment (1870) would extend this right to all male citizens regardless of race. During Reconstruction African Americans were elected to the U.S. Senate and House for the first time. Recognizing the immediate need to educate and retrain millions of new citizens, the Freedman's Bureau established thousands of new schools between 1865 and 1870, and some of these became the black colleges and universities still operating today—Fisk, Morehouse, Howard, Atlanta University, and Hampton, for example.

While the country in general turned its attention toward Reconstruction following the Civil War and the assassination of Abraham Lincoln, white supremacist groups—including The White Brotherhood, Jayhawkers, The Pale Faces, The Knights of the White Camellia, The Rifle Clubs of South Carolina, and the Ku Klux Klan—sprang up to launch a campaign of terror and intimidation against African Americans in the South. Indeed, in the midst of Reconstruction, white rule was restored in one southern state after another; state legislatures enacted Black Codes to restrict black social and political mobility, particularly in the South. The Reconstruction Act of 1867 had been designed in part to outlaw Black Codes and stem the tide of terrorism and racial scapegoating that was gaining momentum, but it was not enough to hold back the fury and determination of humiliated and impoverished southern whites. As anti-black terrorism increased, African Americans left the South—migrating north and west, while some fourteen million European immigrants settled in the Northeast and Midwest between 1860 and 1900. New York City's population grew from five hundred thousand in 1850 to three and a half million in 1900. Chicago's population grew to two million during the same period.

When Reconstruction was officially dismantled, and federal troops were withdrawn from the South, the social and political climate degenerated for black Americans, particularly those living in the South. The decades following Reconstruction have come to be known as the nadir for African Americans in the United States for several reasons. Among these are the legal reversal of gains acquired under the Civil

Rights Acts of 1866 and 1875, the defeat of an important public education bill in 1890, and the systematic demonization of African Americans and blackness in the popular imagination. The latter was represented most notably in Tom Dixon's work, especially *The Leopard's Spots* and *The Klansman*, upon which D.W. Griffith's film *The Birth of a Nation* was based.

Though Booker T. Washington proudly pointed out, among other things, that President McKinley had visited Tuskegee Institute in 1898 (two years after the *Plessy* decision, the same year of the election that sparked the Wilmington, North Carolina, riot that is the subject of Chesnutt's *The Marrow of Tradition*), McKinley and the Republican party had increasingly turned their backs on African Americans and allowed the southern states to solidify their program of Jim Crow segregation and systematic disenfranchisement. Across the South (and in some places in the North) the landscape was dotted with the graves of the tortured, murdered black victims of lynchings. Such social conditions would endure well into the twentieth century, and real change would not come until after mid-century. More African Americans were lynched in post-Reconstruction 1892 than during any other year. Congressman George H. White of North Carolina—one of few elected African Americans still remaining in a state legislature by this time—would introduce the first antilynching bill (which never left the Judiciary Committee) on January 20, 1900. The specter of lynching found its way into novels, poems, plays, essays, and speeches. Certainly it was a topic of conversation among the characters in Frances Harper's *Iola Leroy*, coming as it did during the peak year of mob violence against black Americans and featuring a title character who bears the *pen name* of Ida B. Wells-Barnett, the journalist known for her lynching investigations.

Iola Leroy is a product of miscegenation—though her parents are married to each other. She grows up believing that she is not black, and only learns that she is legally Negro when her parents die and a bigoted paternal cousin enslaves her. Thus, she loses the affluence she has enjoyed for the first part of her life. Though the circumstances of this transformation are unpleasant, Harper chooses not to portray Iola as a tragic mulatta who, like William Wells Brown's Clotel, becomes a tragic victim, plunging to her death in the Potomac in sight of the White House where her father resides. Iola not only survives her enslavement and rescue, but she also dedicates her life to racial uplift—foregoing the chance to marry a white doctor and pass once again into affluent white society. She becomes a teacher, activist, and writer; she marries a black man who shares her sense of dedication to social activism and becomes his equal partner in "the cause."

The sentimental romance form works well in this capacity, as Harper means to portray Iola as an exemplary, extraordinary, idealized human being, able to triumph over the extreme circumstances of her life (though the reader might argue that Iola was actually enslaved for a very short period). Highlighting Harper's admonition that community service—rather than rugged individualism—should rule the day, Iola makes her commitment to racial uplift the core of her path to self-actualization. The novel begins in the midst of the Civil War when Iola must be rescued from slavery. Several enslaved persons discuss their duplicity in planning to escape by joining the Union soldiers even as they pretend to their masters that they know little about the war and are content in their status as slaves. Here, Harper illustrates beautifully the idea of double-consciousness (predating Du Bois) in combination with **masking** (or veiling). After joining up with Union forces, one member of this group, Tom Anderson, calling Iola a great beauty, suggests that they rescue her from a nearby plantation. Many readers will no doubt take issue with the fact that Iola's great beauty is attributed in large part to her near white appearance. A similar problematic exists with William Wells Brown's title character Clotel (chapter 2) and Pauline Hopkins's Sappho Clark in *Contending Forces* (discussed below). After Iola is rescued, she serves as a nurse to the many sick and wounded soldiers. She so impresses the white Dr. Gresham that he proposes marriage—though he knows she is legally black. He wants her to live as a white woman, but she chooses to be black and, so, refuses his offer of marriage.

The story then meanders back to a time twenty years earlier when Eugene Leroy had inherited his parents' estate, which included a number of enslaved persons. He confides to his cousin Alfred Lorraine his plans to educate Marie and make her his wife. Lorraine is appalled. Eugene and Marie marry and have three children, Harry, Iola, and Grace, all of whom could easily pass for white. Grace dies quite young, but Harry and Iola have reached adulthood when they learn of their racial heritage. When Eugene Leroy contracts fever and dies, Alfred Lorraine sues to have Marie and Eugene's marriage declared illegal and causes Marie and Iola (whom he lures away from a northern school) to be sold as slaves. Iola manages to forewarn Harry, who is in school in Maine.

After the war, Iola learns that one of the men who helped rescue her from slavery, Robert Johnson, is her long lost uncle. Both set out in search of other family members, and through a series of coincidences typical of the nineteenth-century sentimental romance, the family is reunited. Before moving to the North, Iola teaches for a short time at a school for newly freed persons, but angry whites burn the school down. In the North, Robert and Iola become part of a black community forum, a *conversazione*, on issues confronting the race; here Harper uses the fictional forum setting to incorporate parts of her own public speeches—a routine occurrence in her fiction. Iola meets her future husband, Frank Latimer, at a *conversazione*. Harper represents them as the perfect couple, soul mates, and equal partners. They marry and move to North Carolina to continue their activism. Indeed, the story ends in two marriages, for Iola's brother Harry marries Lucille Delany. The story of Iola's liberation from slavery and devotion of her life to the cause of racial uplift bears strong similarities (in terms of structure and plot) to the freedom narratives discussed in chapter 1. Though contemporary readers are likely to see the novel as utopian and idealized, it is also grounded firmly in history—its plot mirroring a number of historic events—and it offers straightforward political commentary on the major barriers to black progress and self-determination in the postwar period.

Charles Chesnutt's "The Goophered Grapevine" takes a more humorous approach (at least on the surface) to dealing with issues confronting the black community following the war. Students who have read Victor Séjour's "The Mulatto" (1837) will recognize immediately a similarity in terms of narrative structure to Chesnutt's "The Goophered Grapevine": an elderly black man retelling a story at the behest of an overriding white narrator. (The one divergence is that in Séjour's story, the white narrator never returns after the black man begins to tell the story.)

Julius McAdoo is a formerly enslaved person who has found a way to make a living from the scuppernong grapes that grow on a former plantation. A northern white man, looking for a suitable southern location for his winemaking business, pays several visits to the North Carolina location. On the last visit before purchasing the property, he and his wife encounter McAdoo, who proceeds to tell them a story designed to dissuade them from purchasing the property. Invoking the image of the tar baby from folk tales and perhaps invoking the phrase "I heard it through the grapevine" (since McAdoo has clearly learned of the couple's intentions from someone), he proceeds to tell the story about how the valuable wine-producing grapevines were goophered in order to keep the enslaved population from sampling them at will. To "goopher" is to conjure or cast a spell upon, and conjuring connotes images from the folk tradition that have to do with the ability to invoke through ritual or other means the process necessary for transformation. The owner of the plantation hires Aun' Peggy, a conjure woman, who after certain procedures, pronounces the grapevines goophered and deadly to anyone partaking of the grapes from them.

Julius McAdoo continues with the story, explaining how a series of coincidences involving the deaths of people who have partaken of the grapes lends support to her proclamation, and, consequently, keeps locals away from the grapes. Eventually, a certain newcomer named Henry unwittingly samples the grapes, and Aun' Peggy proposes further suggestions in the form of a "fix" to save him from the effects of the original conjure. Ultimately, Henry displays signs of becoming "one" with the grapevines, graying and becoming old in the late fall and winter, but coming back to life in the spring and summer. Noting the pattern, his owner sees another avenue for capitalistic exploit and begins to sell Henry every spring for a premium price and buy him back at a much lower rate late in the year.

At some point word apparently gets out (perhaps via the "grapevine"), and a man appears who claims that he can show the plantation owner how to improve substantially his grape production; in reality, he sabotages the vines and they, along with Henry, die the following year. Julius McAdoo's point: the grapevines are worthless. The northerner sees through McAdoo's story and buys the plantation, but he hires the elderly man as his coachman, and—though he has no real way of knowing how much money McAdoo was making from the grapes—declares that he believes he is paying him more than he was making before. Thus, one might sum up the story as follows: A self-employed small businessman named Julius McAdoo becomes the servant of a northern white man, and the white man thinks that McAdoo is better off. The surface reader misses the underlying story about slavery, the exploitation of black labor, the hoarding of resources by whites with African Americans literally being kept "out of the garden." The story might also be considered an allegory for the process of colonizing and controlling the means of production for previously self-subsisting societies. The conventional reading of this story, however, posits McAdoo as the **trickster** who manages to secure regular employment (which does not mean he is precluded from continuing his winemaking business).

"The Wife of His Youth" is a more overtly serious story; it concerns a formerly enslaved black man, whose enslavement had been doubly wrong because he was born of free parents and enslaved illegally after they died. The story shares the theme of illegal enslavement with Harper's *Iola Leroy* and Hopkins's *Contending Forces*. Rendered from the third-person point of view, the narrative begins by introducing Mr.

Ryder, who has long since escaped from slavery and become one of the most conservative members of a social organization of affluent African Americans. Though Ryder is easily recognized as Negro, many of the members of the club could easily pass for white; indeed, such clubs as this are sometimes referred to as "blue vein" societies because of the ease at which many members' veins can be seen through their light skin. Ryder is introduced as someone who recognizes the inherent value in group members' proximity to whiteness, and he advocates moving "forward" toward whiteness rather than "backward" toward blackness. He is the group's most eligible bachelor, and the time has come for him to make known his desire to marry one of their own.

On the day of the ball that he has planned in honor of the woman to whom he plans to propose, an aged, dark-skinned, formerly enslaved woman arrives at his home. She is in search of a husband she has not seen since he fled slavery some twenty-five years before; she has been sent to Mr. Ryder because of his past assistance and counsel with others undergoing such searches. The woman tells a heartbreaking story, but Ryder offers her little hope, and she departs vowing to continue her search. That night, when Ryder is to give a response toast, he instead poses to the resplendent group gathered around him the story of a man wrongfully enslaved and then forcefully separated from an older wife who subsequently spent some twenty-five years searching for him. He explains that the man had put the past behind him, changed his name, moved up in the world, and indeed looked nothing like his former self. The supposedly hypothetical question he then asks is whether the man should, upon encountering the old wife, give up the hope of life with a younger woman from his own new social circle, and acknowledge the former liaison. Led by the younger woman in whose honor the ball was held, the group agreed that the hypothetical man should honor the former wife—the wife of his youth. He does, and the story ends there. In effect he is choosing "blackness" over "whiteness"—opting to align himself with "the race" in the most fundamental way possible.

In a striking departure from the racial themes of this period, Alice Moore Dunbar-Nelson's "Sister Josepha" deals more overtly with gender matters. The short story is set in a convent orphanage in New Orleans. Sister Josepha had come to the convent as simply "Camille" at the age of three. Her lack of a last name suggests that she is, at the least, a child of questionable parentage. She grows into a great beauty within the confines of the convent. As a teenager, she is offered the chance to leave the convent via adoption, but the lechery she sees in her potential adoptive father's eyes frightens her deeper into the folds of the

Sisterhood. Even so, she realizes that she yearns for something she can not find within the confines of the convent. In an overheard conversation, Camille hears two older nuns speak with disdain about her limited options. With no last name, outside of the protection of the Church and her vows, she would have little chance to move beyond the limitations of caste. Camille is convinced by story's end that she must remain constrained to her vows and a life that constricts and constrains. The story speaks to the limited options for women and especially for an attractive poor woman of questionable birth living in Catholic, caste-conscious New Orleans at the end of the nineteenth century. The two options presented for Camille, nun or compromised womanhood, suggest that Dunbar-Nelson was well aware of a prevailing ideology (cult of true womanhood) that served to desexualize certain classes of women (white women of privilege) and oversexualize others (women of color and working-class women).

The heroine of Pauline Hopkins's *Contending Forces*, Sappho Clark, also spends time in a New Orleans convent, but for very different reasons than Camille/Sister Josepha. Hopkins's novel returns us to some of the themes from *Iola Leroy*: slavery and freedom, family disruption and reunion, miscegenation and deprivation of birthright, compromised womanhood, and the ever-present problems of lynching, disenfranchise-mint, and social inequality in general. Like Harper, Hopkins uses the form of the sentimental romance, and the story ends happily with marriage. The novel begins in retrospect, taking the reader back to the late eighteenth century when Britain anticipated a gradual end to slavery. The owner of some seven hundred enslaved persons on the British island of Bermuda, Charles Montfort responded by moving his home base to South Carolina in order to manumit his human property more gradually—since the United States lagged decades behind Great Britain in outlawing slavery. Hopkins's narrator explains that intermarriage and mixed breeding had caused much intermixing of African and European blood in Bermuda. Montfort could not be certain that he or his wife Grace were not part African, but neither did it concern him. In Bermuda, it was not altogether uncommon for mulattos to amass substantial wealth and property, including slaves.

Once Montfort's intentions to free his human property became public knowledge, rival planter Anson Pollock murdered him and claimed his wife Grace as his concubine. He uses as justification Grace's questionable racial identity and the fact that Montfort planned to emancipate his slaves; such an act would have violated South Carolina law and custom, which would prove disruptive to the order of things.

Pollock then made slaves of Montfort's sons, Charles and Jesse. Subsequently, Grace escaped through suicide, Jesse fled to the North, and an Englishman purchased Charles, transported him to England, and set him free. Jesse married and his progeny became the Smith family whose South Boston boarding house serves as the setting for most of the present moment (late nineteenth century) action of the story. The beautiful but mysterious Sappho Clark and John Pollock Langley (a descendant of the evil Anson Pollock) are both boarders at the Smith home.

Will Smith, grandson of Jesse Montfort, is a Harvard philosophy student; Hopkins uses W. E. B. Du Bois as a model for Will Smith. Two competing schools of black leadership (represented by Du Bois and Booker T. Washington, the reigning black leader) were emerging at the time. Though Hopkins was known to have been openly critical of Booker T. Washington's accommodationist plan for "racial progress," she displays a certain sympathetic stance toward his views in constructing Dr. Arthur Lewis, a character modeled loosely on Washington. Lewis is the head of a technical school in Louisiana. He eventually wins the hand of Will's sister, Dora, who must first disentangle herself from her engagement with the evil John Pollock Langley. Hopkins draws Langley and his predecessor Anson Pollock as innately evil, unethical men driven by their baser instincts of lust and greed.

Will Smith falls in love with Sappho Clark, who is described as a beautiful mulatta with a secret past. Sappho is in reality Mabelle Beaubean of New Orleans. As an attractive middle-class teenager, she had been kidnapped by her father's white half brother and placed in a house of prostitution for several weeks and subsequently subjected to humiliation and abuse. When she was finally rescued, she was with child. Placed in a convent until the child's birth, Mabelle becomes Sappho, and her child Alphonse is placed with Mabelle's aunt. The nuns tell everyone that Mabelle Beaubean is dead, but she arrives at the Smith boarding house as Sappho Clark. All are drawn to her beauty, which (as with Harper's Iola Leroy) seems to have much to do with her near-white appearance, though she is endowed with certain attractive *internal* qualities—such as grace and an independent spirit.

When John Langley discovers that Sappho has a secret past, he tries to blackmail her into becoming his mistress. She leaves town to avoid harming Will with her "scandalous" past, but she leaves behind a letter that reveals John for the scoundrel he is. Dora subsequently breaks her engagement with John, and a frustrated Will goes abroad to study. John Langley goes west in search of gold and dies in a mining accident. A series of melodramatic coincidences brings Will and Sappho back together, and the story concludes with the marriages of the two Smith siblings. Will exemplifies the qualities of true manhood, and thus he is not deterred by Sappho's past and the fact that she has a child. By depicting Sappho as worthy of the town's most desirable bachelor, Hopkins manages to write her own definition of womanly virtue that closely echoes Harriet Jacobs's almost forty years earlier. Clearly, both women bowed to some extent to literary and social convention, but they equally as clearly demonstrate the hypocrisy underlying the charge that black women lack virtue in regard to their sexual selves.

Hopkins's novel serves as a record of middle-class service to "the race," while refuting the prevailing notion that black women had been so degraded by slavery that they lacked virtue. With Sappho's particular experience, Hopkins graphically depicts the white man's complicity in the sexual degradation of black women. Like other black women of her era, Hopkins used her writing to help counter unflattering images of black women, especially in regard to their sexuality. Such women saw it as their particular task to portray black women as intelligent, hardworking, and sexually virtuous (or chaste) in response to the prevailing ideology that women of color and working-class women in general were innately sexually immoral and therefore available for men's baser needs. Thus, like Harper, Hopkins successfully combined her mission of racial uplift with feminist/womanist consciousness. She also successfully thematizes the Washington/Du Bois debate over the black social and political agenda.

Like the works discussed above, Paul Laurence Dunbar's *The Sport of the Gods* makes use of mainstream literary convention to speak to issues of grave concern to black Americans living in the United States in the postwar and post-Reconstruction years. The Hamiltons, a hardworking black family, have lived and worked on the Oakley estate since slavery times. The black family patriarch, Berry, and his wife Fanny have served the family loyally for some thirty years. The Hamiltons live in a comfortable home with their son and daughter, Joe and Kitty; they eat well, dress well, and even have managed to save a substantial amount of money. Other African Americans envy them, however; when Berry is wrongly accused of stealing money that has in reality been squandered by Oakley's brother, the black community takes delight in Berry's plight. Berry is convicted and sentenced to ten years in prison based largely (and ironically) on the fact and size of his savings account. Scandalized, the remaining Hamilton family members are eventually evicted from the Oakley estate. The black community ostracizes them, and they migrate to

New York City to start over. However, the mean urban environment soon takes its toll on the provincial southerners, who are ill-prepared to deal with the worst that such an environment has to offer. Joe ends up murdering his girlfriend, Kitty becomes part of a vaudeville act, and Fanny is tricked into marrying a gambler who abuses her.

Dunbar also focuses on the impact of the false theft accusation and resulting imprisonment of the innocent Berry on the white family that accused him. Oakley learns from his brother the truth about the money, but to protect family honor, he refuses to do the right thing by Berry, who continues to languish in prison. The moral compromise has a strong adverse emotional and mental effect on Oakley. Finally, Berry is freed from prison when a northern journalist specializing in sensational stories learns of the situation and manages to set into motion the process by which Berry is freed. Conveniently and coincidentally, Fanny's new husband dies, Fanny and Berry remarry, and the couple moves back South to live once again in their cottage on the Oakley estate.

Recurring Themes and Issues

Perhaps more than the literature of any other period, the literature of this period featured themes that dealt directly with the problem of incorporating four million new Americans into the fabric of American life while dealing with an angry, humiliated, hostile South and a largely apathetic and patently racist North. Chesnutt, Dunbar, Harper, and Hopkins all addressed the fragile economic and social situation for African Americans during this period. Harper's *Iola Leroy, or Shadows Uplifted* was released in 1892, the same year that marks the peak for lynchings of black Americans. In addition to the proliferation of lynchings, these authors addressed a number of other issues confronting the black community: temperance, education, criminality, the search for missing family members, women's rights, and the criteria for true womanhood and true manhood. The period also witnessed the beginning of what came to be called the Women's Era, when black women's clubs were organizing for a variety of social causes and especially to formulate a response to attacks on black women's virtue that occurred in popular media. The overwhelming theme of *Iola Leroy* (and other works produced during this unique period) is that of racial uplift, making it the first order of business, even when one might achieve a measure of individual freedom and social status simply by passing for white. As the larger society celebrated the spirit of rugged individualism, Harper and others called for the spirit of cooperation. In *Iola Leroy*, for example, four characters who could easily pass for white and lead lives of relative affluence, choose instead to identify as Negro. The literature also speaks to the quagmire people encountered when they tried to find relatives who had been traded or sold during slavery. Antebellum freedom narratives especially demonstrate that family disruption was an inherent and common aspect of the peculiar institution. The theme is central to Harriet Jacobs's *Incidents in the Life of a Slave Girl* (see chapter 1). Chesnutt's "The Wife of His Youth," beautifully and poignantly illustrates the extent to which one woman would go to find her husband, and what he would give up in turn to honor his original vows. Harper, Hopkins, and Dunbar likewise stress the theme of the black "family reunion," to bring together those families disrupted by the operations of slavery or its aftermath (as in the case of the Hamilton family in Dunbar's novel).

These authors also stress "legitimizing the race" through marriage, education, and economic prosperity. *Iola Leroy* and *Contending Forces* both feature families that are so racially mixed they render absurd the idea of racial purity. Nevertheless, in the United States the norm under chattel slavery was to count African Americans as property and whites as heirs to property, so regardless of who fathered whom, property rights belonged to whites. Harper demonstrates this reality when her title character undergoes a reversal of fortune because a greedy bigot knows she is part Negro. Similar circumstances befall Hopkins's Sappho Clark, who is not enslaved but is, nevertheless, robbed of her birthright.

Time and again Harper used her fiction and nonfiction to warn against the evils of intemperance, and to advocate for strong moral principles to a community that had suffered the degrading effects of enslavement. Realizing that desperation breeds desperate behavior, Harper incorporated key elements of her public speeches and essays into her fictional work. In general, the literature from this period featured characters who espoused the values of morally upright women and men—or in the case of Harper and Hopkins, the values of true womanhood and true manhood.

Dunbar's novel thematizes the unstable social situation of African Americans in late nineteenth-century America. In the end, the Hamilton family chooses the lesser of two poor options. Dunbar's novel was one of the first to discuss the impact of northern migration on rural African Americans. Dunbar uses his plot to represent the popular ideology that African Americans removed from slavery and white paternalism would regress to some subhuman, deviant species. Sadly, the Hamiltons' limited options in freedom render them not free at all. Alice Dunbar-Nelson used a couple of recurring symbols—the closing door, the veil—to represent limited options as well for her aracial female characters like

Sister Josepha. A very light-skinned Creole, Dunbar-Nelson focused less on race and the problems of the color line than the other writers in this group. Their emphasis on miscegenation, passing, morality, and property rights reflects the state of race relations at that historic moment. Their works were, in hindsight, highly prescriptive, designed to address extremely pressing social issues during a very bleak period.

Bibliography

Andrews, William. L., ed. *The African-American Novel in the Age of Reaction: Three Classics*. New York: Mentor, 1992.

Andrews, William L., Frances Smith Foster, and Trudier Harris, eds. *The Oxford Companion to African American Literature*. New York: Oxford UP, 1997.

Bell, Bernard. *The Afro-American Novel and Its Tradition*. Amherst: U of Massachusetts P, 1987.

Brown, Sterling. *The Negro in American Fiction*. Washington: The Associates in Negro Folk Education, 1937.

—. "A Century of Negro Portraiture in American Literature." *Black Insights*. Ed. Nick Aaron Ford. New York: Ginn & Company, 1971.

Brown, William Wells. *The Black Man, His Antecedents, His Genius and His Achievements*. 1863. The Basic Afro-American Reprint Library. New York and London: Johnson Reprint Corporation, 1968.

Butler, Octavia. *Parable of the Sower*. New York: Four Walls Eight Windows P, 1993.

—. *The Sport of the Gods*. 1902. Introd. Kenny J. Williams. New York: Dodd and Mead, 1981.

—. *The Strength of Gideon and Other Stories*. 1900. Introd. Darwin T. Turner. Salem, N.H.: Ayer Company, 1990.

—. *The Uncalled: A Novel*. 1898. Miami: Mnemosyne, 1969.

Dunbar-Nelson, Alice Moore. *The Goodness of St. Rocque and Other Stories*. 1899. Freeport, N.Y.: AMS P, 1975.

Emigration and Migration Proposals: Solutions to the Negro Problem, Part III, Volume II, Anti-black Thought 1863–1925. Series ed. John David Smith. New York and London: Garland P, 1993.

Ernest, John. Resistance and Reformation in Nineteenth-Century African-American Literature. Jackson: UP of Mississippi, 1995.

Foster, Frances Smith, ed. *A Brighter Coming Day: A Frances Ellen Watkins Harper Reader*. New York: The Feminist P, 1990.

Frederickson, George M. *The Black Image in the White Mind: The Debate on Afro-American Character and Destiny, 1817–1914*. New York: Harper and Row, 1971.

Gates, Jr., Henry Louis. *Figures in Black: Words, Signs, and the "Racial Self."* New York and Oxford: Oxford UP, 1987.

Gloster, Hugh M. *Negro Voices in American Fiction.* Chapel Hill: U of North Carolina P, 1948.

Greene, J. Lee. *Blacks in Eden: The African American Novel's First Century.* Charlottesville: U of Virginia P, 1996.

Griggs, Sutton. *The Hindered Hand; or, The Reign of the Repressionist.* 1905. New York: AMS P, 1969.

—. *Imperium in Imperio.* 1899. New York: AMS P, 1975.

Gruesser, John Cullen, ed. *The Unruly Voice: Rediscovering Pauline Elizabeth Hopkins.* Urbana: U of Illinois P, 1996.

Harper, Frances E. W. *Iola Leroy, or Shadows Uplifted.* 1892. College Park, Md.: McGrath Publishing Co, 1969.

—. *Minnie's Sacrifice* (1869), *Sowing and Reaping* (1876–77), and *Trial and Triumph* (1888–89). Ed. Frances Smith Foster. Boston: Beacon, 1994.

—. "The Two Offers." 1859. *A Brighter Coming Day: A Frances Ellen Watkins Harper Reader.* Ed. Frances Smith Foster. New York: The Feminist P, 1990. 105–14.

Harris, Trudier. *Exorcising Blackness.* Bloomington: Indiana UP, 1984.

Hopkins, Pauline E. *Contending Forces.* 1900. Introd. Richard Yarborough. New York and Oxford: Oxford UP, 1988.

—. *The Magazine Novels of Pauline Hopkins.* Introd. Hazel V. Carby. New York and Oxford: Oxford UP, 1988.

Howard, James H. W. *Bond and Free: A True Tale of Slave Times.* 1886. College Park, Md.: McGrath, 1969.

Hull, Gloria. *Color, Sex, and Poetry: Three Women Writers of the Harlem Renaissance.* Bloomington: Indiana UP, 1987.

—, ed. *Give Us Each Day: The Diary of Alice Dunbar-Nelson.* New York: W. W. Norton, 1984.

—, ed. *The Works of Alice Dunbar-Nelson.* 3 Vols. New York and Oxford: Oxford UP, 1988.

Jackson, Blyden. *A History of Afro-American Literature. Vol. 1. The Long Beginning, 1746–1895.* Baton Rouge: Louisiana State UP, 1989.

Johnson, Amelia E. *Clarence and Corinne; or, God's Way.* 1890. Introd. Hortense Spillers. New York: Oxford UP, 1988.

Kelley, Emma Dunham. *Megda.* Introd. Molly Hite. New York and Oxford: Oxford UP, 1988.

Kelley-Hawkins, Emma Dunham. *Four Girls at Cottage City.* Introd. Deborah McDowell. New York and Oxford: Oxford UP, 1988.

Levine, Lawrence W. *Black Culture and Black Consciousness: Afro-American Folk Thought from Slavery to Freedom*. New York: Oxford UP, 1977.

Logan, Rayford. *The Betrayal of the Negro*: *From Rutherford B. Hayes to Woodrow Wilson. 1967*. Introd. Eric Foner. New York: Da Capo P, 1997.

Loggins, Vernon. *The Negro Author in America: His Development to 1900*. New York: Columbia UP, 1931.

Martin, Herbert Woodward, and Ronald Primeau, eds. *In His Own Voice: The Dramatic and Other Uncollected Works of Paul Laurence Dunbar*. Athens: Ohio UP, 2002.

Matthews, Victoria Earle. "The Value of Race Literature." *Massachusetts Review* 27:2 (Summer 1986): 169–91.

McDowell, Deborah E., and Arnold Rampersad, eds. *Slavery and the American Literary Imagination*. Baltimore and London: Johns Hopkins UP, 1989.

Moses, Wilson Jeremiah. *Black Messiahs and Uncle Toms: Social and Literary Manipulations of a Religious Myth*. University Park: Pennsylvania State UP, 1993.

Nelson, John Herbert. *The Negro Character in American Literature*. 1926. New York: AMS P, 1970.

Peterson, Carla L. *"Doers of the Word": African-American Women Speakers & Writers in the North (1830–1880)*. 1995. New Brunswick: Rutgers UP, 1998.

Redding, J. Saunders. *To Make a Poet Black*. Chapel Hill: U of North Carolina P, 1939.

Starke, Catherine Juanita. *Black Portraiture in American Fiction: Stock Characters, Archetypes, and Individuals*. New York and London: Basic Books, Inc., 1971.

Tate, Claudia. *Domestic Allegories of Political Desire: The Black Heroine's Text at the Turn of the Century*. New York: Oxford, 1992.

Wiggins, Lyda Keck, ed. *The Life and Works of Paul Laurence Dunbar*. 1907. New York: Kraus Reprint Company, 1971.

Williamson, Joel. *The Crucible of Race*. New York: Oxford, 1984.

Wilson, Harriet. *Our Nig; or, Sketches from the Life of a Free Black*. 1859. Ed. Henry L. Gates, Jr. New York: Vintage/Random House, 1983.

Yellin, Jean Fagan. *The Intricate Knot: Black Figures in American Literature*, 1776–1863. New York: New York UP, 1972.

Zafar, Rafia. *We Wear the Mask: African Americans Write American Literature, 1760–1870*. New York: Columbia UP, 1997.

Suggested Topics for Writing Critical Essays

1. Conduct a comparative analysis of themes involving property and reparations in two of the novels discussed above.
2. Examine the significance of missing background information and the construction of a specific character or characters as mysterious.
3. How do Harper and Hopkins define "true womanhood"?
4. Explore the theme of racial uplift in any two Chesnutt short stories.
5. Examine some of the strategies used to turn art into propaganda in *Contending Forces.*
6. Trace the running discourse on race and morality in *The Sport of the Gods* and/or *Contending Forces.*
7. Conduct a comparative reading of the theme of "race loyalty" or "family disruption" as represented in Chesnutt and Harper.
8. Explore the theme of religious and/or moral hypocrisy in any of the works discussed above. How does it compare to the way the topic is treated in the autobiographical narratives featured in chapter 1?
9. Contrast Harper's wronged mulatta heroine in *Iola Leroy* with Hopkins's in *Contending Forces.* Decide whether either or both women suggest that whiteness equals beauty. Compare the mulatto figure in either of these two novels with that featured in a novel or story discussed in a previous chapter in this textbook.
10. Examine the use of melodrama in any of the works discussed above. Compare it to the way it is used in any novel or story featured in one of the two previous chapters in this textbook.

Questions to Guide Your Reading

Iola Leroy

1. Construct a family tree showing the relationships among Iola, Robert, Marie, and Harriet.
2. What are Iola's reasons for declining Dr. Gresham's offer of marriage?
3. Who are the major characters in this story? Describe their most dominant traits. Which characters serve as foils for others?
4. Why does Harper take such great pains to reveal the intimate connections between African Americans and white Americans of this period?

5. Do you believe Harper intends to suggest by her depiction of Iola and all the men drawn to her "beauty" that there is innate beauty in Iola's whiteness? Explain.
6. Which four characters give up a chance to pass for white in order to assist in racial uplift?
7. How does Harper incorporate actual historical events and personas into her text?

"The Goophered Grapevine"

1. Who is narrating this story?
2. Whose perspective is presented?
3. Into what subject position does the author place the reader; through whose eyes do we experience the information?
4. What would happen if Julius McAdoo were allowed to reveal his true feelings, or if they were revealed through an omniscient narrator?
5. Is there a moral to this story? What is the point of the story, if there is a point?
6. What does it mean to conjure? Goopher?
7. How does Julius McAdoo's situation change as a result of his encounter with the white northerner? Is he better off or worse off?

"The Wife of His Youth"

1. From what narrative point of view is the story rendered? How does this impact your experience of the subject matter? What if the story had been narrated by the protagonist, or a totally omniscient narrator?
2. Of what importance is the historical context? Could this story exist without the fact of slavery and the Civil War, for example?
3. How does the protagonist's decision to acknowledge the wife of his youth compare to Iola Leroy's decision not to pass for white?
4. What does the story suggest about black family life under slavery?

"Sister Josepha"

1. Who is narrating this story?
2. Is there a secondary story that runs beneath the surface story about a child who grows up in a convent orphanage? What must have happened before?

3. Why does the author not share Sister Josepha's racial identity with the reader? Should we assume that she is white? black? "raceless"?
4. What are Sister Josepha's options, and why are they so limited?
5. What information is missing, but implied, in the story? How does this affect the meaning you derive from the story?
6. How can we discern whether the potential adoptive father of Sister Josepha/Camille truly has lecherous inclinations? Why does Camille decide to stay within the confines of the convent?

Contending Forces

1. Who is Sappho Clark and what is her horrible secret? Why does she come to South Boston?
2. Trace Sappho's lineage. Who were her parents and how did she come to be pronounced dead?
3. Are there absolutely good and absolutely evil characters in this story? Identify them.
4. How many marriages take place during the course of the story?
5. Why does Sappho Clark not fit the description of the tragic mulatta?
6. Trace John Pollock Langley's lineage; Will and Dora Smith's.
7. How does Hopkins incorporate actual historical events and personas into her story?
8. Why does Hopkins take such great pains to reveal the intimate connections between African Americans and white Americans of this period?

The Sport of the Gods

1. Describe the relationship between the Hamiltons and the Oakleys.
2. Why is it so easy for Oakley to believe that Berry Hamilton is a thief?
3. Characterize the Hamilton family as Dunbar portrays them before they leave the South, and after they arrive in the North. How does a change in environment affect family stability?
4. Where does Dunbar use melodrama in this story?
5. How does the story speak to the economic situation for African Americans in the North as well as the South during this period?
6. Why do the Hamiltons return to the Oakley estate? Have they made any progress?

7. What is Dunbar suggesting by this ending—this type of reconciliation?

CHAPTER IV
Fiction 1912–1949

African American literature was very much in transition during the first half of the twentieth century. James Weldon Johnson's *Autobiography of an Ex-Coloured Man* (1912) represents one aspect of the transition from the highly prescriptive literature of the previous decades. Recall that much, though certainly not all, late nineteenth-century fiction featured (in sentimental novel form) a mulatto character or characters whose virtue lies in their willingness to forego the privilege of passing for white, identify as Negro, and serve the cause of racial uplift. Matters of race and identity are important issues in Johnson's novel. His mulatto protagonist must confront his racial heritage and deal with the impact of miscegenation and social inequality, but the difference lies in how Johnson chooses to treat these themes and issues, and indeed in his articulation of the protagonist's central quest. Johnson presents in *Ex-Coloured Man* the episodic quest narrative of an unnamed mulatto who, after learning that he possesses Negro blood, occasionally exploits the advantage offered by the fact that he can pass as white, or *raceless*, for most of the story. He decides finally that it is in his best interest economically to become "white." In effect, Johnson uses the story to thematize what W. E. B. Du Bois first defines as double-consciousness in the essay "Of Our Spiritual Strivings" from *The Souls of Black Folk* (1903). Think of Johnson's novel as a bridge between the mostly sentimental fiction of the previous decades and the variety in fiction that would come in the 1920s, 1930s, and 1940s. Johnson's protagonist is an antihero who can seldom be counted upon to "do the right thing." Unlike his predecessors, Johnson, who would later identify with the younger artists of the New Negro Movement, was less concerned with proving that African Americans were worthy humans than he was with charting new possibilities and directions for the literature—which is not to say that he was apolitical. His work in literature and criticism looked toward a major conversation about the criteria for African American art that would take place in the middle of the next decade during the New Negro Movement.

The highlight of the 1920s in African American literature was, of course, the New Negro Movement, also called the Negro Renaissance, or the Harlem Renaissance. Though the phrase "the New Negro" is most often associated with the period beginning a decade after Johnson's mock autobiography, it appeared decades earlier in an 1895 editorial in the *Cleveland Gazette* in reference to middle-class African Americans who demanded their rights as United States citizens. The previous chapter discusses the contributions of such black Americans, who used their writing to counter prevailing negative stereotypes of African Americans. Author Sutton Griggs used the phrase in *Imperium in Imperio* (1899): "The cringing, fawning, sniffling, cowardly Negro which slavery left, had disappeared, and a New Negro, self-respecting, fearless, and determined in the assertion of his rights was at hand." Also, William Pickens published a collection of essays called *The New Negro* in 1916. The anthology that actually emerged from the energy of the New Negro Movement, and which serves as a sort of inaugural document, however, is Alain Locke's *The New Negro* (1925). First published as an edition of the journal *Survey Graphic*, it contains the work of some of the most talented and memorable artists of that period, including Jean Toomer, Langston Hughes, Zora Neale Hurston, Anne Spencer, James Weldon Johnson, Countee Cullen, and Jessie Fauset. Locke's volume is divided into two parts: "The Negro Renaissance," and "The New Negro in a New World." The volume contains essays, drama, visual art, fiction, and poetry. On the first page of his introduction to the anthology, Locke refers to the "Old Negro" as more myth than man, more formula than human being, a "stock figure perpetuated as an historical fiction partly in innocent sentimentalism, partly in deliberate reactionism." Locke declared the New Negro, vibrant, awake, and progressive.

Younger members of this period would even attempt their own literary magazine, *FIRE!!* Edited by novelist/critic Wallace Thurman, the first and only issue of *FIRE!!* featured drawings, poems, short stories, and essays by Aaron Douglass, Langston Hughes, Helene Johnson, Zora Neale Hurston, Thurman, and others. *FIRE!!* also contained one of the first overtly homosexual works by a black American writer, Richard Bruce Nugent's "Smoke, Lilies and Jade, a Novel, Part I," which was soundly panned by Du Bois. To be sure, the period was not without its debates and controversies surrounding the criteria for the new and progressive literature. The "old guard," made up of such time-tested authorities as W. E. B. Du Bois and Charles W. Chesnutt, felt that African Americans should continue to counter negative portrayals in mainstream American literature and culture by portraying themselves in a positive light. Younger writers, with some exceptions, felt they should not be bridled by such prescriptions. In 1926, *Crisis Magazine* held a multi-edition forum in which artists and critics took turns responding to a predetermined set of questions on the topic of how African Americans should portray themselves in literature and art. Several writers wrote individual essays in 1926 as well. These include (but are not limited to) the following: W. E. B. Du Bois's "Criteria of Negro Art," George Schuyler's "The Negro-Art Hokum," and Langston Hughes's response to Schuyler in "The Negro Artist and the Racial Mountain" (all collected in Angelyn Mitchell's *Within the Circle,* 1994).

After the stock market crashed in late 1929, the bubbling black literary world slowed down to a simmer. Literary production continued nevertheless, with many of the same artists contributing new works and some new artists such as Richard Wright and Ann Petry making their first major contributions in the coming decades. Zora Neale Hurston, one of the brightest stars of the Harlem Renaissance, actually published her best-known work, *Their Eyes Were Watching God*, in 1937 in the midst of the Great Depression. Often referred to as the quintessential folk novel, the story makes use of Hurston's training in anthropology and her field research in folk culture—this, along with the fact that she grew up among the kind of people and settings described in *Their Eyes*. Claude McKay (1890–1948), Countee Cullen (1903–1946), and Rudolph Fisher (1897–1934) also published folk novels in the 1920s and/or 1930s. Jessie Fauset (1882–1961), a major presence during the Harlem Renaissance, added four novels in the period before and after the stock market crash. They featured light-skinned, educated African Americans who sometimes passed for white: *There Is Confusion* (1924), *Plum Bun* (1929), *The Chinaberry Tree* (1931), and *Comedy: American Style* (1933). Nella Larsen's primary contributions came before the depression years: *Quicksand* (1928) and *Passing* (1929). Satirist and sometimes quintessential critic Wallace Thurman (1902-1934) contributed *The Blacker the Berry* (1929) and *Infants of the Spring* (1932); he collaborated with Abraham L. Furman on a third novel, *The Interne* (1932). Richard Wright (1908–1960) weighed in on the criteria for black American literary production in 1937 with "Blueprint for Negro Writing" (collected in Mitchell); he followed up with the short-story collection *Uncle Tom's Children* (1938), the novel *Native Son* (1940), and his autobiography *Black Boy* (1945). Wright did much of his subsequent writing while living abroad, publishing *The Outsider* (1953), *Savage Holiday* (1954), and *The Long Dream* (1958), while he lived in France. He was one of a number of black artists who left America in search of the personal and artistic freedom denied to them at home; others include Claude McKay, Jessie Fauset, Langston Hughes, Chester Himes, and James Baldwin. Wright's *Native Son*, his best known work, is a harsh indictment of American racism; nothing like it had previously been accomplished in African American literature. Along with Ann Petry's *The Street* (1946), it represents the best of the urban realism protest novels of that period. Both novels speak to the injustice and inhumanity of a country that forces its black citizens to live in a climate that is lethally racist.

The four literary decades beginning with Johnson's novel can be characterized by the increasing diversity in the type of fiction produced. Here, we will focus on James Weldon Johnson's *The Autobiography of an Ex-Coloured Man*, selections from Jean Toomer's *Cane* (1923), Nella Larsen's *Passing* (1929), Zora Neale Hurston's *Their Eyes Were Watching God* (1937), Richard Wright's *Native Son* (1940), and Ann Petry's *The Street* (1946). Though Langston Hughes is perhaps the most widely known author from this period, he is best known for his wonderful poetry. We will consider some of his most enduring fiction in the next chapter.

James Weldon Johnson (1871–1938), like most of the writers discussed in this text, possessed many talents. He wrote songs, literary criticism, poetry, and fiction. He was also a diplomat, an English professor, a lawyer, and a journalist. His parents, Helen Louise Dillet and James Johnson, instilled in him a sense of public service. His Bahamian grandfather served in his nation's House of Assembly for some thirty years. Johnson's family moved to Jacksonville, Florida, in 1866, where the father worked as a headwaiter and his mother taught in public school. Within one year of his high school graduation, Johnson founded his own newspaper. Later, he and his brother, Rosamond, wrote compositions for Broadway musicals. They also collaborated on the song later adopted as the Negro National Anthem, "Lift Every Voice and Sing." James Weldon Johnson wrote *The Autobiography of an Ex-Coloured Man* while serving as United States Consul to Venezuela between 1906 and 1909, a post that then power broker Booker T. Washington helped him to secure. *Along This Way* (1933) is the autobiography of Johnson's life. He published a number of other works, including the edited volumes *The Book of American Negro Poetry* in 1922, *The Book of American Negro Spirituals* (1925), and *The Second Book of American Negro Spirituals* (1926). He displays his talent for poetry in *God's Trombones, Seven Negro Sermons in Verse* (1927).

Jean Toomer (1894–1967) was born Nathan Eugene Toomer. His grandfather, P. B. S. Pinchback, served as a lieutenant governor of Louisiana. Racially mixed, Toomer referred to himself as an American, rather than as an African American, or Negro—to use the parlance of the time. When Toomer's parents, Nina Pinchback and Nathan Toomer, divorced five years after Toomer was born, mother and child moved in with grandparents Nina Hethorn Pinchback and P. B. S. Pinchback. After his mother's death, Toomer's grandparents took on the task of rearing him. Toomer attended Paul Laurence Dunbar High School in Washington, D.C.; graduating in 1914, he made the rounds of several major universities but did not stay long enough at any to earn a degree. He did, however, begin *Cane*, which was immediately recognized for its innovation. In the early 1920s, Toomer became part of the literary scene in Greenwich Village, changed his given name from Nathan Pinchback to Jean and took a short appointment as acting principal at a school in rural Georgia. The experience would supply the raw material for *Cane*. Among other things, *Cane* captured the contrasts between southern rural life and northern urban life, and has since come to be considered a masterpiece, though Toomer's own disenchantment with his work is well known. After producing *Cane*, he came under the influence of the Russian mystic and psychologist, George I. Gurdjieff. The association had a profound impact on the type of literature he produced for the remaining years of his life.

Nella Larsen (1891–1964) is best known for her back-to-back novels *Quicksand* and *Passing*. She was born Nellie Walker in Chicago, Illinois. Before Thaddious Davis's 1994 biography of Larsen, it was widely believed that Larsen's Danish West Indian father died when she was quite young and her mother married a Danish man and Larsen grew up the darker-skinned child in a Danish immigrant family. Davis uncovers information that suggests Larsen's family simply chose to pass for white. Larsen attended private school with children who were of German and Scandinavian ancestry. She briefly attended Fisk University Normal High School between 1907 and 1908, and following that she attended the University of Copenhagen for three years. She later returned to the United States to train as a nurse at the Lincoln Hospital School of Nursing in New York City. She took a job at Lincoln and later at Tuskegee Institute's Andrew Memorial Hospital, where she served as head nurse. She eventually found employment with New York City's Board of Health, but left nursing for a time after she married black research physicist Elmer S. Imes in 1919 and moved into the upscale black middle class. She worked for a time at the New York Public Library, but she eventually resigned and worked on her writing. After publishing *Quicksand* in 1928, she was regaled by the Harlem Renaissance literati—led by none other than James Weldon Johnson. *Passing* (1929) received less acclaim initially, but it has recently received the critical attention it deserves. In 1930 Larsen received a Guggenheim Fellowship, but marital problems and a charge of plagiarism (which she vehemently denied) surrounding the publication of her short story, "Sanctuary" (1930), would plague her for the next few years. With the Harlem Renaissance in decline, Larsen became active in other racial matters. She joined other black women writers in the Writers' League against Lynching, and she returned to nursing. She apparently died alone of heart failure in March of 1964.

Zora Neale Hurston (1891–1960) was born in Notasulga, Alabama, but her family later settled in America's first incorporated black town, Eatonville, Florida. She was one of eight children born to John and Lucy Ann Potts Hurston. John Hurston served three terms as the town's mayor. After her mother died in 1904, Hurston left her hometown to attend school in Jacksonville, Florida. Like many other black women of the time, she found work as a maid and even traveled as a lady's maid with an entertainment troupe. She finished high school in Baltimore at Morgan College's preparatory school and then worked service industry jobs while attending Howard University in Washington, D.C. between 1918 and 1924. Alain Locke, Howard professor and editor of *The New Negro*, would become one of her mentors and later select her short story, "Spunk," for the landmark 1925 anthology. Moving to New York after her time at Howard, Hurston became acquainted with Langston Hughes, James Weldon Johnson, Countee Cullen, and several influential white patrons. A scholarship to Barnard brought her in contact with renowned anthropologist Franz Boas, and it was under his direction that she began the extensive research in folk culture that took her to several southern states as well as the Bahamas and Haiti. Attention to some of the details of Hurston's own life reveals that, in writing her best-known novel, *Their Eyes Were Watching God* (1936), she drew upon a number of settings and experiences from her own youth. Much of the plot of the story is centered in a town called Eatonville, and the novel also reflects the author's intimate knowledge of folklore and folk culture. Her *Mules and Men* (1935) is the first known volume of African American folklore published by an American of African descent. She published a second volume of folklore, *Tell My Horse*, in 1938. Hurston also published three additional novels: *Jonah's Gourd Vine* (1934), *Moses, Man of the Mountain* (1939), and *Seraph on the Suwanee* (1948). Her body of work includes a number of essays, plays, and short stories as well. A staunchly independent and assertive woman, Hurston's political views, like her wonderful folk-based writing, often went against the grain. As she would write in one of her more popular essays, "How It Feels to Be Colored

Me," she did not feel "tragically colored"; she understood without question that black Americans were not an inferior brand of human. She is on record as having opposed the Supreme Court's landmark desegregation ruling in *Brown v. Board of Education* (1954), because she understood that desegregation could be a double-edged sword. Her political views and attitudes were decidedly conservative, shaped by her early experience as part of a self-sustaining all-black community and her extensive fieldwork among the "folk." She died penniless in the St. Lucie County Welfare Home in Fort Pierce, Florida.

Richard Wright (1908–1960) was born on a plantation in Roxie, Mississippi (near Natchez, Mississippi) on September 4, 1908. His mother, Ella Wilson Wright, was a schoolteacher, and his father, Nathan Wright, was a tenant farmer. Nathan Wright left the family when Richard was six years old, and this period of poverty and uncertainty in young Richard's life is rendered most vividly in the early pages of *Black Boy* (1945). Wright describes his early years in great detail as a time of almost constant hunger. He would grow up to become one of the world's major authors as well as a highly influential literary "father" to a number of younger artists, including Ralph Ellison, James Baldwin, Toni Morrison, and Charles Johnson. Influenced in his youth by the writing of H. L. Mencken, Wright resolved to use words as a weapon against the social straightjacket in which America placed its black citizens, particularly those who, like Wright, grew up under Jim Crow segregation. In 1927, while the New Negro Movement was in full swing, Wright moved to Chicago and found work as a postal clerk. Four years later, he was, like many in the nation, on relief as a result of the Great Depression; in 1932 he became involved with the Communist Party and began to write poetry. He also joined the editorial staff at *New Challenge* magazine, run by Dorothy West. He worked on the novel *Lawd Today*, which was not published until 1963. In the short-story collection *Uncle Tom's Children* (1938), Wright depicted the thwarted potential of African Americans in the American South. Aided by a Guggenheim fellowship, he completed *Native Son* (1940), which focuses attention on the impact of living in a hostile urban environment. *Native Son* was the most widely read work of African American literature since the freedom narratives; it became a Book-of-the-Month-Club selection. Wright's other published works include the celebrated short story "The Man Who Lived Underground," written in 1944, *The Outsider* (1953), and *The Long Dream* (1958). Though Wright would ultimately break with the Communist Party, he would remain on the Left for the rest of his life. He died in 1960 under mysterious circumstances.

Ann Petry (1908–1997) was born Ann Lane in Old Saybrook, Connecticut, and attended its public schools. Her parents were pharmacist Peter C. Lane and chiropodist/cosmetologist/businesswoman Bertha J. Lane. Petry grew up amid a family of storytellers and all-around successful business people. Her older sister graduated from Brown University; Petry earned a degree in pharmacy in 1931 from Connecticut College (now the University of Connecticut) and joined the family business. She married George Petry in 1938, and they moved to New York City where Petry became a writer. She sold her first short story in 1939. In the early 1940s, she contributed regular items to Adam Clayton Powell's weekly paper, *People's Voice*. Her first novel, *The Street* (1946), is considered a classic of urban realism; it became a best-seller and brought Petry fame as a writer. Her second novel, *Country Place* (1947), focuses on the small-town lives of several white characters, and a third novel, *The Narrows* (1953), follows a doomed interracial love affair. Petry also wrote books for children and juveniles, including *The Drugstore Cat* (1949), *Harriet Tubman: Conductor on the Underground Railroad* (1955), *Tituba of Salem Village* (1964), and *Legends of the Saints* (1970). Like so many of the other authors discussed here, she has received honorary degrees and numerous literary awards.

Contexts and Texts

The first decades of the twentieth century are characterized by the movement of black Americans from the Jim Crow South to the urban North and elsewhere to background music that began as the rural folk form known as the **blues** and transformed into the urban style known as jazz. James Weldon Johnson's unnamed protagonist in *The Autobiography of an Ex-Coloured Man* also provides us with details about how ragtime, whose most significant feature is syncopation, emerged in the late nineteenth century as the first black instrumental music in America. In rural agricultural communities, **sharecropping** and tenant farming kept many African Americans indebted to white landowners. A system of prison labor, often fed through corrupt law enforcement practices, helped to continue the illicit practice of extracting black labor at the lowest possible cost to profiteers.

Though a handful of mostly light-skinned black families had managed to accumulate wealth by the turn of the twentieth century, and a viable black middle-class was beginning to emerge, most black Americans still faced formidable barriers to economic prosperity. Mob violence against African Americans, which included lynchings, continued in the first half of the twentieth century. Black artists produced anti-lynch plays even as the hard core racism of D. W. Griffith's film *The Birth of a Nation* (based on Tom Dixon's *The Leopard's Spots* and *The Clansman*) played to sold-out audiences. In the fifteen years following the death of Booker T. Washington in 1915, black Americans migrated to northern cities in droves. Fed up with decades of Jim Crow segregation and homegrown terrorism, huge numbers of black Americans gave up on the South and cast their lot with the North. The influx of new immigrants to northern cities fed color discrimination and mob violence against African Americans for a variety of reasons, including their use as union breakers. Recall from the previous chapter that Paul Laurence Dunbar's *The Sport of the Gods* (1902) depicts the hazards some African Americans encountered making the transition from South to North in the late nineteenth century. Later literary works, such as Wright's *Native Son* (1940) and Petry's *The Street* (1946) depict the urban North as a socio-economic straightjacket that severely limits the mobility of their respective protagonists. A number of African Americans, including Richard Wright, flirted with socialism and/or communism as attractive alternatives to the racism operating in America's economic sphere. Black nonfiction from this period reveals, among other concerns, a concern with mob violence against African Americans and limited employment opportunities. Black male unemployment in urban areas was very high. In the North and the South, domestic work was the most prevalent type of non-agricultural employment available to black women.

Despite the general climate of social inequality, African Americans in the North and South persevered, and some managed to prosper. For a brief period before the economic downturn of the 1930s, however, Harlem (as well as other urban areas) flourished. Harlem, in particular, was a place of hope and celebration. The era of the *New Negro*, which Sutton Griggs alludes to in *Imperium in Imperio* (1899), began in earnest with many black Americans determined to move away from the old mentality of fear, accommodation, and acquiescence toward one of celebration, progress, and racial pride. Artists and critics—even the "Old Guard"—felt comfortable drawing upon their own black cultural heritage. Certain members of the literary vanguard (including Du Bois and an older Charles Chesnutt) believed that Negro art should always serve the purpose of racial progress. In "The Criteria for Negro Art," Du Bois makes a strong argument that all art is potentially propaganda; he notes that African Americans had as much right to define Beauty as anyone, and he suggests a participatory black presence in the formation of an aesthetics of Beauty. He reminds African Americans of their valued past. He also points out that mainstream literature continues to distort the truth about African Americans and the mainstream paying audience reaffirms the distortions by continuing to pay for the literature. His concern is that such distortions will only serve the purpose of continued discrimination. For Du Bois, the artist had a duty to be political. The topic served as fodder for a question-and-answer series in *Crisis* magazine in 1926 and also as the subject of numerous essays (and a few works of fiction).

Younger artists (including Langston Hughes in "The Negro Artist and the Racial Mountain") expressed the feeling that artists should not be burdened by thoughts of who would or would not be pleased by their end products. Wallace Thurman did not believe that art should come with an agenda. Claude McKay denounced the prizegiving and official grooming of artists; neither did he condone Du Bois's reasoning that all art is propaganda. Like Thurman, McKay felt that the artist who set out with a political agenda had already undermined his true artistic expression. For Alain Locke, politics was present in the existence of the black artist and his work. Locke wanted African Americans to follow that approach while writing about their own experiences in those forms. A plethora of other artists and critics—including Jesse Fauset and Countee Cullen—weighed in on this important issue. Author/critic George Schuyler went so far as to suggest in "The Negro Art Hokum" (1926) that there was no such thing as Negro art. Nevertheless, during the extreme social conditions of the two decades between 1955 and 1975, architects of the Black Arts Movement would once again find it necessary to call for art with a deliberately political purpose, though the new reasoning was more an amalgamation of both the "old guard" and the younger artists of the Harlem Renaissance, combined with the revolutionary energy generated by postcolonial and nationalist movements around the world (see chapter 5). The writers featured in this chapter largely resisted the prescriptions of the past; though much of the literature fell under the heading of protest, the increased artistic freedom opened up a storehouse of talent and an outpouring of literature before, during, and following the New Negro Movement.

James Weldon Johnson's initially anonymously published *The Autobiography of an Ex-Coloured Man* (1912) serves as a transitional work signaling a new turn in African American fiction—a break with the past in keeping with the modernist idea. The fictional autobiography was Johnson's first published work. When it first appeared, many readers believed it to be a true story. Continuing the exploration of identities shaped by miscegenation and passing, Johnson presented to the world the story of an unnamed black male protagonist, an antihero, who spends the first nine years of his life thinking that he is "not a Negro." In effect, Johnson's novel thematizes W. E. B. Du Bois's notion of double-consciousness and reinforces Du Bois's observation that the problem of the twentieth century would be the problem of the color line. The novel also highlights questions of identity.

The title of Johnson's *The Autobiography of an Ex-Colored Man* should warn readers that Johnson's unnamed protagonist will not "do the right thing" as so many mulatto characters before him had done in choosing blackness (and service to the race) over whiteness. Clearly, Johnson intends his novel as a "break with the past"; however, the novel serves also as a wonderful illustration of Du Boisian double-consciousness. He does not simply see his black self through the eyes of whites, he *becomes* white, assumes whiteness. Both a literal and psychological odyssey, the episodic novel charts the life and adventures of an anonymous protagonist whose ability to pass for white is his ticket to wealth. Having lived an idyllic early childhood in rural Georgia with his mulatto mother (who was occasionally visited by his white father), the protagonist spent his formative years thinking that he was "standard" in relation to black people, with black people clearly being Other. His calm is disturbed after they move to Connecticut. During school one day, the principal asks all the white scholars to stand; the protagonist stands only to be told that he should sit and stand with the other Negroes. Disturbed by the information, he confronts his mother, who verifies that he is part Negro. For the first time, the narrator looks closely at his face in the mirror and recognizes his *blackness*. He stares in the mirror searching for signs of difference; significantly, he senses nothing inherently different about himself. The protagonist's mother conveniently dies just before he graduates from high school. After his mother dies, he leaves home for historically black Atlanta University and (seemingly inadvertently) falls into a period of fluid identity, moving back and forth between being white (or "raceless") and being Negro.

On his way South to attend Atlanta University, the protagonist stupidly leaves his tuition money in the chest that he has stored at a rooming house. When he returns, the money is missing, and he ends up going to work rolling cigars at a Jacksonville, Florida, cigar factory. Thus begins another episode in his life, and after three years there he travels to New York City. He learns to gamble and indeed becomes addicted for a time. Fortunately, he also becomes very adept at ragtime, a style of music that was gaining in popularity at the time, and he catches the eye and ear of a wealthy white benefactor. While traveling with his benefactor through Europe, he spots his father in a Paris theater with his half sister, and the chance encounter makes him more aware than ever of his "illegitimacy" and disinheritance. He finally decides to return to the United States, identify as Negro, and do what he can to help his "race." This plan also goes awry.

He eventually travels south to collect songs from among the rural black folk, and also to become a composer. Here, and throughout the novel, the protagonist makes note of class differences among African Americans. One night he witnesses a brutal lynching of a black man; that act, the brutal taking of a man's life because that man was black, cinched it for Johnson's protagonist. He decides at that moment that he does not want to identify with a race of people who could be so harshly treated at will. Like literacy obtained for the enslaved Frederick Douglass, discovering the meaning of his blackness is a double-edged sword for Johnson's protagonist, who decides ultimately to allow the world to assume that he is white. Thus, he begins a new episode—that of using America's erroneous assumption about his skin color to accumulate wealth. He marries a white woman who bears him two children and conveniently dies. His children are light enough to pass for white, and one assumes that they will live their entire lives with part of their personal history closed off to them. The protagonist, despite his wealth, is left with the problem of diminished ability to assert himself as a subject in the world. The reader understands that race, and America's preoccupation with race, is the real culprit. In the end, the protagonist remains ambivalent about his final choice and wonders whether he sold his birthright for something inherently less valuable.

The novel thus explores issues involving race, identity, and subjectivity, at a time when the races were segregated by law and black Americans were systemically denied equal opportunity access to resources. It is also a meditation on the phenomenon of "passing" and reveals several of the reasons why mixed-race persons chose to identify as white when they had that option. Clearly, not all mulattos declared their undying loyalty to "the race." This differing attitude brings us to Jean Toomer, who is said to have gone from refusing to identify solely as Negro because he was of mixed heritage, to asserting that his grandfather, P. B. S. Pinchback, had only been pretending to be black when he ran for political office during Reconstruction. Therefore, he (Toomer) was also white.

Cane (1923) is composed of six prose vignettes, seven fully developed stories, fifteen poems, and one short play. The setting is the 1920s in the United States North and South, but primarily the South.

Parts I and III are set in rural Georgia, a region where Toomer had worked as a school principal. The title refers to Georgia's sugar cane industry. Part II is set in Chicago and Washington, D.C. The stories in the first part focus on women in the South, whose lived experiences contrast with bourgeois expectations. Their names are Karintha, Becky, Carma, Fern, Esther, and Louisa. Toomer represents them all in terms of their sexuality and sensuality, and as beautiful as the prose pieces are, one might easily read into the portraits either a very narrow or a very precise perspective on these women's lives. Generally speaking, Toomer casts Karintha and her sister southern protagonists in *Cane* as creatures of instinct.

Karintha, depicted as an exceedingly sexy vixen, gives birth to an "illegitimate" child, whom she subsequently incinerates. Contemptuous of men, she sleeps with them—old or young—for money. Becky is a white woman who commits the sin of bearing two black children. Her story speaks to the white South's continued denial of the fact of interracial sexual relationships and miscegenation, whose evidence is in the varying hues of African America. Becky falls below the rank that whiteness normally guarantees her in society not only because she has sex with black men but also because her mulatto children personify the taboo relations. Like Mag Smith of Harriet Wilson's *Our Nig* (1859), Becky and her sons are ostracized by the white community; they live a lonely, reclusive impoverished existence in a cabin by the railroad—though the community "secretly" helps them out by leaving food. The boys grow into sullen men, and eventually leave home. One day Becky's cabin burns to the ground, and the townsfolk assume that Becky was in it.

In "Carma," the subject is infidelity, and it turns on a series of incongruities. Carma *sleeps around* while her husband, Bane, is away working. When he returns and learns of her activities, he threatens her; she grabs a gun and heads for the cane field. Bane hears a shot, and thinking that Carma is wounded, gathers a search and rescue party. He locates a seemingly injured Carma, and another man helps him carry her home. Once there, however, he realizes that she has once again deceived him. An angry Bane slashes the man who had just helped him. Based on the information presented, we can only think of Bane as a hardworking and loving husband who ends up in prison. Carma, who is described as very strong, and whom no one blames for taking lovers during her husband's long absences, responds to her situation with a startling lack of emotional maturity. Toomer depicts both characters as driven by their emotions and lacking a sense of measured reasoning.

"Fern" is the story of Fernie May Rosen, the illegitimate offspring of a white Jewish man and a black woman. Fern is beautiful, and men find her irresistible, but she lives a doubly tortured existence symbolized by her Jewishness and her blackness. She exists in a state of blues so deep and tragic that the mood of the story and its central character might be characterized as indigo. Nothing that her many suitors do for her can fill her unfulfillable desire. Louisa, the protagonist of "Blood-Burning Moon," has two lovers, one white, and one black. The black man, a laborer, is lynched after killing his white rival. Aside from the commentary on the still widespread custom of lynching at the time, the story speaks to the realities of a white sovereignty that circumscribes black existence. Louisa's murdered black lover could not expect to maintain exclusive access to Louisa, nor could he expect to continue to exist once he had challenged her white lover's sovereignty in that domain.

Several poems and the short story "Esther" make up the remainder of *Cane*'s first section. The second section of *Cane* is composed of sketches and stories set in Washington, D.C., with the exception of the last story, "Bona and Paul," which is set in Chicago. The third section contains the impressionistic play, "Kabnis." Protagonist Ralph Kabnis (whose situation bears a strong resemblance to Toomer's own as outsider in rural Georgia during his brief teaching stint) returns to rural Georgia from New York to teach. His mission is one of racial uplift, but the community he wants to save sees him as an outsider and thus a potentially disruptive force in the delicate social arrangement they have negotiated as southern African Americans in a hostile white society.

Larsen's *Passing* (1929) opens with Irene Redfield receiving a letter from childhood associate Clare Bellew. Irene immediately recalls via a flashback the last time she had seen Clare two years before when both women had been passing for white in order to take refreshment at a Chicago hotel. The chance encounter results in Irene visiting Clare's home where she had discovered to her chagrin that Clare's husband was not only white, but he was also a virulent bigot and did not know that Clare was part Negro. Irene does not betray Clare, but she leaves angry wanting nothing further to do with the situation. Reading Clare's letter two years later, she resolves simply to ignore it. Clare, who misses having contact with the black community, arrives at Irene's Harlem home uninvited and insinuates herself into their lives. Larsen reveals in Irene the kind of character who carefully plans and measures each phase of her life. Though she is strongly attracted to Clare's wreckless "freedom," she is too careful and too pragmatic to allow it too much force and influence in her own carefully crafted world. At least one major scholar has suggested that characters in this story pass not only for white, but also for heterosexual (see McDowell).

The language Larsen uses to describe the attraction between the two women is indeed sensual and suggests the presence of homoerotic desire. Clearly, the two women are drawn to each other, but the desire seems rooted in the lifestyle and personal choices the other has made. Clare clearly longs for the black self (life, heritage, identity, culture—recall Johnson's ex-coloured man) she has given up in order to be married to a white man, and Irene secretly desires the freedom to be "not black," unburdened by America's preoccupation with race. On the surface, however, Larsen's novel suggests (and Irene suspects) that Clare is having an affair with her husband Brian. Despite the undercurrent of what seems to be homoerotic desire, Irene values over all else her status and affluence and the continued security of her offspring; she sees the affair as a definite threat to her black middle class security.

Larsen effectively makes use of the unreliable narrator in this masterpiece of ambiguity. Because most of the plot is filtered through Irene's consciousness, and because Irene clearly has her own *issues*, we can never know for sure what's what. Toward the end of the novel, Clare's husband Jack tracks her to a Harlem benefit. Just as he enters the room, Clare falls from a window to her death. The final moments of the story center on Irene's mental and emotional response to Clare's fall and her reaction upon learning that Clare died during the fall. Irene, who had wanted to rid herself of Clare's influence, wonders whether she might have caused the tumble out of the window. The ending suggests that regardless of whether Irene actually caused Clare's death, Irene is relieved to be rid of the woman who threatens the safety of her heterosexual existence. The question has to do with whether it is the homoerotic desire that Clare awakens in Irene, the heterosexual desire that Clare awakens in Brian, both, or neither, that causes Irene's *dis-ease*. The novel is a tightly woven masterpiece of ambiguity that undermines pat interpretations.

Zora Neale Hurston's *Their Eyes Were Watching God* (1937) broke with established black literary convention in several ways. First of all, Hurston chose to foreground the personal quest of a black woman. She also refuses to depict black Americans as racial victims. Further, she depicts a heroine who not only leaves her first marriage, but she also lives and makes love to a man who is not her husband. In portraying Janie, Hurston breaks with the literary convention of the *proper black lady* from an earlier generation of writers, as well as that of the tragic mulatta figure. She manages all this while adhering to, and thus celebrating, a rural southern black vernacular. The overt protest in Hurston's novel is registered not against racism, but against the limitations placed on black women's potential for self-actualization.

The novel opens with Janie Crawford's return to her community of Eatonville. The neofreedom narrative she recites orally to her friend Phoeby Watson begins with an adolescent kiss, traverses through three heterosexual relationships, and culminates in a self-aware woman who is prepared to face life alone and on her own terms. Thus, the narrative unfolds through retrospect, from the moment Janie's grandmother, Nanny Crawford, becomes aware of Janie's burgeoning sexuality. The grandmother wants to protect Janie from the pitfalls of being black, female, and comely. In her own life, Nanny had served as the concubine for her former owner, and indeed Janie was the product of miscegenation. Nanny had raised her, and Janie had grown up literally in the white folks' backyard playing with white children, thinking herself "standard" in much the same way that James Weldon Johnson's ex-coloured man imagines himself before receiving the shocking truth that he is, in actuality, Negro. When Janie comes of age, Nanny insists on her marriage to Logan Killicks, a respectable black man of property. Killicks can offer Janie the protection she needs from sexual exploitation and the social and economic catastrophe of unwed motherhood. Janie enters into the unwanted marriage, only to abandon it when a more desirable prospect arrives in the form of Jody Starks. She marries a second time, and she and Jody help to found the all-black town of Eatonville. The marriage sours, however, as Joe Starks becomes more and more concerned with money and prestige, to the detriment of intimate and interpersonal relationships. If Logan Killicks had tried to make Janie into a mule, Joe Starks tried to place her on a pedestal—even as he berated her for being *merely a woman*. With this representation, Hurston illustrates the weakened sense of self that comes with accepting the pedestal.

Older than Janie, Joe becomes ill and eventually dies, making it possible for Janie to develop beyond the constraints of that relationship. One day a sexy *slacker* called Tea Cake appears on Janie's doorstep; he appeals to the latent adolescent in Janie. The pear blossom Hurston uses as a metaphor for Janie's sexuality resurfaces. Janie and Tea Cake begin an organic and passionate affair, leaving Eatonville to travel south and work among common laborers—literally in the muck. There, amidst the ravages of nature, Janie's sexuality is fully expressed; and this is an important aspect of the novel. It features a sexually desiring and active black woman who lives to tell about it, who does not die of shame or the sinfulness associated with sexual pleasure. During a flood that follows a hurricane, a rabid dog bites Tea Cake, who subsequently attacks Janie. She shoots him in self-defense and must stand trial for murder. Acquitted, she returns alone to Eatonville and, fortunately, the money she had the good sense not to spend during her affair with Tea Cake. The novel ends with her reciting her story to her sister-friend, Phoeby. She has found a way to stand on her own two feet, with or without a man in her life. Janie's story contains attributes of what Alice Walker and others would later call a womanist text (see Walker's *In Search of Our Mothers' Gardens*, 1983, or Katie Cannon's *Katie's Canon*, 1995). The male-dominated black literary establishment largely panned the novel for its perceived lack of attention to racial matters. Others failed to see the womanist politics driving Janie's quest.

Richard Wright's *Native Son* (1940) helped to usher in a new era of black American writing. The novel presents the life and impending death-by-execution of protagonist Bigger Thomas, whose fear and rage permeate this story about his overdetermined, doomed existence. Bigger is a twenty-year-old black man who lives with his religious mother, his timid sister Vera, and his less rebellious younger brother Buddy in a rat-infested tenement on Chicago's South Side. Other characters are Mr. Dalton, Bigger's employer and the man who owns the rat-infested tenement, his blind wife, their very liberal daughter Mary, Mary's communist boyfriend Jan Erlone, and Boris Max, Jan's communist friend who defends Bigger during his trial for murder. The story is set during the Great Depression, the 1930s. Wright uses snowfalls, ice, and blizzards to symbolize the cold, hostile white society. Bigger, officially a petty thief, takes a job as the Dalton's chauffeur. One of his duties is to drive Mary to and from her university, but, on his first day of work, Mary directs Bigger to take her to meet her communist boyfriend instead. Subsequently, the three get drunk and Bigger is forced to carry Mary to her room, but before he can exit, the blind Mrs. Dalton enters. All too aware of the racist American image of the black-man-as-sexual-beast, a panicked Bigger fears being caught in the room; in order to stifle Mary's drunken bantering, he places a pillow over her face and inadvertently kills her. In this and subsequent fear-and-panic-driven acts, Wright highlights the systemic malaise governing black-white interactions. Correctly discerning that no one will believe his version of the story, and feeling somehow inherently guilty, Bigger cuts off Mary's head and burns her body in the furnace. The police eventually find her bones.

Bigger subsequently confesses the murder to his black girlfriend, Bessie Mears, and as the net draws closer around him, he murders Bessie (after first raping her) to keep her from "spilling the beans." A bludgeoned Bessie actually freezes to death trying to escape from the air shaft into which Bigger had thrown her supposedly lifeless body. Bigger is eventually caught after a chase sequence eerily reminiscent of King Kong's capture in the famous film. The third and final part of the novel covers the inquest and trial. In jail, Bigger learns from newspaper accounts, which bear strong similarities to true-life accounts of the case of Robert Nixon carried in the *Chicago Defender* during that time, that he is indeed the "typical nigger"; he has fulfilled his destiny by doing just what the dominant culture expects of him. In a disturbingly horrifying spectacle, prosecutors introduce Bessie's body during the inquest to support their erroneous assumption that Bigger had also raped Mary Dalton, affirming in part Bigger's initial fear of being caught in the white woman's bedroom. Authorities also take Bigger to Mary's room for a *demonstration* of the rape, but Bigger refuses to oblige them and continues to insist on his innocence in that regard. Boris Max's defense at trial is that Bigger's environment trapped him like the proverbial rat (as symbolized in the novel's opening page). He reasons that it was the totality of Bigger's impoverished and oppressed life in hostile, racist America that made him commit murder. In depicting Max's *misreading* of the situation, Wright critiques the liberal mentality that paints African Americans as hapless victims and denies them a sense of agency. Bigger is convicted and sentenced to the electric chair; the appeal of his death sentence fails. The novel's horrible irony is that the rapid spiral downward all began with Bigger's very real fear of being discovered in a young white woman's bedroom. Equally ironic is the fact that Mary's wealthy parents offered Bigger the job in the first place as a gesture of charity. They end up sacrificing much more than they could have imagined, and setting in motion a chain of events that would also cost Bigger his life.

Lutie Johnson of Ann Petry's *The Street* (1946) also suffers from her lack of perception. Petry's novel is set primarily in Harlem in the 1940s. Lutie Johnson arrives in Harlem with the idea that she will pull herself up by her bootstraps. Lutie is a divorced mother, who, as a married woman, had returned home from an extended period of work to find that her husband had replaced her with a lover. Taking her son, she moves to New York; dazzled by the idea of the American Dream, however, Lutie lacks the ability to see beyond the myth. She believes that, with a little hard work, anyone can buy a nice home with a white picket fence in the suburbs. Thus, Petry's novel is first and foremost a critique of the myth of the American Dream and equal-opportunity access to that dream in the first half of the twentieth century.

In Harlem Lutie settles for an apartment that she considers beneath her, feeling that she will soon do better. Confronted with the multiplied effects of race, class, and gender discrimination, she is effectively immobilized in terms of economic progress, however. Lutie and, by default, her son eventually fall victim to schemes perpetrated by a variety of thieves and opportunists. Several characters try to exercise control over Lutie's sexuality: the mentally challenged building superintendent, the "neighbor" who is also a madam, Junto, the nightclub owner, and Boots Smith, a small-time hustler who works for Junto. After Lutie refuses the superintendent's advances and is warned against further advances by the building Madam, the man tricks her son into stealing mail. The child becomes enmeshed in the criminal justice system, and Lutie's desire to free her son from the criminal justice system leads to a confrontation with Boots that ends in his death. Boots had previously tricked Lutie out of her wages as a singer, and when she learns that he is only willing to help her if she makes herself sexually available, she kills him, takes money from his wallet, and flees town without having resolved her young son's situation. Boots functions merely as an intermediary—as a procurer/pimp for Junto, the white man who controls the economic means in Lutie's community. Junto wants to make Lutie his concubine. After killing Boots, Lutie simply takes the first train out of town, leaving her son behind. The novel ends on that note, but Petry has established the link between Junto (symbolic capitalist), his economic control in Harlem, and the multiple oppressions that operate on Lutie's existence. She has much in common with Bigger Thomas. Each protagonist suffers as a result of limited perception, and while it is easy to understand how both are oppressed based on their race and economic class, it is less obvious that both protagonists' sexual lives are circumscribed. Bigger proves to be the rapist that society expects him to be, though his rape is inflicted on the body of a black woman, not the white woman white society expects him to rape. Lutie works so hard to reject the label of sexually licentious black woman that she is effectively de-sexualized in the process. Both novels raise serious questions about healthy expressions of sexuality.

Recurring Themes and Issues

Questions about race and self-identity are central to Johnson's *The Autobiography of an Ex-Coloured Man* and Larsen's *Passing*. Both novels illustrate that with whiteness comes improved access to resources, but claiming the privileges of whiteness means closing off a part of the self. Johnson's unnamed protagonist uses his ability to pass for white to amass a small fortune in real estate. Larsen's Clare Kendry passes for white in order to marry a very wealthy white man. Economic opportunity and social mobility elude Wright's Bigger Thomas and Petry's Lutie Johnson. Both fall prey to the overdetermined social conditions of hostile urban environments. Lutie Johnson foolishly believes that she needs only to work hard to achieve her American Dream. Like Bigger Thomas, her epiphany comes too late.

Movement and mobility are also strong features in these works, produced as they were during a period of increased migration, especially from North to South. Johnson's protagonist begins his life in the South, moves to the North, graduates from high school, and moves back to the South. Arriving in Atlanta, he is robbed of his college funds and decides to travel to Florida. He remains in Florida for a time, but eventually moves North, travels to Europe, then back to the American North to make his way South, from which he flees after witnessing a brutal lynching toward the end of the novel. The setting for *Cane* moves from South to North and back South again (though if one begins, as some critics suggest, by reading the second part of the novel first, the movement is North to South). Toomer creates the impression that an invisible observer is moving back and forth (across the southern landscape, to various venues in northern cities, and from South to North and back South) with each setting change.

All of Janie Crawford's movement takes place in the South. She leaves her grandmother's home to live with new husband Logan Killicks, travels to Eatonville with Jody Starks, heads south into the Florida swampland, and finally travels back to Eatonville. Though Ann Petry represents Lutie Johnson as someone overly constrained by the race, class, gender, and predatory heterosexism she encounters in Harlem, the story also reveals a preoccupation with movement and lack of movement in terms of geography and economics, respectively. Like Wright's Bigger Thomas in *Native Son*, Lutie's social mobility is greatly impeded by an overdetermined, lethal environment that narrows avenues of escape. Nevertheless, she does manage to move from the South to the North and later to flee Harlem on a train.

Though Hurston sets her work in the midst of rural southern folk culture, it is interesting to contrast her depictions of rural southern folk with Toomer's. Jean Toomer represented the lushness of the southern rural landscape and southern rural lifestyles in *Cane* (1923) as one might expect of an incredibly sensitive outsider. The work (which some call a novel) is dominated by its attention to sexual and sensual matters. Finally, black writers were beginning to talk about sex. Sex, sexuality, and sensuality had been taboo topics in the literature of previous decades. Toomer's southern women, however, seem instinct driven, whereas Hurston's Janie Crawford emerges as a multidimensional character. Hurston comes across as an insider among rural southern black folk.

Sex and sexuality issues are explored to some extent in all the works discussed in this chapter. Though matters of sensuality are largely muted in Johnson's *Ex-Coloured Man*, it becomes part of the southern rural landscape in *Cane*, which focuses on everything from adultery, interracial sex ("Carma"), and miscegenation ("Fern") to the red-hot lust of a lynching scene ("Blood-Burning Moon"). In *Passing*, Irene Redfield seems oddly attracted to her childhood friend Clare Kendry in a way that she is not attracted to her own husband. The words Larsen uses to describe Clare—as seen through Irene's eyes—are filled with sensual desire. The cool, sweet, seemingly homoerotic desire expressed in the polite *Passing* gives way to Janie Crawford's search for a way to experience the fullness of her sexual passion. Sexuality becomes rape and charges of rape in Wright's brutal *Native Son*. Bigger Thomas rapes and murders his black girlfriend, Bessie Mears, and is accused of raping Mary Dalton. Similarly, in *The Street*, the topic of sexuality manifests itself in predatory and violent terms. Lutie Johnson is considered and treated as sexual prey by several characters, and she ends up killing one of them. Clearly, the fiction produced in the first half of the twentieth century continued to cover old ground even as it opened up new areas of inquiry for the novel and paved the way for the flowering that was yet to come.

Bibliography

Andrews, William L., Frances Smith Foster, and Trudier Harris, eds. *The Oxford Companion to African American Literature*. New York: Oxford UP, 1997.

Baker, Jr., Houston A. *Modernism and the Harlem Renaissance*. Chicago, U of Chicago P, 1987.

Bloom, Harold, ed. *Bigger Thomas*. New York: Chelsea House, 1990.

—. *Richard Wright*. New York: Chelsea House, 1987.

—. *Richard Wright's Native Son*. New York: Chelsea House, 1988.

Bontemps, Arna. *Black Thunder*. 1936. Boston: Beacon, 1968.

Bontemps, Arna. *The Harlem Renaissance Remembered*. New York: Dodd and Mead, 1971.

Bontemps, Arna, and Langston Hughes, eds. *The Book of Negro Folklore*. New York: Dodd and Mead, 1958.

Brown, Sterling. *The Negro in American Fiction*. Washington, D.C.: The Associates in Negro Folk Education, 1937.

Brown, Sterling, Arthur P. Davis, and Ulysses Lee, eds. *The Negro Caravan*. 1941. New York: Arno P, 1969.

Butler, Robert J, ed. *The Critical Response to Richard Wright*. Westport, Conn.: Greenwood P, 1995.

Campbell, James. *Exiled in Paris: Richard Wright, James Baldwin, Samuel Beckett and Others on the Left Bank*. New York: Scribner, 1995.

Cannon, Katie Geneva. *Katie's Canon: Womanism and the Soul of the Black Community*. Continuum: New York, 1995.

Davis, Arthur P., and Michael Peplow, eds. *The New Negro Renaissance*. New York: Holt, Rinehart & Winston, 1975.

Davis, Thadious M. *Nella Larsen, Novelist of the Harlem Renaissance: A Woman's Life Unveiled*. Baton Rouge: Louisiana State UP, 1994

Du Bois, W. E. B. *The Souls of Black Folk*. 1903. Ed. Henry Louis Gates, Jr., and Terri Hume Oliver. New York: W. W. Norton, 1999.

Dundes, Alan, ed. *Mother Wit from the Laughing Barrel: Readings in the Interpretation of Afro-American Folklore*. U of Mississippi P, 1990.

Ervin, Hazel Arnett. *Ann Petry: A Bio-Bibliography*. New York: G. K. Hall, 1993.

Fabre, Michel. *The Unfinished Quest of Richard Wright*. 1973. Urbana: U of Illinois P, 1993.

Fauset, Jessie Redmon. *The Chinaberry Tree*. New York: Frederick A. Stokes, 1932.

—. *Comedy: American Style*. New York: Frederick A. Stokes, 1933.

—. *Plum Bun*. New York: Frederick A. Stokes, 1929.

—. *There Is Confusion*. New York: Boni & Liverright, 1924.

Felgar, Robert. *Student Companion to Richard Wright*. Westport, Conn.: Greenwood P, 2000.

—. *Understanding Richard Wright's Black Boy: A Student Casebook to Issues, Sources, and Historical Documents*. Westport, Conn.: Greenwood P, 1998.

Fisher, Rudolph. *The City of Refuge: The Collected Stories of Rudolph Fisher*. Ed. w/Introd. John McCluskey, Jr. Columbia: U of Missouri P, 1990.

—. *The Conjure-Man Dies: A Mystery Tale of Dark Harlem*. 1932. Ann Arbor: U of Michigan P, 1992.

—. *The Walls of Jericho*. 1928. New York: Arno Press, 1969.

Gates, Jr., Henry Louis. "The Trope of the New Negro and the Reconstruction of the Image of the Black." *Representations* 24 (Fall 1988): 129–55.

Gates, Jr., Henry Louis, and K. A. Appiah, eds. *Richard Wright: Critical Perspectives Past and Present*. New York: Amistad, 1993.

Gayle, Addison. *Richard Wright: Ordeal of a Native Son*. 1980. Gloucester, Mass.: P. Smith, 1983.

Hakutani, Yoshinobu, ed. *Critical Essays on Richard Wright*. Boston: G. K. Hall, 1982.

—. *Richard Wright and Racial Discourse*. Columbia: U of Missouri P, 1996.

Harris, Trudier. *Exorcising Blackness*. Bloomington: Indiana UP, 1984.

—. "Our People, Our People." *Alice Walker and Zora Neale Hurston: The Common Bond*. Ed. Lillie P. Howard. Westport, Conn.: Greenwood P, 1993. 31–42.

Holladay, Hilary. *Ann Petry*. New York: Twayne, 1996.

Huggins, Nathan. *Harlem Renaissance*. New York: Oxford UP, 1971.

Huggins, Nathan, ed. *Voices from the Harlem Renaissance*. New York: Oxford UP, 1976.

Hurston, Zora Neale. "Art and Such." 1938. *Reading Black, Reading Feminist: A Critical Anthology*. Ed. Henry Louis Gates, Jr.. New York: Meridian, 1990. 21–26.

—. "Characteristics of Negro Expression." *Negro: An Anthology*. Ed. Nancy Cunard. London: Wishart, 1934. 39–46.

—. "How It Feels to Be Colored Me." *World Tomorrow* 11 (May 1928): 215–16.

—. *Jonah's Gourd Vine*. Philadelphia: J. B. Lippincott, 1934.

—. *Moses, Man of the Mountain*. Philadelphia: J. B. Lippincott, 1939.

—. *Mules and Men*. 1935. New York: Harper and Row, 1990.

—. "The 'Pet Negro' System." *American Mercury* 56 (March 1943): 593–600.

—. *Seraph on the Suwanee*. New York: Charles Scribner's Sons, 1948.

—. *Spunk: The Selected Short Stories of Zora Neale Hurston*. Berkeley: Turtle Island Foundation, 1985.

—. *Their Eyes Were Watching God*. Philadelphia: J. B. Lippincott, 1937.

Johnson, James Weldon. *The Autobiography of an Ex-Coloured Man*. 1912. Introd. Henry Louis Gates, Jr. New York: Vintage/Random House, 1989.

Joyce, Joyce Ann. *Richard Wright's Art of Tragedy*. Iowa City: U of Iowa P, 1986.

Kinnamon, Keneth. *The Emergence of Richard Wright: A Study in Literature and Society*. 1972. Ann Arbor: UMI Books on Demand, 1998.

Kinnamon, Keneth, ed. *Critical Essays on Richard Wright's Native Son*. London: Prentice Hall International, 1997.

—. *New Essays on Native Son*. New York: Cambridge, 1990.

—. *A Richard Wright Bibliography: Fifty Years of Criticism and Commentary, 1933–1982*. New York: Greenwood P, 1988.

Kramer, Victor, ed. *The Harlem Renaissance Re-examined*. New York: AMS P, 1987.

Larsen, Nella. *The Complete Fiction of Nella Larsen*. Ed. Charles R. Larson. New York: Anchor Books, 2001.

—. *Passing*. 1929. Introd. Ntozake Shange. New York: Modern Library, 2000.

—. *Quicksand*. 1929. Ed. Introd. Thadious M. Davis. New York: Penguin Books, 2002.

Larson, Charles R. *Invisible Darkness: Jean Toomer and Nella Larsen*. Iowa City: U of Iowa P, 1993.

Lively, Adam. "'Passing': A Question of Identity." *Masks: Blackness, Race and the Imagination*. New York: Oxford UP, 2000. 161–202.

Locke, Alain, ed. *The New Negro*. 1925. Introd. Arnold Rampersad. New York: Atheneum, 1992.

McClendon, Jacquelyn Y. *The Politics of Color in the Fiction of Jessie Fauset and Nella Larsen*. Charlottesville: UP of Virginia, 1995.

McDowell, Deborah. "Introduction." Nella Larsen. *Quicksand and Passing*. Boston: Beacon, 1986.

Mitchell, Angelyn, ed. *Within the Circle*. Durham: Duke, 1994.

Mitchell, Hayley R., ed. *Readings on Native Son*. San Diego: Greenhaven P, 2000.

Petry, Ann. *The Street*. 1946. Boston: Houghton Mifflin, 1974.

Pickens, William. *American Aesop; Negro and Other Humor*. 1926. New York: AMS P, 1969.

—. *The New Negro: His Political, Civil and Mental Status, and Related Essays*. 1916. New York: Negro Universities Press, 1969.

—. *The Vengeance of the Gods, and Three Other Stories of Real American Color Line Life*. 1922. New York: AMS Press, 1975.

Roberts, John W. *From Trickster to Badman: The Black Folk Hero in Slavery and Freedom*. Philadelphia: U of Pennsylvania P, 1989.

Roses, Lorraine, and Ruth Elizabeth Randolph, eds. *Harlem Renaissance and Beyond: Literary Biographies of 100 Black Women Writers, 1900–1945*. Boston: G. K. Hall, 1990.

Rowley, Hazel. *Richard Wright: The Life and Times*. New York: Henry Holt and Company, 2001.

Shockley, Ann Allen. *Afro-American Women Writers, 1746–1933*. New York: New American Library, 1989.

Singh, Amritjit, William Shiver, and S. Brodwin, eds. *The Harlem Renaissance: Revaluations*. New York: Garland, 1989.

Somerville, Siobhan B. *Queering the Color Line: Race and the Invention of Homosexuality in American Culture*. Durham: Duke UP, 2000.

Stepto, Robert. *From Behind the Veil: A Study of Afro-American Narrative*. 1979. 2nd ed. Chicago: U of Illinois P, 1991.

Thurman, Wallace. *The Blacker the Berry: A Novel of Negro Life*. 1929. New York: AMS P, 1972.

—. *Infants of the Spring*. 1932. Introd. Amritjit Singh. Boston: Northeastern UP, 1992.

Thurman, Wallace et al., eds. *FIRE!!* 1926. Metuchen, N.J.: The Fire!! Press, 1982.

Toomer, Jean. *Cane*. 1923. Norton Critical Edition. Ed. Darwin T. Turner. New York: W. W. Norton. 1988.

Turner, Darwin. "Introduction." Jean Toomer. *Cane*. 1923. Norton Critical Edition. New York: W. W. Norton, 1988.

Walker, Alice. *In Search of Our Mothers' Gardens: Womanist Prose*. New York: Harcourt Brace & Company, 1983.

Walker, Alice, ed. *I Love Myself When I Am Laughing...And Then Again When I Am Looking Mean and Impressive: A Zora Neale Hurston Reader*. New York: The Feminist P, 1979.

Walker, Margaret. *Richard Wright, Daemonic Genius: A Portrait of the Man, a Critical Look at His Work*. New York: Warner Books, 1988.

Wall, Cheryl, ed. *Their Eyes Were Watching God: A Casebook*. New York: Oxford, 2000.

—. *Women of the Harlem Renaissance*. Bloomington: Indiana UP. 1995.

Washington, Mary Helen. *Invented Lives: Narratives of Black Women 1860–1960*. New York: Anchor Books, 1987.

West, Dorothy. *The Living is Easy*. 1948. Old Westbury: Feminist P, 1982.

Wintz, Cary D. *Black Culture and the Harlem Renaissance*. Houston: Rice UP, 1988.

Wright, Richard. *Black Boy: A Record of Childhood and Youth*. 1945. HarperPerennial, 1993.

—. *How "Bigger" Was Born: The Story of Native Son*. New York: Harper & Brothers. 1940.

—. *Lawd Today*. 1963. Boston: Northeastern UP, 1993.
—. *The Long Dream*. 1958. Boston: Northeastern UP, 2000.
—. *Native Son*. 1940. New York: HarperPerennial, 1993.
—. *The Outsider*. 1954. New York: HarperPerennial, 1993.

Suggested Topics for Writing Critical Essays

1. Compare and contrast the use of the theme of passing in Johnson's and Larsen's novels.
2. Conduct a gendered analysis of Du Boisian double-consciousness in Larsen's novel.
3. Write a paper in which you explore the varying ways that passing is represented in Larsen's novel.
4. Compare and contrast Clare Kendry to Iola Leroy in Harper's novel of the same title (chapter 3).
5. Use gender to compare and contrast the impact of societal forces on the lives of Bigger Thomas (*Native Son*) and Lutie Johnson (*The Street*).
6. Explore the various ways that sex, sensuality, and/or sexuality are represented in *Their Eyes Were Watching God*, or any of the other novels featured in this chapter. Alternatively, examine the inclusion of sexuality in contrast to its exclusion in any story or novel featured in the previous chapters.
7. Examine closely Hurston's novel's use of folklore and folk forms.
8. Compare and contrast the use of landscape in *Cane* and *Their Eyes*.
9. Compare and contrast the use of the mulatto figure in a work featured in this chapter with one of the works featured in a previous chapter.

Questions to Guide Your Reading

The Autobiography of an Ex-Coloured Man

1. Is there a "tragic mulatta" in this story? What "types" or "archetypes" do you find?
2. What is the narrator's central quest? For what is he searching? How is Du Boisian double-consciousness played out in this story?
3. What does the narrator gain by *passing*? Does he lose anything by *passing*?

4. How does the narrator divide black Americans in terms of class? Are the class biases revealed in the text those of the narrator/protagonist, those of the author, or both? Explain.
5. The story is told in episodes. Can you tell when one episode ends and the next begins? Describe an episode.
6. How does the legacy of slavery factor into the narrator's story? Is this story fiction or autobiography? What point of view does the narrator use?
7. What does the narrator reveal about the history of black American music and the patronage system for black artists at the turn of the twentieth century?
8. What does the story reveal about economic opportunity for black Americans during this period?
9. How is Du Boisian double-consciousness depicted in this story? Cite at least two passages from the text to back up your answer.
10. How does the narrator benefit from passing? Cite specific passages in your response.
11. Using specific textual evidence, explain how "slavery" and "freedom" are defined in this story. Is the narrator "enslaved" in some sense during all or part of this narrative? Is he "free" at the end of the narrative?

Cane

1. Identify the spatial and temporal settings for each of the stories in *Cane*. Where does the "action" take place, and what is the historical context or backdrop? How is the title of the text related to these matters?
2. Characterize the author's relationship to the subject matter and characters in each of the stories. What judgments, if any, are apparent?
3. Identify recurring themes and tropes, or motifs, in the stories. Note the author's engagement with the southern rural landscape and relations between the races. How does he characterize such relationships? Where does violence occur?
4. Identify the narrative point of view for each story. Characterize the mood of each story. How does the mood affect your ability to engage actively with the plot and characters?
5. Speculate as to why Toomer focuses so intently on female characters in his stories. Are his representations realistic? Explain why you feel the characters are, or are not, well-defined.

Passing

1. McDowell writes in the introduction to the text that *Passing* is not simply about hidden racial identity, it is also about hidden sexual identity. Do you agree or disagree? Explain. Other than the charade of passing for white, what other charades take place in the story?
2. As you read, mark passages that include expressions of homoerotic desire. Define the "nameless, shameful impulse" that Irene Redfield mentions.
3. Describe Clare Kendry based on the information provided through Irene's recollection and observation of her. Can we trust Irene's information? Irene clearly thinks of herself as quite different from Clare. Do you agree? Explain. What is the effect of having information filtered through Irene's consciousness?
4. What differences in Clare's and Irene's backgrounds help to account for their different approaches to the "race problem"?
5. Mark passages that deal with issues of class in the novel. Compare and contrast the Redfield household/marriage with the Bellew household/marriage. Why does Clare refuse to hire a black maid? Characterize the relationship between Irene and Kulena.
6. Why do you suppose the author leaves ambiguous the question of whether Clare falls or gets pushed to her death? Explain.
7. How does Clare's rationale for passing compare to that of the ex-coloured man in Johnson's text? Is money their only motivation? Do you think Irene wants to pass? How is Du Boisian double-consciousness played out in this story?
8. Using specific textual evidence, explain how "slavery" and "freedom" are defined in this story. Is anyone "enslaved" at the beginning of the text and has anyone been "liberated" by the end?

Their Eyes Were Watching God

1. What is the narrative point of view? Does this narrative in any way resemble a freedom narrative or neofreedom narrative?
2. How does Hurston's language use affect your reading of the text?
3. What men play important roles in Janie Crawford's life? Compare and contrast these men both in terms of how they are similar and/or different from one another and in terms of how each views Janie.

4. Is this a quest narrative? Explain. If it is a quest narrative, who is on a quest and for what is she searching? Would you conclude that progress is made? Where is the evidence?
5. Who is Phoeby, what is her role, and why is she important to the story?
6. Hurston makes abundant use of folklore, gossip, storytelling, and oration in general in this story. Note the various places where this occurs.
7. Of what importance is "voice" and "speaking" in the novel?
8. Trace Hurston's use of trees as metaphor throughout the story.

Native Son

1. What is Bigger Thomas's home environment like at the outset of the story? Do his surroundings "improve"?
2. What is the symbolic nature of the rat in the opening pages of the novel? Who owns the tenement in which Bigger and his family live? Describe the Thomas family.
3. Why does Bigger kill Mary Dalton? Why does he murder Bessie Mears? For which crime or crimes is he convicted? Note the varying ways Bessie's body is used in the story.
4. How many major characters are figuratively blind in this story? Literally blind? When does Bigger finally "see"?
5. Why is Bigger Thomas a thief? Why is he afraid to steal from white people? What is his attitude toward white people?
6. Profile Mary Dalton and her boyfriend. What kind of white people are they? What are their political inclinations?
7. What is the economic climate like during the time period in which this novel is set?
8. Characterize Bigger's capture and arrest.
9. What is the dominant metaphor or trope for Bigger's story?

The Street

1. What are Lutie Johnson's economic options?
2. What settings other than the Harlem street, where Lutie and Bub live for most of the novel, are represented? How are these other settings related to Lutie's belief that she can achieve the so-called American Dream?
3. Identify Lutie's oppressors and predators. What do they want from her? Why do they wish to control her body?
4. What is Bub's situation vis-à-vis his mother's? What is the dominant metaphor or trope for this story?

5. Describe Lutie in relationship to the other women characters in Petry's novel.
6. How do Lutie's race, gender, and class factor into her possibilities for achieving the so-called American Dream?
7. Characterize America's economic situation the time period in which this novel is set?
8. How is this situation reflected in the novel through plot and theme?

CHAPTER V
Fiction 1950–1970

Artists and critics writing before, during, and immediately after the New Negro Movement, like their predecessors, paved the way for the flowering of African American literature that would take place in the coming decades, particularly in the last two decades of the twentieth century. In the twenty years between 1950 and 1970, Americans saw the legal death of Jim Crow and the establishment of the nation's first Black Studies program at San Francisco State University in 1968. Gwendolyn Brooks became the first black American woman to be awarded a Pulitzer Prize, and Ralph Waldo Ellison's *Invisible Man* (1952) gained acceptance in established literary circles. Still, W. E. B. Du Bois's prediction in *The Souls of Black Folk* (1903) that the problem of the color line would plague America throughout the twentieth century is highly apparent in much of the literature produced in relation to the social, cultural, and political movements of these two decades.

In African American literary circles, critical concerns about the criteria for black art would once again take center stage. The energy generated by the Civil Rights and Black Power Movements gave rise to the Black Arts Movement, out of which flowed some of the most vocal and consistently revolutionary and nationalist consciousness-raising art that black Americans had ever produced. Much of the literature took the form of poetry and drama and featured the remarkable talent of Amiri Baraka, Nikki Giovanni, Sonia Sanchez, Haki Madhubuti, Jayne Cortez, and Lucille Clifton, to name just a few. Some early work was published in the leftist journals *Freedomways* and *Liberator*, and, as in previous periods, African Americans founded journals and magazines devoted solely to bringing the work of black artists and critics into print. These include *Black Dialogue*, *Journal of Black Poetry*, *Black Scholar*, and *Negro Digest* (later *Black World*). Two presses, Broadside Press in Detroit and Third World Press in Chicago, played integral roles.

Important critics from this period, such as Larry Neal, Addison Gayle, Jr., and Stephen Henderson, sought (as their predecessors had done) to articulate an aesthetic in relation to the production of African American art: Larry Neal, Addison Gayle, Jr., and Stephen Henderson. Larry Neal and Amiri Baraka would produce *Black Fire* (1968), a landmark anthology featuring fiction, drama, poetry, and essays. Three years later, Addison Gayle, Jr., would publish *The Black Aesthetic* (1971). Students interested in understanding the goals and objectives of the artists and critics identified with the Black Arts Movement should begin with these two texts. Some of the prescriptive aspects of this movement have received sharp criticism, both from among authors who were part of it and others who, while not a part of it, nevertheless benefited either directly or indirectly from the fact of its existence. The art produced as part of the Black Arts Movement was designed to be revolutionary at a time when a revolution in American life and culture was considered by many to be well overdue. Black Arts Movement authors asserted that black people must and should determine their own set of criteria for judging their art. Ironically, one of the most celebrated texts to come out of the decade immediately preceding the Black Arts Movement was produced by Ralph Ellison, whose best known work (*Invisible Man*, 1952) stands as a treatise on the dangers (and limitations) of unquestioned loyalty to any ideology or aesthetic. *Invisible Man* should be read and considered in conjunction with such texts as Frederick Douglass's 1845 *Narrative*, James Weldon Johnson's *The Autobiography of an Ex-Coloured Man* (1912), Richard Wright's *Native Son* (1940) and *Black Boy* (1945), Randall Kenan's *A Visitation of Spirits* (1989), Charles Johnson's *Middle Passage* (1990), and even Alice Randall's *The Wind Done Gone* (2001).

If *Invisible Man* can be defined as black consciousness written on paper, then Gwendolyn Brooks's *Maud Martha* (1953) can be defined as "black female consciousness written on paper"; even more specifically it can be defined as "dark-skinned, coarse-haired, heterosexual black female consciousness on paper." As had been the case with Hurston's *Their Eyes Were Watching God* some sixteen years earlier, the male-dominated black literary establishment yawned at Brooks's representation of black female self-discovery (see Washington). Gender matters were expected to take a backseat to race matters (and this would become the basis for much controversy a couple of decades later). Initially published by Harper and Row, *Maud Martha* was reissued in 1993 by Chicago's Third World Press. Students should read the novel with Brooks's poetry, particularly *Annie Allen*. This story of self-discovery (bildungsroman) also fits in well among texts such as Harriet Jacobs's *Incidents in the Life of a Slave Girl* (1861), Zora Neale Hurston's *Their Eyes Were Watching God*, Paule Marshall's *Brown Girl, Brownstones* (1959), Toni Morrison's *The Bluest Eye* (1970), Audre Lorde's *Zami* (1982), and Alice Randall's *The Wind Done Gone* (2001).

Go Tell It on the Mountain (1953), a novelized spiritual autobiography, is James Arthur Baldwin's contribution to the *bildungsroman*. Other works include a groundbreaking story about homosexuality in *Giovanni's Room* (1956), the best-selling critique of America as a prejudice-laden "democracy" in *Another Country* (1962), and the somewhat optimistic (in terms of race relations and fluid sexuality) *Tell Me How Long the Train's Been Gone* (1968). The latter text depicts the potential for real love and intimacy between African Americans and whites in America. The last two novels, in particular, reflect Baldwin's growing concern with the pervasiveness of racism, sexism, heterosexism, and classism in America. His treatment of black homosexuality in his fiction had few precedents. During the Harlem Renaissance, Richard Bruce Nugent had published "Sadji" (1925) and the more explicit "Smoke, Lilies, and Jade" (*FIRE!!* 1926). Several years later, author/critic Wallace Thurman would include several black gay characters in *Infants of the Spring* (1932). Langston Hughes's poem "Cafe 3 A.M." and his short story "Blessed Assurance" feature gay characters, as does Owen Dodson's 1951 novel *Boy at the Window*. In *Tell Me How Long the Train's Been Gone*, Baldwin combines his concerns about racism and compulsory heterosexism by depicting loving, nurturing bisexual relationships among a black artist, his white female confidante and friend, and his militant young black male lover. As *manhood* has almost always been a recurring issue in African American literature, Baldwin received harsh criticism both for his views on sexuality and his personal sexual orientation from those who felt that heterosexuality was a necessary correlate to manhood. Baldwin expended considerable energy in an effort to disabuse American society of that notion; he held out his literary representations as examples of the potential for overcoming socially constructed barriers to love and positive interactions among human beings. An author clearly ahead of his time, Baldwin's work is currently enjoying a period of renewed interest.

Both Alice Childress (1916–1994) and Langston Hughes (1902–1967) would underscore the value of laughter in collections of short, oftentimes humorous (but always insightful) conversations that provide telling commentary on contemporaneous issues. Childress's *Like One of the Family...Conversations from a Domestic's Life* (1956) contains sixty-two short conversations between heroine Mildred Johnson and her friend Marge. Hughes collected several volumes of Simple stories from his earlier *Chicago Defender* series, including *The Best of Simple* (1961). The short sketches typically feature conversations between Jesse B. Simple (Simple) and Boyd, the narrator. Both Mildred Johnson and Jesse

B. Simple provide commonsense observations about everyday issues related to being black and working-class in America.

Samuel R. Delany (b. 1942), the first known black American author to make science fiction his specialty, published several early works during this period. They include *Jewels* (1963), *The Fall of the Towers* trilogy (1963–1965), *The Ballad of Beta-2* (1965), *Babel 17* (1966), *The Einstein Intersection* (1967), and *Nova* (1968). Delany's later works of the 1970s and 1980s are deemed superior to these early offerings. Chester Himes (1909–1984), famous for his work in the detective-story genre, would publish some of his most famous novels during this period, including *The Big Gold Dream* (1960), *All Shot Up* (1960), *Cotton Comes to Harlem* (1965), *The Heat's On* (1966), and *Blind Man with a Pistol* (1969). Himes uses the standard detective-story formula with a twist: He demonstrates the cause-and-effect relationship between oppression and black "criminality." It might be fruitful to consider certain of his works in conjunction with Richard Wright's *Native Son* (1940) and Ann Petry's *The Street* (1946). At least two of Himes's novels have been made into movies.

Also during this period, John Alfred Williams (b. 1925) published several works, including *One for New York* (1960), *Sissie* (1963), and *The Man Who Cried I Am* (1967). In the first two novels, Williams presents characters who struggle against an oppressive culture but find a way to reconcile themselves to America's inherent racism. In the latter novel, however, the protagonist is compelled to respond through violence. Kristin Hunter's *God Bless the Child* (1964) also depicts black Americans vis-à-vis oppressive social conditions, depicting characters in a tragic quest for material success. Protagonist Rosie Fleming literally and figuratively succumbs to consumption in this very unflattering, at times pathological, portrait of urban African Americans trying to achieve their version of the American Dream by almost any means necessary.

Celebrated contemporary author John Edgar Wideman published his first novel, *A Glance Away,* in 1967, partly as an attempt to distance himself from the Black Arts Movement. Subsequent works have reflected a shift in this early strategy. Ishmael Reed, who is as much a critic as he is a brilliant and innovative novelist, published *The Freelance Pallbearers* and *Yellow Back Radio Broke-Down* (which parodies the American western) in 1967 and 1969, respectively. In addition to novels and poetry, he has written operas, songs, essays, and plays. A master of parody, Reed was a very active presence in the Black Arts Movement, but he is careful to avoid any aesthetic that is overly prescriptive or dogmatic, regardless of its source. We will look more closely at his work in the next chapter. The multitalented Clarence Major is an incredibly important author whose novel *All-Night Visitors* (1969) falls within this period, as does the important essay, "A Black Criterion" (1967). In literary circles Major, who is also an accomplished visual artist, is best known for his metafictional novels, though he produces poetry and short fiction as well. John Oliver Killens also began publishing books during this period. His first novel, *Youngblood*, appeared in 1954. His other novels include *And Then We Heard the Thunder* (1963), *Sippi* (1967), *The Cotillion; or, One Good Bull is Half the Herd* (1971), *The Great Black Russian; A Novel on the Life of Alexander Pushkin* (1988, published posthumously). He also produced a fictionalized account of Denmark Vesey's life, His Great Gittin' Up Morning (1972), and a book on the life of John Henry, *A Man Ain't Nothin' But a Man: The Adventures of John Henry* (1975).

Literary style and technique vary widely among the authors. Brooks's *Maud Martha* reads more like poetry than fiction. Other works, including that of Wideman, Reed, and Major, often fit under the rubric of metafiction, a product of the postmodern impulse that recalls certain experiments by British writers as the novel came into existence in the eighteenth century as a new form. At the height of the Black Arts Movement, Major (and others) dared to emphasize the fragmented nature of experience and, therefore, identity; with *All-Night Visitors* and later works Major suggests that contemporary society affords no possibility for anything like a coherent identity. Baldwin's realistic three-part narrative begins in the present, takes the reader through the personal histories of several characters, and then returns to the present. The chronological narrative of Ellison's surrealistic *Invisible Man* comes pouring out of the unnamed protagonist's consciousness. In addition to experiments and innovation in narrative form and subject matter, gender (or the specificity of black women's experience) became a central concern in black women's writing, at least for the women who wrote about these experiences. This is especially apparent in the work of Brooks, Childress, and Marshall.

In this chapter we will focus on the following representative works: Ellison's *Invisible Man*, Brooks's *Maud Martha*, Baldwin's *Go Tell It on the Mountain*, *Childress's Like One of the Family*, Marshall's *Brown Girl, Brownstones*, and Langston Hughes's *The Best of Simple*. All these works have in common a preoccupation with the myth of the American Dream; they are not represented as the "best" of what is available from the period, as much as they represent what students are likely to encounter in a typical undergraduate course. It goes without saying that many equally representative works must be omitted. Students should be aware of two other works that, while they do not fall into the fiction genre, speak eloquently to urban black America's disillusionment with the myth of the American Dream. They are the poems in Langston Hughes's *Montage of a Dream Deferred* (1951) and Lorraine Hansberry's famous play, *A Raisin in the Sun* (1959).

Ellison's *Invisible Man* (which won several major awards, including a National Book Award) has long been seen as the novel of black male experience in America to be bested. The great-grandson of formerly enslaved persons, Ellison was born in Oklahoma City, Oklahoma, on March 1, 1914, to Ida Milsap and Lewis Alfred Ellison. His mother and father had been born in Georgia and South Carolina, respectively. His father died after having served the United States military in China, Cuba, and the Philippines; Ellison's mother worked at various domestic jobs to support the family. Educated in segregated schools in Oklahoma, Ellison vowed early not to allow America's racial prescriptions to limit his chances for self-actualization. As had happened with W. E. B. Du Bois almost half a century earlier, Ellison received a scholarship to attend a black college so that he would not try to attend one of the large predominantly white universities in his state. He attended Tuskegee Institute, the school founded by Booker T. Washington in 1881. Ellison would use a Tuskegee-like setting and a Washingtonesque figure to satirize the kind of ideological programming African Americans were apt to receive at such institutions. Ellison left Tuskegee after meeting several figures in the black literary establishment (including Arna Bontemps, Langston Hughes, and Richard Wright) in New York during the summer of his junior year. He wrote the five words that begin his masterwork—"I am an invisible man"—in 1945 while he was serving with the merchant marine. Ellison also published two collections of his essays: *Shadow and Act* (1964) and *Going to the Territory* (1986). He died on April 16, 1994. His second novel, *Juneteenth* (published in part as a short story of the same name in 1965), and some previously unpublished short stories have since been published. Ellison's writing reflects his concern with the interplay between black American and European American culture. He attributes his literary awakening to T. S. Eliot's *The Waste Land*, but he was also influenced by Henry James, James Joyce, Hemingway, Dostoyevsky, and others. His first break came when he wrote a book review for a magazine for which Richard Wright served as editor.

Like James Weldon Johnson's *Autobiography of an Ex-Coloured Man* (1912), *Invisible Man* features an anonymous black male protagonist whose quest leads him through a series of episodes that finally offer no real resolution to the issue of identity at the root of his quest. In the novel's prologue, Ellison immediately establishes a blues mood and a question about the black past by using Louis Armstrong's words: "What did I do to be so black and blue?" Speaking from an urban basement illuminated with power pilfered from the highly symbolic Monopolated Light & Power company, the hero sets up the foundation for the story of how he came to be in that basement. His story spans some twenty years and is composed of twenty-five chapters plus prologue and epilogue. The first-person narrative begins in the South, where the hero was born and "educated," and brings us full circle through the narrator's odyssey back to the northern urban hole from whence it begins—where the hero is in hibernation with only his black American "self" as company.

Author Gwendolyn Brooks was born three years after Ellison, on June 7, 1917, in Topeka, Kansas, to schoolteacher Keziah Corinne Wims and janitor David Anderson Brooks. The family moved to Chicago five weeks later. Like Langston Hughes, Brooks is best known for her poetry. A number of her poems were (like Hughes's Simple stories discussed below) published in the black *Chicago Defender*. Her first poem appeared in *American Child* magazine when Brooks was only thirteen. Three years later James Weldon Johnson had read and critiqued her poetry. (Langston Hughes would later become her friend and mentor as well.) When she graduated from high school in 1935, she was already a regular contributor to the weekly variety column of the *Chicago Defender*. In 1936 Brooks graduated from Wilson Junior College and then worked for a short time as a maid and secretary. Two years later she joined Chicago's NAACP Youth Council, and a year later she married Henry Lowington Blakely, II. Brooks and her husband actually lived in a kitchenette apartment (similar to the one described in *Maud Martha*) at 63rd and Chaplain in Chicago above a real estate agency. She studied poetry with Inez Cunningham Stark at a community art center on the Southside of Chicago. Brooks would later teach creative writing to one of the Southside's best-known youth "gangs," the Blackstone Rangers. Winning the Midwestern Writers' Conference poetry award in 1943 led ultimately to the publication of her first collection of poems, *A Street in Bronzeville*, in 1945. Other volumes include *Annie Allen* (1949)—for which she won a 1950 Pulitzer—*Maud Martha* (1953), *The Bean Eaters* (1961), and *In the Mecca* (1968). During this period she also wrote reviews and articles that were published in the *New York Times*, *Negro Digest*, and the *New York Herald Tribune*.

Brooks's literary career took a decided turn after she attended a Black Writers' Conference at Fisk University in 1967 and interacted with a number of artists involved with the Black Arts Movement. She credits these younger artists with helping her gain greater awareness about American society and about herself. In the 1970s, she became a consultant in American literature for the Library of Congress and was named Poet Laureate of Illinois. Brooks has taught in a number of colleges and universities, including Chicago's Columbia College, the University of Wisconsin at Madison, and City University of New York. She represented in a variety of poetic forms the human condition from a black perspective. Much of her work concentrates on the people who live in a small Chicago community. Her career as author, teacher, and community activist spanned almost seventy years. She died on December 3, 2000.

Comparable to Ellison's *Invisible Man*, Brooks's *Maud Martha* represents a pending break with the naturalistic and deterministic tone set by Richard Wright in *Native Son* (1940) and Ann Petry in *The Street* (1946). In some ways *Maud Martha* is more akin to the realism of Hurston's classic *Their Eyes Were Watching God* (1937) by its focus on a woman's journey of self-discovery and her growing awareness of her own agency. Certainly *Maud Martha* and Paule Marshall's *Brown Girl, Brownstones* help to connect the relatively few previously published and available quest narratives with black female protagonists to the proliferation of women-centered texts that would appear in the final decades of the twentieth century.

Set before, during, and after World War II and divided into thirty-four sketches—some of which are as short as three pages—*Maud Martha* thematizes (in a manner similar to James Weldon Johnson in *Autobiography of an Ex-Coloured Man*) the Du Boisian notion of double-consciousness. Brooks expands on the idea of double-consciousness, however, by presenting a title character and protagonist who must overcome her feelings of rejection in a world that values whiteness (light skin), maleness, European features, and "good hair" over blackness (dark skin), femaleness, African features, and coarse hair. In effect, she experiences "multiple consciousness." In 1970, Toni Morrison would advance this theme in *The Bluest Eye*.

Similar to *Maud Martha*, James Baldwin's first novel, *Go Tell It on the Mountain*, is also somewhat autobiographical. Baldwin's novel is based loosely on events surrounding the first fourteen years of the author's life. Born August 2, 1924, Baldwin was the son of Emma Berdis Jones and the stepson of David Baldwin. He grew up in Harlem where he attended Frederick Douglass Junior High and Dewitt Clinton High School. Like many of the other writers discussed in this volume, he was an avid reader who was quite enamored of literature. He decided as a teenager that he would become a writer. At the age of fourteen he underwent a conversion similar to that of his protagonist John Grimes in *Go Tell It on the Mountain*. After high school he worked for a time in Trenton, New Jersey, and he used this period as the backdrop for *Notes of a Native Son* (1955) which, in part, revisits the strained relationship between Baldwin and his stepfather and recounts the man's death and funeral.

Baldwin then lived in Greenwich Village for several years before leaving America for Paris. Following the example set by other African American artists—including Josephine Baker, Chester Himes, and Richard Wright—Baldwin left America in an attempt to increase his options for realizing a greater measure of his potential. In the title essay from *Notes of a Native Son*, Baldwin writes of the near catastrophic experience that precipitated his flight away from America. Best appreciated during his lifetime for the fiery nonfiction that displayed his razor sharp intellect, Baldwin published six novels—the four mentioned above and two others: *If Beale Street Could Talk* (1974) and *Just Above My Head* (1979). He also published a collection of short stories titled *Going to Meet the Man* (1965), and he collected his nonfiction in *The Price of the Ticket* (1985). He was at his home in St. Paul de Vence, France, when he died in 1987.

The Great Depression is the time frame for *Go Tell It on the Mountain*. The year is 1935 and the protagonist needs to reconcile his naturally burgeoning sexuality with his dogmatic religious teachings that forbid all but heterosexual relations within marriage. In addition, he lacks much of the information he needs to grapple with the central question of his identity. No one who is able to do so has provided John Grimes with his personal background, with the story of his past that he needs to express himself as an active subject in the world. The first part of the novel reveals the Grimes family's economically impoverished status and general family life. The second part reveals the intimate details of John's personal background through the personal histories of his parents and his Aunt Florence. The third part centers on John's conversion experience and a partial, temporary resolution to his problems.

The waning years of the Great Depression, World War II, and the years that follow represent the setting for Paule Marshall's first published novel, *Brown Girl, Brownstones* (1959). Born Valenza Pauline Burke in Brooklyn, New York, Marshall is the daughter of Samuel and Ada

Clement Burke Marshall. Her parents were from Barbados and had lived in the United States for ten years when Marshall was born in 1929. She graduated Phi Beta Kappa from Brooklyn College in 1953. She also attended Hunter College. Before she became a writer, she worked for the New York Public Library and as a journalist for *Our World* magazine. She has taught English and creative writing at a number of colleges and universities, including Columbia, Virginia Commonwealth University, Yale, the University of Iowa, The University of California-Berkeley, and the University of Massachusetts-Boston. Marshall's other works include *Soul Clap Hands and Sing* (1961)—four novellas tied by a common theme; *The Chosen Place, Timeless People* (1969); *Praisesong for the Widow* (1983); *Reena and Other Stories* (1983); *Daughters* (1991); and *The Fisher King* (2000). Like the Boyce family represented in *Brown Girl, Brownstones*, Marshall's family was part of the West Indian American community trying to realize a part of the American Dream while holding on to valued aspects of their own culture. In her writing, Marshall explores these conflicts and tensions as well as those between black West Indians and other Americans of African descent.

Brown Girl, Brownstones is the coming of age story of Selina Boyce. Selina is a first-generation Barbadian caught up in the family paradox of a mother who wants to fight *tooth and nail* to realize the elusive American Dream and a father whose dream is to earn enough money to return to his homeland. She must come of age amidst this harsh family conflict and eventually choose her own path in life. The story centers on Selina Boyce's journey of self-discovery. Selina is the daughter of Silla and Deighton Boyce, first-generation Barbadians living in a tight-knit West Indian community in Brooklyn, New York. Selina comes of age amid family turmoil brought on by her parents' competing desires: her mother wants to own her own American brownstone, and her father wants only to accumulate enough money to return to his homeland. The story raises and grapples with complex issues about identity, manhood, womanhood, integration, and so forth. *Brown Girl* is, like *Maud Martha*, one of very few black American novels published prior to the 1970s which focuses on a young black female protagonist and her intimate everyday life. Though Gwendolyn Brooks raised the issue of mother-daughter conflict in *Maud Martha*, Marshall takes the issue to much deeper levels in *Brown Girl*. The novel was adopted for television in 1960 by CBS Television Workshop.

If the four texts discussed above take on a somber, almost foreboding tone in representing the elusive nature of the American Dream, then Alice Childress and Langston Hughes provide comic relief while grappling with the same issues in *Like One of the Family* and *The Best of Simple*, respectively. Their critiques of America are no less scathing, however. Mildred Johnson and Jesse B. Simple serve up mother wit, or common sense, in huge doses with each carefully crafted vignette.

Alice Childress was born October 12, 1916, in Charleston, South Carolina. Her grandmother, with whom she went to live at the age of five, would expose young Alice to the arts and teach her the art of storytelling. Though Childress would eventually be forced to drop out of high school following the deaths of her mother and her grandmother, she loved reading and was a frequent visitor at the public library. Literacy and a firm foundation bore Childress through various mundane jobs in sales, domestic work, and the insurance business. In 1940, she appeared as Dolly in John Silvera and Abram Hill's *On Strivers' Row*, based on the famous Harlem community. The following year she joined the American Negro Theatre (and is considered one of its founders) and subsequently appeared in a number of plays, including an adaptation of *Rain* as Sadie Thompson. She received a Tony nomination for her role as Blanche in *Anna Lucasta*, which had a good run on Broadway in the 1940s. Known primarily for her work in drama, Childress wrote several plays, including *Florence* (1949), which anticipated the drama of the Black Arts Movement; *Just a Little Simple* (1950), a musical and dramatic restructuring of Langston Hughes's *Simple Speaks His Mind*; *Trouble in Mind* (1955); *Wedding Band: A Love/Hate Story in Black and White* (1966); and *Wine in the Wilderness* (1969). In 1952 she became the first black American woman to produce a professional play, *Gold through the Trees*. In 1956, she became the first woman to receive an Obie (the award for off-broadway plays), for *Trouble in Mind*. Her novels include *A Hero Ain't Nothin' but a Sandwich* (1973), which was made into a film premiering in 1978; *A Short Walk* (1979); *Rainbow Jordan* (1981); and *Those Other People* (1989). Childress is remembered as someone who used her writing to critique American society and to champion the cause of the poor and the working class.

Like One of the Family . . . is composed of vignettes from Childress's weekly column, "Here's Mildred," which ran briefly in Paul Robeson's *Freedom* before the *Baltimore Afro-American* picked it up. It features the feisty common sense of Mildred, a domestic worker, whose outspokenness stands in stark contrast to the self-effacing, long-suffering, tolerant black maids depicted in white American literature. Mildred is no stereotypical "mammy" of *Gone with the Wind* (1936). Her heroism derives from her indignance and "mother wit" in the face of her employers' racism, inhumanity, and outright stupidity. Through

Mildred's stories, Childress successfully combines humor and satire in a continuing quest to portray accurately the lives of poor people and to struggle against the ignorance upon which prejudice is built.

Langston Hughes accomplishes similar feats with his Simple stories. Many high school students and most college students encounter Hughes's poetry at some point; he is perhaps America's best known black poet. Born to Carrie Langston Hughes and James Nathaniel Hughes in Joplin, Missouri, Hughes grew up primarily in Lawrence, Kansas. Largely through his association with his maternal grandmother, Hughes absorbed a strong appreciation for his rich cultural heritage. He inherited his literary talent from maternal relatives, including his great-uncle John Mercer Langston, who wrote an autobiography titled *From the Virginia Plantation to the National Capital* (1894). Hughes's timely enrollment at Columbia University in New York City just as the New Negro Movement was about to take off proved especially fortuitous. Though he left Columbia in 1922 to travel and work, he eventually graduated from Pennsylvania's historically black Lincoln University in 1929.

Hughes's accomplishments in the literary realm are many and varied. His literary career began with the publication of "The Negro Speaks of Rivers" in the June 1921 issue of *Crisis* Magazine, edited at the time by W. E. B. Du Bois. He rose to prominence as one of the younger artists writing during the period dubbed the New Negro Movement (also called the Harlem Renaissance) discussed in the previous chapter. He eventually published several collections of poetry, including *The Weary Blues* (1926), *Fine Clothes to the Jew* (1927), *One Way Ticket*, (1949), *Montage of a Dream Deferred* (1951), and *Ask Your Mama* (1961). He also published a novel, *Not Without Laughter* (1930); two autobiographical works, *The Big Sea* (1940) and *I Wonder as I Wander* (1956); several volumes collecting his Simple stories written for the *Chicago Defender*; children's stories; and plays, including *Mulatto*, which had a Broadway run during the Great Depression. His very important essay "The Negro Artist and the Racial Mountain," published in *The Nation* in 1926, expresses his philosophy concerning the responsibility of the artist to her or his art vis-à-vis the black community.

We will focus here on the Simple stories because they exemplify so well an aspect of black American culture seldom taught: humor as survival strategy—the ability to laugh in the face of oppression, to find comedy in the tragically ironic. Hughes's most obvious predecessor in this regard (in the short-story form) is Charles Chesnutt, who—in some of his short stories—drew upon a storehouse of folklore and knowledge of black vernacular and culture to invoke humor while muting his more serious critiques of American racial attitudes. Hughes makes his objective much more obvious. He created Simple in the early 1940s to give voice to the paradox of black Americans fighting for democratic ideals abroad when they were denied the benefits of democracy at home. He collected the Simple stories in *Simple Speaks His Mind* (1950), *Simple Takes a Wife* (1953), *Simple Stakes a Claim* (1957), *The Best of Simple* (1961), and *Simple's Uncle Sam* (1965). Akiba Sullivan Harper edited *The Return of Simple* in 1994. The fact that Hughes was able—in subsequent decades—to collect several volumes of the Simple stories attests to the popularity of Jesse B. Simple as a character. In the 1960s, the column found its way into the *New York Post*, and in the 1990s, noted Hughes scholar Arnold Rampersad would refer to Jesse B. Simple (Simple) as black America's most lovable and enduring comic character.

Contexts and Texts

All of the works featured in this chapter were set in whole or in part during the Great Depression of the 1930s. Their collective plots take us from the second decade of the twentieth century through World War II and into the early years of the 1950s. Likewise, they are set in a large urban city, though Ellison's novel begins in the South, where sharecropping was common. Ellison's Trueblood character represents this aspect of black rural life, just as Ellison's too-wise black veteran character represents the many African Americans who served the country during World War II (and in previous wars) and came home to face the same old racism. Brooks's *Maud Martha* also visits this issue briefly.

It would take the social movements of the 1950s, 1960s, and early 1970s to effect the legal and systemic changes necessary to guarantee some measure of equal opportunity for the majority of African Americans living in America. Ralph Ellison's *Invisible Man* (1952)—whose ending eerily forecasts the urban uprisings of the 1960s—came into print just two years before the landmark 1954 Supreme Court decision in *Brown*, which effectively dealt the legal death knell to the "separate but equal" doctrine codified by the 1896 *Plessy* decision. Harry S. Truman was ending his tenure in the White House, but Eisenhower would soon take over. The Montgomery bus boycott (1955–1957) that began with Rosa Parks's defiant act of refusing to give up her seat on a segregated bus in that Alabama city, helped to set the Civil Rights Movement ablaze. Though black women were clearly the catalyst for the Montgomery boycott, it was the event that introduced Martin Luther King, Jr., to America and subsequently to the world. Civil rights issues took center stage as Democrat John F. Kennedy was elected over Eisenhower's vice president Richard M. Nixon in 1960. Thurgood Marshall, who had represented plaintiffs in the famous *Brown* case, was appointed to the United States Supreme Court as its first black member. Lyndon Johnson, who took over the presidency after John F. Kennedy was assassinated on November 22, 1963, spearheaded new government efforts to "level the playing field" in regard to equal opportunity access for African Americans. Thurgood Marshall would later note Johnson's precedent-setting record on civil rights, despite his questionable decisions surrounding the escalating Vietnam conflict. Johnson's decision not to seek a second term helped pave the way for the Nixon years. Some national civil rights organizations that came into existence during these two decades were the Student Nonviolent Coordinating Committee (SNCC, pronounced SNICK), the left-leaning Students for a Democratic Society (SDS), and in the late 1960s the Black Panthers. Malcolm X also came to prominence as a leader in the Nation of Islam and as a model for the Black Power Movement of the 1960s.

However, these events occurred after Ellison's *Invisible Man* (which ends in a full-scale race war) appeared in 1952. The immediate context for Ellison's novel is the period between Booker T. Washington's heyday, which ended with his death in 1915, and the end of World War II. A neofreedom narrative, Ellison's text revisits slavery via the narrator's dying grandfather and the impact of the man's *narrative* on the protagonist's life. Ellison felt that so much of African American literature had previously been directed to whites as a way to protest discrimination and unequal opportunities for African Americans. To Ellison, this often took the form of pleading the case for black humanity, which implied that African Americans could actually be less than fully human. In *Invisible Man* he tries to write in a way that embraces and illustrates the promise and uniqueness of black experience.

Though the novel had its vocal critics, it was generally hailed as evidence of a new and necessary direction in African American literature. Its chief metaphors and tropes are "invisibility," "light," and the "absence of light" (blindness) which controls degree of vision, knowledge, enlightenment, and self-awareness. "Blackness" and "whiteness" also figure prominently. The protagonist's life follows a scheme similar to that of the central subject in a freedom narrative—moving from slavery to freedom—though in this case the author has centered the focus on perceptual and ideological freedom. Thus, the entire story is presented through the anonymous protagonist's consciousness. Following the prologue, in which the hero states that the purpose of his narrative is illumination, he offers a story that is not so much his own as it is that of a typical black American (whose perspective is decidedly male). He invokes black vernacular and cultural forms, including the blues and jazz, most obviously in the Louis Armstrong song mentioned in the prologue and the unforgettable Trueblood episode from the second chapter. The novel is so complexly layered that it could be used as the sole text for a course.

An excellent student and a "credit to his race," the first-person narrator of *Invisible Man* receives as his reward for having attained that status a scholarship to a *Negro* college. Before he receives the scholarship, however, he is forced to compete in a humiliating and bloody mock game of (literally) blind capitalist pursuit as entertainment for the town's white leaders. Chapter 1 is set in the South and contains the narrator's memory of the event, which is dubbed the "Battle Royal." In a stark illustration of the elusive black quest for a piece of the American economic pie, blindfolded adolescent males battle for coins on an electrified rug before an audience of drunken, highly amused, tuxedoed white men—the town's finest. Before the free-for-all, during which the teenagers are encouraged to beat and bloody their rivals, a blond female stripper performs for the entertainment of the white men and as a reminder of what lies outside the reach of black men. Think of the Battle Royal as an initiation rite, an emasculation rite, or a combination of the two in which black males are encouraged to *knock one another off*. After the entertainment, the hero is presented with the college scholarship he had been promised. Swallowing his own blood, he delivers a speech that echoes the "wisdom" of Booker T. Washington's 1895 Atlanta Exposition Speech (included in *Up from Slavery*), but caught up in the excitement, he utters the phrase "social equality" rather than "social responsibility." The overzealous narrator is quickly corrected. He acknowledges his mistake, apologizes, and completes the speech to thunderous applause. (Students should compare the circumstances surrounding this speech with those surrounding the other speeches the narrator makes during the course of his story). With scholarship in hand, the narrator enrolls at an all-black college that Ellison models (ideologically) after Booker T. Washington's Tuskegee Institute.

After delivering a speech praising the model of Booker T. Washington, he is awarded his scholarship and a briefcase. Scholarship in hand, the hero goes to a southern black college, and manages to live up to what is expected of him—for a time. Having been primed by his grandfather's outmoded advice to don the mask of the grinning slave in order to survive, the hero of *Invisible Man* initially fares well under the Washingtonesque Dr. Bledsoe, the college president who is both minstrel and tyrant. Bledsoe grins in the faces of the college's white sponsors while running roughshod over the student body and punishing those who stray from his dictates. When the narrator—assigned by Bledsoe to chauffeur visiting sponsor Mr. Norton—inadvertently ventures off the beaten path (strays from prescription) and shows the sponsor some of the more harsh realities of black experience, Bledsoe sends him packing. First, he provides the narrator with several letters addressed to rich white men in New York City; the naive narrator believes they are letters of recommendation. His venturing off the *prescribed* course effectively set into motion his journey toward self-knowledge. As with Baldwin's John Grimes, the narrator needs to understand his past in order to respond in the present to the question: Who am I? Or perhaps a better question is, "What did I do to be so black and blue?"

In New York City, he goes from rich white man to rich white man with Bledsoe's letters, thinking that surely one of them will offer him a job. His "luck" changes when one of the men is out of town and he meets instead with the man's son, a Mr. Emerson—who, as it happens, bears the last name of Ellison's namesake Ralph Waldo Emerson. Emerson is surprised that the narrator had not actually read the supposed recommendation; he shares the contents of the letter with him. Disillusioned, because the letters direct the addressees to stifle the narrator's progress, he follows up on a job lead that Emerson-the-younger provides. He secures employment at a paint factory where his job is to mix a small amount of black paint into a white base to create "optic white." Here Ellison comments on a history of miscegenation and illusions surrounding race and racial purity. As with the life-altering stint as Mr. Norton's chauffeur, the narrator soon strays from the script and creates something other than optic white—finding once again that he has been assigned to control what he can not control, and once again, he is banished. The other side of this "coin" is, however, that the narrator seems to have a natural resistance to strict programming, and wherever he goes his inability to adhere to the prescriptions of rigid ideology causes a disruption in the system. This basic aspect of the narrator is most closely related to Ellison's own distrust of formula, dogma, and prescription.

Next, the narrator is assigned to the boiler room of the paint factory, and he ends up hospitalized from the explosion that results from his presence there. When he awakens in his hospital bed, he realizes that his doctors are discussing plans for a lobotomy. He "escapes" this fate, is dismissed from the hospital, and sets off on a series of encounters with a variety of ideologues and groups; he joins an interracial radical, socialist organization called The Brotherhood and eventually earns their contempt for his inability to follow their script. What becomes clear is that the narrator, like the story's author, can not be counted on to "follow the herd." Just as he veered off Bledsoe's prescribed course in college, and could not be counted on to follow the proper directions in mixing optic white paint, he strays once again from the prescribed ideology.

It is important while reading this challenging text to think of the protagonist as *black American consciousness*. Ellison uses characters and organizations such as Bledsoe, Ras the Exhorter/Destroyer, and The Brotherhood to represent ideological solutions available to African Americans coping with the social, economic, and political conditions of pre-1950 America, and at some point the protagonist manages to get on the bad side of them all. He is finally driven underground during the violent Brotherhood-orchestrated race war that ends the novel. The story is, thus, eerily prophetic. In the epilogue, we are reminded that the protagonist has been speaking to us from his basement hole for some five hundred pages. Alone there with only the self he managed to rescue, he continues his symbolic siphoning of "power and light." *Invisible Man* is ultimately about the value of self-knowledge. The hole into which the protagonist settles to hibernate serves as a sort of isolation chamber shielding him from the immediate influences of the prescriptions and formulas to which he seems to have an innate aversion. Ellison's overarching agenda in *Invisible Man* thus makes it a closely related predecessor to such texts as Ishmael Reed's *Mumbo Jumbo* and Charles Johnson's *Oxherding Tale*. Its themes, tropes, and subject matter also connect the novel to Douglass's 1845 *Narrative*, Johnson's *Autobiography of an Ex-Coloured Man*, Richard Wright's *Native Son* and *Black Boy*, and Charles Johnson's *Middle Passage* (1992).

Gwendolyn Brooks's *Maud Martha* deals with the developing consciousness of a young girl living in a northern city during the period before, during, and after World War II. Composed of thirty-four very poetic sketches, the novel provides an application of double-consciousness that expands Du Bois's definition to take into consideration the fact not only of race, but also those of gender, caste, and color. For most of the story, Maud Martha Brown is overly preoccupied with the way others (a domineering mother, a chauvinistic husband, boys who prefer light-skinned girls with good hair, and white society in general) see her. Brooks renders the somewhat autobiographical narrative from the third-person limited omniscient perspective.

The novel opens with a description of the young girl who is Maud Martha, and introduces the metaphor of the dandelion (a common thing of undervalued "beauty") to which Maud compares herself. The overwhelming emotion depicted in this opening sketch that reveals the protagonist's central quest is naturally that of desire, or longing. Brooks uses the second sketch to provide detail about a spring landscape and to depict children at play in the schoolyard in the morning. The day is cool and blustery and the overwhelming mood is one of anticipation and possibility. With few exceptions, the remaining sketches are just as tightly rendered, and each one advances Maud Martha further along toward adulthood. The third vignette provides insight into Maud's parents' relationship and Maud's paradoxical relationship with her mother. The death of Maud's grandmother is the focus of the fourth vignette, which evokes feelings of vulnerability and disgust. In the fifth sketch, Maud's feelings of racial inferiority surface as she anticipates a visit from a white classmate. From Maud's perspective, he is the entire white race sitting in judgment of her, the entire black race. The dominant emotion: self-loathing. In the thirteenth vignette, titled "Low Yellow," she explores the definition of "pretty" and how it is defined in terms of skin color and hair texture. Dark-skinned, coarse-haired Maud realizes she does not fit the prevailing definition of "pretty."

The remaining vignettes take us through Maud's somewhat uneventful adolescence, her marriage to Paul-the-bargain-hunter, and the birth of her daughter Paulette. Always the driving force is *desire and yearning*, but Brooks uses each vignette to highlight other moods, attitudes, and emotions, including intrigue, anxiety, shame, resolve, despair, resignation, and optimism. Especially poignant is the vignette "kitchenette folks," which describes the people who live in the building where Maud and Paul's disappointing kitchenette apartment is located. Several experiences eventually help her toward a sense of self that is not based on others' perceptions. A stint as a domestic worker helps her to better understand her husband's attitudes, but a major turning point comes when she gives birth and realizes that she is responsible for the life of another human being. She stands up to her mother for the first time, she realizes that she need not envy her "prettier," more desirable sister Helen, and she even musters up enough self-confidence to confront both a pushy salesperson and a white Santa Claus who tries to snub her child. Thus, Brooks ties motherhood to the protagonist's self-development. The novel ends on a note of optimism as Maud looks forward to the birth of her second child. The reader is left with the feeling that Maud Martha is finally in touch with her own creative power, her natural love of life, and her capacity for self-definition. Though *Maud Martha* received scant attention when it was first published, black feminist critics would resurrect the novel in the 1980s. It represents the multiplied effects of both the perception and the reality of being on the bottom rung of society's race, class, gender, caste, and color hierarchies.

Go Tell It on the Mountain is part spiritual autobiography and part neofreedom narrative. (See chapter I for definitions.) Early working titles of James Baldwin's *Go Tell It on the Mountain* included "Crying Holy" and "In My Father's House." Its ultimate title is taken from a Christian hymn that announces the birth of Jesus, the Christian savior who, Christians believe, died to redeem humankind. The semi-autobiographical story is told in three parts. Part I, titled "The Seventh Day," is told through protagonist John Grimes's third-person limited omniscient perspective. The Seventh Day refers to the biblical creation story; major characters' names are taken from the Bible and usually have some biblical significance, though not necessarily paralleling their biblical counterparts. John's father Gabriel's quest for an heir aligns him with Abraham of Old Testament fame, rather than the angel Gabriel, for example. The story begins on the morning of John's fourteenth birthday. The setting is 1935 (the middle of the Great Depression) in a Harlem tenement. John's immediate familial and communal relationships are established in this opening section. Raised by a domineering stepfather and a loving, but acquiescent mother, John lives his life in a state of ongoing guilt about his sexuality. He also must endure the constant disapproval of his stepfather, Gabriel, who has his own demons. The quest at the center of the narrative, however, is similar to that of the previous two works and has to do with identity and the acquisition of self-knowledge. Similar to Linda Brent in Harriet Jacobs's *Incidents in the Life of a Slave Girl* (1861), John has no real options for freedom because he is forced to choose between two undesirable alternatives. A product of a restrictive and stiflingly poor household in 1935 America, John understands his options to be a relatively short-lived existence on the streets as a hustler or a dogmatic existence in the Pentecostal church his family attends.

Part II of the novel features three prayers: Elizabeth's, Gabriel's, and Florence's, with Gabriel's falling structurally at the center of the novel. Part of the answer to the question, "Who am I," so essential to young John, lies within these intimate, personal histories to which he is not privy. Here Baldwin probes the memories of John's mother, stepfather, and aunt to illuminate the past and to explain how it is that each character came to exist in that way, at that moment. All three are in need of redemption. Elizabeth lives with the guilt that her husband is not her one true love Richard, John's biological father, and that she might have saved Richard from suicide had she told him she was carrying his child. Her preoccupation with these facts is her most obvious barrier to redemption. Gabriel's guilt is based on his squandered opportunities, a promiscuous past, an adulterous affair, and the subsequent denial of his firstborn son. Lack of humility stands between Gabriel and redemption. Florence, raised in the shadow of her favored and undeserving brother, Gabriel, bears a deep resentment for the value society places in men over women. She also ran from the scene when white men attacked and subsequently raped her friend Deborah (whom Gabriel married in an effort to redeem himself), and she left home for the North while her mother lay dying. Her inability to forgive Gabriel stands in the way of her redemption. The individual prayers of these three characters shed light on John's history and the "why" of his current situation, but only for the reader. John remains "in the dark." One understands that unconditional love is in very short supply among the three adults in John's life.

In the final part of the novel, "The Threshing Floor," John chooses what he considers the better of the two options presented to him. Still missing important insights about the past that has so strongly impacted his present situation, he undergoes a spiritual transformation that effectively relieves him of the power that Gabriel has exercised over his life up to that point. In a sense, he, like Gabriel before him, chooses religion as a way to reinvent himself and manipulate the people around him. The novel closes on an ambiguous note, leaving readers wondering about John's so-called conversion. John has found a temporary remedy. Students can best understand the parallels to Baldwin's real life by reading the essays titled "Down at the Cross" and "Notes of a Native Son," both of which are collected in *The Price of the Ticket*. Here Baldwin admits that he saw in his official entry into the Church a way of immobilizing his stepfather, whom he considered incomprehensible and brutal.

Alice Childress's often hilarious *Like One of the Family . . . Conversations from a Domestic's Life* (1956) also provides a take on the American Dream from the vantage point of a struggling domestic worker. The volume is composed of vignettes from Childress's weekly column, "Here's Mildred," which ran briefly in Paul Robeson's *Freedom* before the *Baltimore Afro-American* picked it up. It features the feisty common sense and mother wit of the outspoken Mildred, a domestic worker with a strong sense of self.

The heroic Mildred is often indignant in the face of her employers' racism, inhumanity, and outright stupidity. In "The Pocketbook Game," she tells her friend Marge about the peculiar ways of a particular employer:

> "Marge, she's got a big old pocketbook with two long straps on it . . . and whenever I'd go there, she'd be propped up in a chair with her handbag double wrapped tight around her wrist, and from room to room she'd roam with that purse hugged to her bosom . . . . Yes, girl! This happens every time! No, there's *nobody* there but me and her . . . . Marge, I couldn't say nothin' to her! It's her purse, ain't it? She can hold onto it if she wants to! (26)

Mildred finally figured out how to make her point. Sent to fetch the building superintendent, she exited the apartment and waited a few minutes in the hall before rushing back to the door and knocking frantically. When the woman answered the door and inquired as to whether Mildred saw the super, Mildred responded breathlessly, "I was almost downstairs when I remembered . . . *I left my pocketbook!*" (27). Later, when the woman says to Mildred, "I hope that you don't think I distrust you . . . ," Mildred explains that she understands. She adds, "Cause if I paid anybody as little as you pay me, I'd hold my pocketbook too!" (27). Mildred's deceptively simple mother wit reveals the protective stance of her employer in regard to her property. Mildred is thus the black woman forced by a history of unequal social and economic opportunity to clean her floors and toilets, and whom she believes to be inclined therefore to steal. In a larger sense, Mildred (like Childress's vignette) literally and figuratively speaks volumes about property and power in a capitalistic economy.

In Paule Marshall's *Brown Girl, Brownstones*, Selina's mother, Silla Boyce, is determined to realize her American Dream to purchase one of the brownstones she craves. With World War II as a backdrop, the conflict between Silla's objectives and those of her husband Deighton make for an unpleasant adolescent experience for Selina. Deighton, an unskilled and uneducated factory worker with a fun-loving personality, wants to make enough money to return to Barbados and purchase property in his homeland. That is his American Dream. He takes and completes an accounting course only to realize that it will not gain him entry into the predominantly white world of accounting. It is a bitter realization for the usually resilient Deighton, but the ever-loyal Selina is his comrade through it all, his buffer in the ongoing conflict with Silla. Selina is caught between the two.

On the one hand, Silla is depicted as mean-spirited and unbending, while Deighton seems to lack the fortitude required for success in the United States. His personality is a striking contrast to Silla's. When Deighton inherits property in Barbados, he is set to return home. Land ownership in Barbados represents manhood realized to Deighton, but Silla wants him to sell the property so that she can make a down payment on a brownstone. The situation is hopeless. Silla forges Deighton's signature on some legal documents and sells the property, but Deighton finds out. He tricks Silla into giving him the check so that he can deposit it in the bank, but instead he spends the money. The marital relationship is irreparably shattered. Deighton subsequently crushes his arm in a factory accident, and that serves as the last straw. He gives up and joins an ascetic cult, a closed community that cuts ties to marriage and all earthly attachments. An angry Silla reports his illegal alien status to authorities and has him deported. Deighton dies within a few miles of Barbados when he falls, jumps, or is pushed overboard.

Selina has lost the lightness that helped to balance her mother's overbearing personality. She begins a painful process of self-discovery. Selina eventually comes of age and buys her own brownstone. Ultimately, she realizes that she is more like her mother than she ever knew, and that it is what she inherited from her mother that bears her up when life is most difficult. Several friends and associates, including the bohemian Suggie and hairdresser Miss Thompson, offer support along the way. She also meets a lover, Clive Springer, an artist who served in the war. He inspires her to fight against racism and sexism. Finally, she leaves everyone behind to go off on her own to Barbados. She reaches out to her Barbadian roots for the strength she needs to develop in order to face what is ahead.

In crafting his Simple stories, Langston Hughes successfully adapted time-tested comedy routines in which two quick-talking comedians play against each other. Each of the Simple tales is comprised almost entirely of dialogue between Jesse B. Simple and Boyd, the straight man who allows Simple's wit to shine. Boyd speaks in Standard English, while Simple speaks in a rich folk idiom characteristic of Harlem. Jesse B. Simple was "born" with the February 13, 1943, issue of the *Chicago Defender* in Hughes's "Here to Yonder" column. Though some of the Simple episodes take place on the street and in the apartment building where he lives, the typical setting is a Harlem bar. The narrator—who speaks perfect Standard English—and Simple—who speaks in a black urban idiom—discuss everything from Simple's ever-vigilant landlady, to his relationship with his current and/or former love interests. Hughes declared that the Simple episodes are simply conversations with himself. By representing the dialogue in two voices, Hughes brilliantly and candidly reveals his own sometimes conflicting ideas, beliefs, fears, and desires. More importantly, he continues to represent the most intimate aspects of black life for black people or anyone else who cares to read his stories, for Simple's issues are human issues told from the seriocomic perspective of an urban working-class black man. The Simple stories are a practical application of the philosophy Hughes espoused in "The Negro Artist and the Racial Mountain" (1926)—to represent in his art black American life as he saw it. Students interested in Hughes's work should become familiar with that short essay. Jesse B. Simple is a quintessential Harlem blues person.

Recurring Themes and Issues

Questions surrounding identity continue to be important throughout this period and beyond. Ellison's Invisible Man did not know where he was going because he did not know where he had been. Similarly, James Baldwin's John Grimes is shut off from information that he requires to proceed through life as a confident subject. Even if we accept as a fact that identity is at best fragmented and always in the process of forming, the protagonists in *Invisible Man* and *Go Tell It on the Mountain* are both missing key information about their pasts that will assist in procuring their release from perceptual blindness. Both novels suggest that historical subjectivity is indeed important.

Music (blues, jazz, and/or gospel) permeates the work of Hughes, Ellison, and Baldwin. Hughes, who uses both the blues as form and ethos in his poetry, also uses the blues ethos (or mood) in his Simple stories. The blues, as Ralph Ellison and others have noted, is an impulse to deal with the worst that life has to offer without being defeated by it (see, Ellison's "Richard Wright's Blues" in *Shadow and Act*). Ellison's novel is framed by Louis Armstrong's classic song, "What Did I Do to Be So Black and Blue?" His Trueblood character is depicted in blues singer mode, sharing his general tale of hardship and revealing that he has impregnated both his wife and his daughter. Langston Hughes's Simple character deals with a harsh, meddling landlady, a dearth of employment opportunities, and never-ending woman problems with the down-but-not-out attitude of the blues singer: "It will be better in the morning." Baldwin developed a strong appreciation for gospel music in his youth that stayed with him throughout his life, and he makes this aspect of his life a major element of the semi-autobiographical *Go Tell It on the Mountain.*

Double-consciousness is used as a theme or trope in many of the works. Brooks ties Maud Martha's self-image problems to societal hierarchies that accord value on the basis of gender, hair texture, skin color, economic class, and so on. They are nevertheless barriers to her "freedom" because she must find a way to see her dark-skinned, coarse-haired, female self in a positive light—through her own eyes, not the eyes of others. Brooks makes motherhood a signal event in her protagonist's life and self-development. Her most noteworthy predecessor in this regard is Harriet Jacobs's pseudonymous narrator Linda Brent in *Incidents in the Life of a Slave Girl*; her most noteworthy successor is Sethe Suggs in Toni Morrison's *Beloved.* Double-consciousness figures most prominently in Ellison's *Invisible Man*, for many of the narrator's problems are related to his problems of perception. For Childress's straightforward domestic worker, Mildred, double-consciousness drives her ability to dispense generous helpings of mother wit.

All the works featured in this chapter have in common the discourse they provide on the subject of the elusive American Dream, particularly during the period of the Great Depression and immediately following it. All focus attention on the idea of "freedom" in a literal and/or figurative sense of that concept, and several of the novels are properly categorized as neofreedom narratives. Invisibility and blindness are themes and tropes in several of the works. Alienation figures prominently as well. The plight of black domestic workers, economic hardship, and the strain on family relations are all prominent issues.

Bibliography

Andrews, William L., Frances Smith Foster, and Trudier Harris, eds. *The Oxford Companion to African American Literature*. New York: Oxford, 1997.

Baldwin, James. *The Price of the Ticket*. New York: St. Martin's/Marek, 1985.

Baker, Jr., Houston A. *Blues, Ideology, and Afro-American Literature: A Vernacular Theory*. Chicago: U of Chicago P, 1984.

Benston, Kimberly W., ed. *Speaking for You: The Vision of Ralph Ellison*. Washington: Howard UP, 1987.

Berry, Faith. *Langston Hughes: Before and Beyond Harlem*. Seacaucus, N.J.: Carol Publishing Group, 1983.

Bloom, Harold, ed. *Modern Black American Fiction Writers*. New York: Chelsea House, 2000.

—. *Modern Critical Views: Gwendolyn Brooks*. New York: Chelsea House, 2000.

—. *Modern Critical Views: James Baldwin*. New York: Chelsea House, 1986.

—. *Modern Critical Views: Ralph Ellison*. New York: Chelsea, 1986.

Bobia, Rosa. *The Critical Reception of James Baldwin in France*. New York: Peter Lang, 1997.

Booker, M. Keith. *The Caribbean Novel in English: An Introduction*. Portsmouth, N.H.: Heineman, 2001.

Brooks, Gwendolyn. *Report from Part One*. Detroit: Broadside P, 1972.

—. *Report from Part Two*. Chicago: Third World P, 1996.

Busby, Mark. *Ralph Ellison*. Boston: Twain, 1991.

Childress, Alice. "Knowing the Human Condition." *African American literature and Humanism*. Ed. R. Baxter Miller, 1981. 8–11.

Christian, Barbara. *Black Women Novelists: The Development of a Tradition 1892–1976*. Westport, Conn.: Greenwood P, 1980.

Coser, Stelamaris. *Bridging the Americas: The Literature of Paul Marshall, Toni Morrison, and Gayl Jones*. Philadelphia: Temple UP, 1995.

Dace, Tish, ed. *Langston Hughes: The Contemporary Reviews*. New York: Cambridge UP, 1997.

Denniston, Dorothy Hamer. *The Fiction of Paule Marshall: Reconstructions of History*. Knoxville: U of Tennessee P, 1995.

DeSantis, Christopher C., ed. *Langston Hughes and the Chicago Defender: Essays on Race, Politics & Culture 1942–62*. Urbana: U of Illinois P, 1995.

Dundes, Alan, ed. *Mother Wit from the Laughing Barrel: Readings in the Interpretation of Afro-American Folklore*. University of Mississippi P, 1990.

Ellison, Ralph. *Invisible Man*. 1952. Introd. Ralph Ellison. 1981. New York: Vintage: Random House, 1995.

—. *Shadow and Act*. New York: Random House, 1964.

Emanuel, James A. *Langston Hughes*. New York: Twayne, 1967.

Evans, Mari. *Black Women Writers 1950–1980*. New York: Anchor Books, 1984.

Gates, Jr., Henry Louis and K. A. Appiah, eds. *Langston Hughes: Critical Perspectives Past and Present*. New York: Amistad, 1993.

Guillory, Elizabeth Brown. "Alice Childress: A Pioneering Spirit." *SAGE* 4 (Spring 1987): 104–9.

Harper, Donna Akiba Sullivan. *Not So Simple: The "Simple" Stories by Langston Hughes*. Columbia: U of Missouri P, 1995.

Harris, Trudier. *Black Women in the Fiction of James Baldwin*. Knoxville: U of Tennessee P, 1985.

— *From Mammies to Militants: Domestics in African American literature*, 1982.

—. *New Essays on Baldwin's Go Tell It on the Mountain*. Cambridge: Cambridge UP, 1996.

Haskins, James S. Always Movin' On: The Life of Langston Hughes. Trenton, NJ: Africa World P, 1993.

Hersey, John, ed. *Ralph Ellison: A Collection of Critical Essays*. Englewood Cliffs, NJ: Prentice, 1974.

Hughes, Langston. *The Big Sea: An Autobiography*. New York: Knopf. 1945.

—. *I Wonder as I Wander: An Autobiographical Journey*. New York: Rinehart, 1956.

Hughes, Langston, and Arna Bontemps. *Book of Negro Folklore*. New York: Dodd, 1957.

Jennings, LaVinia D. *Alice Childress*. New York: Twayne, 1995.

Jones, LeRoi (Baraka, Amiri). *Black Music*. New York: William Morrow, 1967.

—. *Blues People: The Negro Experience in White America and the Music That Developed from It*. New York: William Morrow, 1963.

Kent, George E. *A Life of Gwendolyn Brooks*. Lexington: U of Kentucky P, 1990.

Leeming, David Adams. *James Baldwin: A Biography*. New York: Knopf, 1994.

McBride, Dwight, ed. *James Baldwin Now*. New York: New York UP, 1999.

Meltzer, Milton. *Langston Hughes: A Biography*. New York: Crowell, 1968.

Mikolyzk, Thomas A. *Langston Hughes: A Bio-bibliography*. New York: Greenwood, 1990.

Miller, R. Baxter. *The Art and Imagination of Langston Hughes*. Lexington: UP of Kentucky, 1989.

Mootry, Maria K., and Gary Smith, eds. *A Life Distilled: Gwendolyn Brooks, Her Poetry and Fiction*. Urbana: U of Illinois P, 1987.

Mullaney, Janet Palmer, ed. *Truthtellers of the Times: Interviews with Contemporary Women Poets*. Ann Arbor: U of Michigan P, 1998.

Nelson, George. *Hip Hop America*. New York: Viking, 1998.

Oakley, Giles. *The Devil's Music: A History of the Blues*. New York: Taplinger, 1977.

O'Meally, Robert. *The Craft of Ralph Ellison*. Cambridge: Harvard UP, 1980.

O'Meally, Robert, ed. *New Essays on Invisible Man*, 1988. New York: Cambridge UP, 1988.

Osofsky, Gilbert. *Harlem: The Making of a Ghetto: Negro New York, 1890–1930*. 2nd ed. New York: Harper, 1971.

Ostrom, Hans, ed. *A Langston Hughes Encyclopedia*. Westport, Conn.: Greenwood P, 2002.

—. *Langston Hughes: A Study of the Short Fiction*. New York: Twayne, 1993.

Ottley, Roi, and William J. Weatherby. *The Negro in New York: An Informal Social History*. New York: New York Public Library, 1967.

Pettis, Joyce Owens. *Toward Wholeness in Paule Marshall's Fiction*. Charlottesville: U of Virginia P, 1995.

Porter, Horace A. *Stealing the Fire: The Art and Protest of James Baldwin*. Middletown, Conn.: Wesleyan UP, 1989.

Rampersad, Arnold. *The Life of Langston Hughes*. 2 vols. 1986–1988. New York: Oxford UP, 1986.

Reilly, John M., ed. *Twentieth-Century Interpretations of Invisible Man: A Collection of Essays*. Englewood Cliffs, N.J.: Prentice, 1970.

Rose, Tricia. *Black Noise: Rap Music and Black Culture in Contemporary America*. Hanover, N.H.: UP of New England, 1994.

Ruff, Shawn Stewart, ed. *Go the Way Your Blood Beats: An Anthology of Lesbian and Gay Fiction by African-American Writers*. New York: Henry Holt, 1996.

Rummell, Jack. *Langston Hughes*. New York: Chelsea House, 1988.

Rushdy, Ashraf. *Neo-Slave Narratives: Studies in the Social Logic of a Literary Form*. New York: Oxford, 1999.

Scott, Lynn. *James Baldwin's Later Fiction: Witness to the Journey*. East Lansing: Michigan State UP, 2002.

Somerville, Siobhan B. *Queering the Color Line: Race and the Invention of Homosexuality in American Culture*. Durham: Duke UP, 2000.

Standley, Fred L., and Louis H. Pratt, eds. *Conversations with James Baldwin*. Jackson: UP of Mississippi, 1989.

Stepto, Robert. *From Behind the Veil: A Study of Afro-American Narrative*. Urbana: U of Illinois P, 1979.

Sundquist, Eric. *Cultural Contexts for Ralph Ellison's Invisible Man*. Boston: Bedford/St. Martin's, 1995.

Tracy, Steven C. *Langston Hughes and the Blues*. Urbana: U of Illinois P, 1988.

Trotman, James. *Langston Hughes:The Man, His Art, and His Continuing Influence*. New York: Garland, 1995.

Washington, Mary Helen. *Invented Lives: Narratives of Black Women 1860–1960*. New York: Anchor Books, 1987.

Watts, Jerry G. *Heroism and the Black Intellectual: Ralph Ellison, Politics, and Afro-American Intellectual Life*. Chapel Hill: U of North Carolina P, 1994.

Wright, Stephen Caldwell, ed. *On Gwendolyn Brooks: Reliant Contemplation*. Ann Arbor: U of Michigan P, 1996.

Suggested Topics for Writing Critical Essays

1. Analyze the author's use of double-consciousness in *Invisible Man*. Compare it to the way that Johnson uses it in *The Autobiography of an Ex-Coloured Man* (chapter 4).
2. Compare and contrast the use of double-consciousness in *Invisible Man* and *Maud Martha.*
3. Explore the trope of blindness in *Invisible Man*. Compare it to the use of blindness in *Native Son*.
4. Discuss Brooks's use of conventions of poetry in constructing the sketches that make up the narrative of *Maud Martha*.
5. Compare and contrast the use of humor as social and political commentary in *The Best of Simple* and *Like One of the Family*.
6. Compare the use of humor in Hughes or Childress to its use in Chesnutt (chapter 3).
7. Compare and contrast the image of the "American Dream" as it is represented in any two of the works featured in this chapter. Alternatively, compare and contrast the situation of Lutie Johnson (*The Street*) and Silla Boyce (*Brown Girl, Brownstones*) vis-à-vis their quest for the so-called American Dream.
8. Examine a work or works in terms of how they speak to the historical context out of which they were produced. Consider the aftermath of World War II, the impact of black migration to northern cities of previous decades, the impact of the Great Depression, and other societal influences.

Questions to Guide Your Reading

Go Tell It on the Mountain

1. Are there homoerotic undertones in this novel? Explain. What is the nature of John Grimes's longing and desire? How much of his guilt is associated with sex, dirt, and skin color?
2. Note the role of religion, the church, and gospel music. Compare the novel with the information provided in *The Fire Next Time* and *Notes of a Native Son*.
3. What statement about sexuality in general does Baldwin make in the novel? Do any of the four major characters (John, Gabriel, Elizabeth, Florence) find the redemption they seek? For what does each seek redemption? Why are they "standing in the need of prayer"?
4. Are Florence and Gabriel two sides of the same coin? Who was Richard? What happened to him? What information is provided about the past of the three adults who figure prominently in John Grimes's life? Is John privy to that information?
5. If you have read *Invisible Man* and/or *Their Eyes Were Watching God*, do you notice any similarities in the source of outdated or useless advice obtained from an elder—advice that no longer suits the needs of the protagonist?
6. How is "manhood" defined in Baldwin's novel? Does the novel seem to suggest or identify certain essential qualities in men, or, for that matter, in women?
7. What statement does the novel make about the degree of difficulty inherent in John Grimes's search for identity?

Invisible Man

1. How does the narrator define "invisibility" and "hibernation"? What is the purpose of the prologue? What does the author accomplish with the prologue and the epilogue?
2. Why does the protagonist/narrator call himself an Invisible Man? What, to him, is the nature of his invisibility?
3. Place the Battle Royal under a microscope. Who are the key players, and how does the "competition" function as allegory?
4. Ralph Waldo Emerson is known as an American transcendentalist. Why do you suppose that Ellison weaves so many references to Emerson into the story?
5. If asked to interpret the overall meaning of *Invisible Man* in approximately one hundred words, what would you write?

Would you focus on transcendence, identity, black consciousness, the quest narrative, all these, or something else?

6. Do you believe that the issues raised in the novel have "universal" significance?
7. Examine the relationship between the narrator and Mary Rambo, Trueblood, Mr. Norton, Lucius Brockway, Mr. Emerson, The Brotherhood, Ras the Destroyer, Rinehart, Tod Clifton, or Bledsoe.
8. What is the symbolic value of the items the narrator collects in his briefcase? Of Tod Clifton's sambo doll? Of birds? What is High John the Conqueror? What is the figurative meaning of the narrator's allusion to draining off power from Monopolated Light & Power?
9. Analyze the "black is, black ain't" sermon on pages 9-12? How is oration used in this novel? How many speeches are included altogether?

Maud Martha

1. Why do you suppose Brooks divides *Maud Martha* into thirty-four sections?
2. Read any section and see if you can determine what quality, state, or emotion is depicted in it. What emotion dominates Maud Martha's life?
3. Who is Maud Martha? What is the nature of her relationship with her sister, her mother, her husband, her daughter, the larger society?
4. Do any of these relationships change? Explain.
5. Describe Maud Martha's kitchenette apartment. Where is it located?
6. What does Maud Martha want? What is her quest? How does she feel about herself? Does her self-image change during the course of the novel?
7. Does skin color matter in this story? How does Brooks reveal prejudices within the black community?
8. Is there humor in *Maud Martha*? Where? *Maud Martha* is autobiographical in some respects.
9. What is the novel's point of view? Why tell the story of a very average, brown-skinned woman (Maud Martha Brown) living in a kitchenette apartment in the early twentieth century? Of what significance is her story?

Brown Girl, Brownstones

1. Characterize the relationship between Deighton and Silla Boyce. Describe the dynamics of the Boyce household.
2. Compare and contrast the "American Dreams" of Deighton and Silla Boyce. What does each want ultimately? With which parent does Selina most identify? How are matters of race and prejudice addressed in the story?
3. What is the time period covered by the novel's plot, and what point of view is represented? What significant events mark turning points in the story and in Selina's coming of age?
4. How is the backdrop of the Civil Rights Movement represented in the novel? What role does Selina play? How does this affect her relationship with her family? What impact does it have on her own personal development?
5. How would you characterize the author's feelings toward the primary characters in the novel? Which are treated more sympathetically? Less sympathetically?

Like One of the Family

1. Who is Mildred and what does she do for a living? Where does she live? To whom does she tell her stories?
2. What is "mother wit"? Does Mildred possess it? Explain.
3. What is the general economic and social setting for Mildred's stories?
4. Where does she gather the material for the stories she tells?
5. In one hundred words or less, explain Mildred's philosophy of life.
6. Does she feel inferior to anyone? Explain.

The Best of Simple

1. Would you characterize Jesse B. Simple as an "Everyman"? What are his attributes, and with whom does he converse in the Simple stories?
2. Describe Simple's relationship with his landlady. Where is his favorite place to be?
3. Why is he always singing the blues?
4. Other than the narrator and his landlord, what other people play prominent roles in Simple's life?
5. How would you characterize Simple's way of looking at life? How does he deal with his never-ending problems?

6. Where does Simple live? How does his life fit into a blues mood or ethos?

CHAPTER VI
Contemporary Fiction

Bolstered by the energy of mid-century social and political movements, the literature of African Americans experienced a new renaissance in the last three decades of the twentieth century. By the late 1990s, African American literature had become a major field of study, one in which university graduate students could earn doctorate degrees. A literature whose existence and value had long been questioned by those in academia—who reasoned that if they were unaware of certain texts, then those texts either did not exist or were not worthy of their attention—had come of age. In the face of such condescension, an energetic community of authors and scholars continued to write and publish. Except for the writings of a few authors, such as Wright, Ellison, and Baldwin, the literature initially entered the college or university classroom primarily through Black Studies programs and departments. As critical interest and scholarship in the literature increased throughout the last two decades of the twentieth century, so also did its presence in English and Literature departments. Whispered stories abound of academicians previously ignorant of African American literature suddenly turning their full attention to it, even as the search continues for buried and neglected works from previous centuries. The appearance of the *Oxford Companion to African American Literature* and two comprehensive anthologies by major presses just before the new millennium signaled that the tradition had achieved new prominence.

For a variety of reasons, black women's literature received more attention than black men's literature during the 1970s and 1980s, and this preference caused not a small amount of discord within the ranks of people who had previously seen themselves as bound together against a common oppressor. The particular set of societal conditions that culminated in the flowering of black women's literature after 1970 had no precedent in this country. Toni Cade Bambara, Gayl Jones, Paule Marshall, Toni Morrison, Gloria Naylor, Alice Walker, Sherley Anne Williams, Ntozake Shangé, Jamaica Kincaid, Octavia Butler, Pearl Cleage, Marita Golden, Carlene Hatcher Polite, Jewelle Gomez, Audre Lorde, and Carolivia Herron are just a few of the writers who have contributed to the recent proliferation of literature. Though Toni Morrison and Alice Walker are perhaps the most recognized authors among this group, the most prolific is Octavia Butler, a brilliant author of science fiction.

The fact that during this period the publishing industry was initially more enchanted with black women fiction writers than it was with black men fiction writers does not mean that black men were producing and publishing literature of a lesser quality. Authors such as John A. Williams, Ishmael Reed, Clarence Major, John Edgar Wideman, Charles Johnson, Samuel Delany, Randall Kenan, and David Bradley have all contributed toward a substantial body of work. Differences between the literature men produced and the literature women produced could be found both in the form and substance/content.

Indeed, some of the *gender matters* that have resulted from the unique circumstances of the 1970s and 1980s are based on charges that certain black women writers were betraying "the race," or "conspiring with the enemy" when they used their novels and stories to "air dirty laundry." Some claimed that black women's stories were not intellectually rigorous, were not innovative, and did nothing to advance the novel as a form. Others claimed that black women were exploiting their own victimization and playing to America's race problem. Even as contemporary black women's literature is celebrated in academic circles, novels such as Trey Ellis's *Platitudes* (1988) and Charles Johnson's *Middle Passage* (1990) lampoon some of its most celebrated authors. On occasion, black male authors have been labeled misogynist for the ways they represent women in their work. Another criticism has been that they ignore women altogether. Even discussions about the difference between criticism and theory took on sexist overtones—with the suggestion that black women simply did not *do theory.* Some social critics see the *gender debate* as a diversion from more pressing issues. Regardless of the debate—which actually became the theme of Trey Ellis's *Platitudes*—African American literature did not go unnoticed this time around.

For literature depicting gay, lesbian, bisexual, and/or transgender life, the process has been slower. The contemporary Gay and Lesbian Rights Movement, whose pivotal event was the Stonewall uprising in the late 1960s, helped to bring gay and lesbian literature to wider audiences, though clearly, compulsory heterosexuality was never a prerequisite for the ability to produce fine literature. Richard Bruce Nugent and James Baldwin are among the very few openly gay black authors publishing work before the 1970s who chose not to lock themselves or their characters in a sexual closet, and who attempted to depict gay life in a realistic way. Ann Allen Shockley's *Loving Her* (1974) and *Say Jesus and Come to Me* (1982) were two of the earliest published extant black women's novels in which the author attempted to represent authentic black lesbian life. Audre Lorde's autobiographical *Zami: A New Spelling of My Name* (1982), which depicts the author's coming of age as, among other things, a lesbian, has become a staple in women's studies and black women's literature courses. Anthologies such as Joseph Beam's *In the Life: A Black Gay Anthology* (1986), Essex Hemphill's *Brother to Brother: New Writings by Black Gay Men* (1991), *Go the Way Your Blood Beats*, and *Afrekete: An Anthology of Black Lesbian Writing* (1995) helped to make gay and lesbian writers more visible. E. Lynn Harris's contemporary popular novels of gay and lesbian experience enjoy a large readership. Samuel Delany perhaps stands alone among male writers in his innovative depictions of queer characters and their lives for his science fiction narratives.

The authors and works featured in the previous chapter had in common the fact that they all worked toward dissecting the myth of the American Dream. It is much more difficult to find a common rubric for any such group of writers since 1970 without omitting some key authors. The sheer volume of literature produced and published during this period renders the task of offering representative texts extremely difficult. The task becomes even more difficult when we consider the wide range of approaches, the varied themes and issues, the deliberate efforts to write simultaneously against and within a larger tradition, and the overlapping categories of literature. Such categories include black masculinist literature, black feminist/womanist literature, gay literature, lesbian literature, nationalist (Afrocentric) literature, postmodern literature, neofreedom narratives, and science fiction. One must also include the growing body of literature with a more popular appeal by writers such as Walter Mosley, E. Lynn Harris, and Terry McMillan. In addition, in-depth critical, contextual, biographical, and bibliographical information about the authors whose works I will discuss below is readily available online through a variety of reference materials simply by doing a keyword search on the Internet. For these reasons, I will diverge slightly from the format of the first five chapters in order to provide a larger sampling of works. My objective here as before is to consider those works most likely to be encountered in undergraduate courses, with some attention to balance in terms of gender, sexuality, and subgenre. I am also concerned with their connections to what has come before.

We will focus on the following works in this chapter: Ishmael Reed's *Mumbo Jumbo* (1972), Alice Walker's *The Color Purple* (1982), Gloria Naylor's *The Women of Brewster Place* (1982), Toni Morrison's *Beloved*

(1987), Randall Kenan's *A Visitation of Spirits* (1989), Charles Johnson's *Middle Passage* (1990), Octavia Butler's *Parable of the Sower* (1993), *Afrekete* (1995), and Alice Randall's *The Wind Done Gone* (2001). Reed's *Mumbo Jumbo* is included for its innovative use of **parody** and for its thematization of **neohoodooism**. Walker's *The Color Purple* is included for several reasons, including its status as a Pulitzer Prizewinning novel, its use of the epistolary form to tell a story of intraracial gender conflict and a black woman's journey toward self-knowledge, and its expression of Walker's womanist principles. *The Women of Brewster Place* is celebrated author Gloria Naylor's first novel and the only composite novel of this group. The individual stories of seven women are bound together by the fact that they live in the same dead-end community. The most celebrated and most taught writer of this group is Toni Morrison. *Beloved* garnered (or helped to garner) for her the two most prestigious awards in literature: the Pulitzer Prize and the Nobel Prize. Kenan's extraordinary first novel, *A Visitation of Spirits* (which might have been titled *Invisible Gay Teenager*, to invoke Ellison's *Invisible Man*), speaks to the potential harm of following convention blindly. Kenan's story tracks the short life of a gay black southern rural teenager so steeped in conventions of family, religion, and community that his journey toward self-discovery can only end in his death by suicide rather than in self-acceptance. Charles Johnson's prize-winning, masculinist *Middle Passage* (1990) is included for its use of parody to illuminate the limitations and silences of previous works. Johnson uses the tall tale format to thematize his own ideas about fluidity and process in regard to identity. Similarly, Octavia Butler's woman-centered *Parable of the Sower* (1993) beautifully represents the science fiction subgenre. Butler uses botany and thermodynamics to explore the extremes of capitalism and consumption in the context of an increasingly lethal earth environment that has resulted from the mix of unchecked capitalist greed, and unchecked environmental pollution that has led to global warming.

The short fiction anthologized in *Afrekete* (1995) provides a variety of perspectives on black lesbian life, and in some cases (though certainly not all), the writing seems to address itself to *straight* audiences. Alice Randall's novel is included for its newness and for the way it invokes the tradition from which it emerges. The first-person narrative of Cynara, a formerly enslaved mulatto woman, *Wind* is composed of diary entries. Cynara's presence in history has been obscured by a larger dominating presence. Cynara writes herself into existence by writing to herself and leaving the diary behind to be shared with ensuing generations. Cynara's *freedom narrative* connects Randall's text to the entire tradition from which it emerges. First, and most obviously, it invokes the autobiographical tradition. A product of miscegenation, the protagonist also invokes central mulatto characters (and issues related to race and passing) from the nineteenth-century novels of William Wells Brown, Frances Ellen Watkins Harper, Pauline Hopkins, and Charles Chesnutt. Issues of race and passing continued in the twentieth century with novels such as Johnson's *The Autobiography of an Ex-Coloured Man* (1912), Larsen's *Passing* (1929), and a number of others. Randall has also created a character and a story that responds to the obvious gender issues raised by Ellison's masterwork, *Invisible Man* (1952): Where is the Black Woman and what is her place in American history? Finally, as we shall see, Randall's work is closely related to two of the most recognized women's novels in the field: *The Color Purple* and *Beloved.*

Contexts

With America's increasing involvement in Vietnam in the late 1960s, antiwar protests increased. People of color in general protested their overrepresentation among the ranks of the foot soldiers on the front lines. College students protested on their campuses, and in some cases (at Jackson State and Kent State, for example) government forces killed them. Such a volatile climate gave rise to forced violent confrontations between activists and police. A number of murders and political assassinations took place in the fifteen years leading up to 1970. Some of the murdered and assassinated included Emmett Till in 1955, Patrice Lumumba in 1961, Medgar Evers in 1963, four little girls in the bombing of an Alabama church in 1963, President John F. Kennedy in 1963, Malcolm X in 1965, and Robert F. Kennedy and Martin Luther King in 1968. COINTELPRO, FBI director J. Edgar Hoover's counter-intelligence program designed to attack and destroy (through covert operations) what it identified as organized revolutionary exploits, targeted in particular The Black Panther Party. A number of Party members, including Fred Hampton, were murdered during this time.

On another front, attorney Milton Henry (Gaidi Obadele) and his brother Richard (Imari Abubakari Obadele), both of whom had been acquainted with Malcolm X, established the Republic of New Africa in 1968 and declared their allegiance to the provisional government. The organization also became a an FBI target, with meetings raided and members repeatedly jailed. After Imari Obadele was released from prison in 1980, he earned a Ph.D. in political science. After earning his Ph.D., Obadele published books and articles, taught at various universities, and continued the call for reparations, acquisition of land, and the establishment of an autonomous black nation. The Republic of New Africa is now based in Washington, D.C.

Urban uprisings took place in a number of cities across the country during the summers of 1964 to 1968. In 1968, Angela Davis moved to Los Angeles and joined the Communist Party. She had abruptly halted her doctoral studies at the Johann Wolfgang von Goethe University in Frankfurt, Germany, the previous year. She began teaching philosophy at UCLA in 1969, but she was fired once her Communist affiliation became known. A court overturned the dismissal, but the school refused to renew her contract. Davis would later become a strong activist for black political prisoners. She eventually made the FBI's ten most wanted list—charged with a crime she did not commit, but for which she nevertheless served sixteen months in prison.

The Kerner Commission, which investigated major urban uprisings in Los Angeles, Newark, and Chicago, issued its report in 1968. It concluded that people were committing acts of violence out of frustration related to the harsh realities of American racism—effectively echoing the point of Richard Wright's *Native Son* almost thirty years earlier, and Ralph Ellison's *Invisible Man* less than two decades earlier. The Kerner Commission report also warned that the country was moving toward two separate and unequal societies—one black and the other white—this pronouncement coming after almost a century of Jim Crow segregation! With his past record on civil rights, and despite his questionable handling of the Vietnam conflict, Lyndon Johnson might have heeded the warning; however, his record in office particularly in regard to Vietnam, led him to choose not to run for reelection in 1968. With Richard Nixon in charge, America was still in Vietnam when the 1970s began, headed toward the Watergate debacle.

The energy and innovation of the culturally nationalist Black Arts Movement, whose chief architects were Amiri Baraka, Larry Neal, and Askia Toure, had a profound impact on the subsequent production of scholarship about African American literature. It is, after all, the body of criticism about it that gives a literature its cachet. The articulation of a Black Aesthetic assisted in this project, as did research and scholarship that revealed flaws, omissions, and gaps in conventional scholarship, while revealing evidence of African Americans' positive contributions to American culture. Authors exhibited increased willingness to use African and African American folk forms in their works. Fiction writers used strategies and techniques that called attention to gaps and omissions. Writing against the conventional linear Western historical narrative, Toni

Morrison would, for example, create the circular, meandering narrative of *Beloved* (1987) to address historical gaps and omissions. More recently, Alice Randall's *The Wind Done Gone* (2001) revisits and revises misrepresentations and myths associated with Margaret Mitchell's American classic, *Gone with the Wind* (1936).

The new writings also increasingly represented and acknowledged African American **identity** and experience in multiple terms rather than monolithic ones. Barbara Smith's groundbreaking essay, "Towards a Black Feminist Criticism" (1977), paved the way for what has since become a cottage industry in black feminist literary scholarship, though her lesbian reading of the relationship between Sula Peace and Nel Wright in Toni Morrison's *Sula* (1973) was not generally well-received. Charles I. Nero offers in "Toward a Black Gay Aesthetic" (1991) a critique of heterosexism among black American intellectuals. Literary critics have noted the generally counterdiscursive relationship that African American literature often enjoys with Anglo American literature (see, for example, J. Lee Greene's *Blacks in Eden* or Henry Louis Gates, Jr.'s *The Signifying Monkey*). Tensions and conflicts between Afrocentrists and post-structuralists, and between critics and theorists, have been played out in a variety of forums. One of the more famous of these happened during a series of exchanges among Joyce Ann Joyce, Henry Louis Gates, Jr., and Houston Baker, Jr. in several issues of *New Literary History* in 1987. Barbara Christian's "The Race for Theory" (1987) speaks to the problem of continuing to build a tradition of black literary criticism in a climate that increasingly valued post-structuralist theoretical paradigms. She offered that black women writers had long been theorizing through their literature. Certainly, the same can be said for numerous black male writers, including Ishmael Reed.

Ishmael Reed and *Mumbo Jumbo* (1972)

If one of Ralph Ellison's goals in *Invisible Man* was to warn against formulaic thinking or buying wholesale into a given ideology, then Ishmael Reed seems to take that idea a step further by making it his goal as a writer to attempt what has never been done before. Reed began his career as a novelist by parodying Ellison's novel (even as it was being canonized) in *The Freelance Pallbearers* (1967), a novel that also satirizes America's political situation vis-à-vis the Vietnam War.

Reed was born on February 22, 1938, in Chattanooga, Tennessee, but he grew up in Buffalo, New York. He attended Millard Fillmore College and later the University of Buffalo, but he lacked the financial support to complete the degree program. He became involved with the Umbra

Workshop (a group of nationalist-minded black writers integral to the formation of the Black Arts Movement) and *Umbra Magazine* after moving to New York City in 1962. Before moving to New York City, he had worked as a correspondent for a black Buffalo newspaper, the *Empire Star Weekly,* and as a co-host of a local radio show. In New York City, he helped found the famous underground newspaper, the *East Village Other*. Later, Reed would work in several efforts to focus attention on American literatures often excluded, overlooked, or marginalized in establishment circles. One early effort was the journal, *The Yardbird Reader*, and in the late 1970s, he helped found the Before Columbus Foundation, an organization dedicated to promoting a wider and more inclusive vision of American literature.

Reed describes his philosophy of art in terms of neohoodooism (with "hoodoo" being the African American version of the African religious practices known as "voodoo"). Reed's satirist and parodist forefathers include George Schuyler, Wallace Thurman, and Rudolph Fisher; all three men were part of the New Negro Movement of the 1920s. Other contemporary authors who use satire and/or parody include Charles Johnson, Trey Ellis, Carolivia Herron, Paul Beatty, and Alice Randall. Reed has published a total of nine novels. His second novel, *Yellow Back Radio Broke-Down* (1969)—a satire of the American western—introduces us to the concept of neohoodooism. Reed's particular genius is his ability to use satire and parody to demystify Western myths and historical narratives. He resists the demand from Western culture that black culture subordinate itself to it. His concerns are not unlike those represented in Morrison's *The Bluest Eye* (and other works), though his methods, strategies, and techniques are significantly different. Like many writers from Douglass forward, Reed defines Freedom as being able to tell his own story in his own way. He has been very vocal about the role that the publishing industry's bottom line and other such power interests play in shaping representations of African American culture—in determining what gets published and, therefore, what gets read.

Mumbo Jumbo is in simplest terms a mystery novel and a detective story, but (like Toni Cade Bambara's *The Salt Eaters*, 1980) it is one of the most complex tales you will ever read. The central character is PaPa LaBas, a private investigator who searches in vain for an ancient HooDoo Text (an alternative to the Christian Bible) that contains the explanation for Jes Grew. Jes Grew is purportedly evident in spontaneous eruptions of black music and artistic production such as occurred during the New Negro Movement, the Black Arts Movement, and (to extend the argument) the current renaissance and worldwide popularity of black American culture from so-called high art to hip-hop.

The novel thematizes neohoodooism by constantly suggesting that Western civilization's reliance on unchanging texts and formulaic procedures works against life. Ultimately, Jes Grew keeps appearing in its various ever-changing manifestations because the text explaining those appearances is missing (and ultimately destroyed). Had LaBas been successful in finding and codifying the sacred HooDoo Text, Jes Grew would eventually suffer a similar fate, become staid and repetitive, and lose its vibrant resilience and regenerative element. This concept parallels the idea that once a Movement becomes formulaic and prescriptive (as Reed and others believe was the case with the Black Arts Movement), it loses its regenerative creative powers. Reed is grappling with the same issue that Langston Hughes was addressing in "The Negro Artist and the Racial Mountain" (1926): how to be innovative, creative, and true to the artist's self when social conditions call for certain prescribed, formulaic responses.

Toward the end of *Mumbo Jumbo*, LaBas lectures on black religious history, beginning in Egypt with Osiris and explaining how it was that we in the West ended up with Christianity as a dominant Text rather than the HooDoo Text that would explain Jes Grew. LaBas's history of the world according to hoodoo centers the black (male) subject. According to the text, Moses, a descendant of Osiris's selfish brother, mates with the former's wife, Isis, and extracts from her the Osirian mysteries that explain Jes Grew. The mysteries, according to *Mumbo Jumbo*, were subsequently distorted and resulted in the Bible. The true text was hidden. LaBas is able to trace the text to New York City, but before he can put his hands on it, the Black Nationalist Abdul destroys it. According to LaBas, the spontaneous recurring appearance of Jes Grew in its various manifestations represents the death and regeneration of Osiris. The idea is that because Jes Grew is not codified, it will always be innovative, novel, new.

Alice Walker and *The Color Purple* (1982)

Alice Walker was born on February 9, 1944, in Eatonton, Georgia, to sharecroppers Willie Lee and Minnie Lou Grant Walker; she was their eighth child. When she was eight years old, a brother shot her in the right eye with a BBgun. The wound caused her to lose sight in her right eye, a physically and emotionally scarring experience that made her turn inward. She began recording her emotions surrounding the loss of her eye, and later included some of this material in her published work. In

1961, she graduated at the top of her high school class, and for the next two years she attended Spelman College in Atlanta on a Georgia Rehabilitation scholarship. In 1963, she transferred to Sarah Lawrence College. After receiving her B.A. from Sarah Lawrence, she moved to New York City where she worked for the Welfare Department. She married civil rights attorney Melvyn Roseman Leventhal in 1967; the couple moved to Mississippi where Walker became active in the Civil Rights Movement, and also taught as writer-in-residence first at Jackson State College and later at Tougaloo College. She gave birth to her only child, Rebecca Grant (now a writer and part of the *third wave* of black feminism), on November 17, 1969. Walker and Leventhal divorced in 1977.

Walker has collected several volumes of her poetry, including *Once* (1968), *Revolutionary Petunias* (1973), and *Good Night, Willie Lee, I'll See You in the Morning* (1979), and *Her Blue Body Everything We Know* (1991). Her novels include *The Third Life of Grange Copeland* (1970), *Meridian* (1976), *The Color Purple* (1982), *The Temple of My Familiar* (1989), *Possessing the Secret of Joy* (1992), and *By the Light of My Father's Smile* (1998). Walker's short stories are collected in *In Love & Trouble: Stories of Black Women* (1973) and *You Can't Keep a Good Woman Down* (1981); her children's books include *Langston Hughes, American Poet* (1974), *The Life of Thomas Hodge* (1974), and *To Hell with Dying* (1988). *In Search of Our Mother's Gardens* (1983) is a collection of "womanist prose"; its articles, essays, and reviews elaborate on Walker's views on "womanism," or black feminism. Other nonfiction prose is included in *Living by the Word* (1988), *The Same River Twice* (1996), and *The Way Forward Is with a Broken Heart* (2000). In 1993 and 1994, Walker and Pratibha Parmar produced the documentary film *Warrior Marks* and the accompanying book of the same title.

If Langston Hughes's "Negro artist" had to confront the "racial mountain," then Walker and other black women artists have had to confront the "racial and gender mountain." In some thirty years of publishing, Walker has been plagued by almost constant criticism for her depictions of intraracial abuse, for her depictions of black women, and, most soundly, for her depictions of black men. In some cases the same people who insist on artistic freedom and innovation criticize Walker for veering off the recommended course. Others charge her and other black women writers of being in collusion with the powerful, oftentimes invisible forces that shape American society—particularly since the most recent renaissance in African American literature was initially sparked by a renaissance in black women's writing that obviously benefited from the publishing industry's willingness to publish their work.

When *The Color Purple* appeared in 1982, it was immediately the subject of controversy for its representations of abusive and generally problematic relationships between black men and women. When it was adapted and released on film a few years later, the controversy became even more heated. The novel tracks the torturous journey of Celie, a rural black female adolescent, toward womanhood and self-awareness. It is composed of letters Celie writes to God and, later, letters between Celie and Nettie. Nettie is Celie's younger sister who becomes a missionary in Africa. The story is set for the most part in rural Georgia, but Celie moves to Memphis for a time, and Nettie's letters take us to an African village.

Celie's first letter, written when she is fourteen, tells the story of her sexual and emotional abuse at the hands of the man she believes to be her father. He not only impregnates her, but he also refuses to allow her to keep either of the two children he fathers; he admonishes her to tell no one but God. The situation invokes the slaveholder/bondwoman relationship of freedom narratives. After Celie's mother dies, her stepfather marries her off to Albert, an older man for whom she serves as housekeeper, child-rearer, and sexual surrogate (a stand-in for Shug Avery, the woman Albert desires but can not possess). In her pre-enlightenment letters, Celie refers to Albert as Mr. ______ because she does not learn his first name until Shug arrives. Left alone to fend off her "father's" advances, Celie's beloved younger sister Nettie comes to live with Celie. Albert soon sends her packing after she soundly rebuffs his sexual advances. Nettie is, coincidentally, taken in by the family that is raising Celie's "stolen" babies; she subsequently travels with the family to Africa as a missionary.

Years later Celie finally meets Shug Avery when Albert brings the very ill woman home. Celie nurses Shug to health, and they become first friends and then lovers. Walker stresses reciprocity in the relationship between Shug and Celie; each woman helps the other toward the physical, psychological, and spiritual transformation they require. Shug, a woman who lives life on her own terms, helps Celie locate a cache of letters from Nettie that Albert has been hiding over the years. The discovery of the cache of letters hardens Celie toward Albert and becomes a major turning point in her developing self-knowledge, her enlightenment. She eventually leaves Albert and moves to Memphis with Shug Avery and starts a unisex pants-making business. When Alphonso, her first rapist and the man she believed to be her father, dies, she learns that he was only her stepfather and that she is an heiress to property left by her real father who had been lynched by a white mob. Celie moves with her business back to her former community. She has come of age and is her own woman. In a parallel movement that many of her sharpest critics seemed to miss, Walker depicts the personal evolution of Albert. By novel's end, he and Celie are like old friends, equals sitting side-by-side on the front porch, sewing (though some see this as evidence of Albert's emasculation). The experience has been transformative for them both, and their new relationship is one based on mutual respect, rather than the previous hierarchy of one dominating the other. In an almost too-happy-to-be-true but nevertheless satisfying ending for the reader, Celie is reunited with her sister and two children. Walker's womanist fable comes full circle.

Gloria Naylor and *The Women of Brewster Place* (1983)

Gloria Naylor was born on January 25, 1950, in New York City to Albert McAlpin and Roosevelt Naylor. Her parents had migrated north from Mississippi. The family moved several times, living for a time in the upper Bronx, in Harlem, and in Queens. In Queens, Naylor's mother joined the Jehovah's Witnesses, and Naylor herself became a Witness minister in 1968. From 1968 to 1974 she lived with her parents and worked as a switchboard operator, and after that she traveled in North Carolina and Florida as a preacher and "pioneer" for the Jehovah's Witnesses. In 1975, she was back in New York suffering an emotional breakdown. She had left the Jehovah's Witnesses, and the following year, she moved away from her parents' home. In 1977 she read the first novel by a black woman that she had ever read: Toni Morrison's *The Bluest Eye* (1970). Naylor and Morrison would later discuss their roles as artists in a July 1985 dialogue in *Southern Review*. Naylor was married briefly between 1980 and 1981. She published her first novel, *The Women of Brewster Place*, in 1982, a year after graduating from Brooklyn College. In 1983, she received an M.A. in Afro-American Studies from Yale. Her subsequent novels include *Linden Hills* (1985), *Mama Day* (1988), *Bailey's Café* (1992), and *The Men of Brewster Place* (1998). She has taught at George Washington University, the University of Pennsylvania, New York University, Princeton University, Boston University, and the University of Kent, Great Britain. Her writing has earned her numerous awards.

The Women of Brewster Place begins with an epigraph from Langston Hughes's poem "Harlem," which begins with the line "What happens to a dream deferred?" The novel is really composed of seven stories about seven different women connected by setting and dreams deferred and drying up like raisins in the sun. The opening and closing sections, "Dawn" and "Dusk," respectively, frame the stories and provide details about the birth and death of Brewster Place. The seven featured women are Mattie Michael, Etta Mae Johnson, Kiswana (Melanie) Browne, Lucielia Louise Turner (Ciel), Cora Lee, Theresa, and Lorraine. Each woman's story sheds light on her personal past, explains how she arrived at Brewster Place, and characterizes her position vis-à-vis the rest of the community.

As a rural teenager, Mattie Michael had been seduced by the local smooth-talking male, impregnated, and subsequently sent packing by her strict father. With the help of an older woman, she finds a home for herself and her pampered son Basil. She even manages to acquire property in a good neighborhood. She loses the property when her now young adult son leaves town after she uses the property to post his bail in a criminal case. Brewster Place is thus the end of the line for Mattie; but even Brewster Place has its pillars, and Mattie is as strong as they come. Other characters lack Mattie's fortitude.

Etta Mae Johnson is Mattie's best friend. An independent and sensual woman fond of music and loving, Etta pays a high price for refusing to follow society's prescribed rules for proper women. After a string of unsuccessful liaisons with men, she settles at Brewster Place near her friend Mattie, whose unconditional love and support provide just the balm she needs. Lucielia (Ciel) Louise Turner is the granddaughter of a woman who once took Mattie in and indirectly helped her become a property owner. Ciel is married to a man who does not want to be married to her or any woman (though we do not learn the reason why until we read *The Men of Brewster Place*, 1998). Emotionally tortured by the unstable relationship, she almost loses her will to live after her young daughter dies in a household accident while she and husband Eugene are engaged in yet another argument. Completing the circle of reciprocity that began when Ciel's mother rescued Mattie and the infant Basil from the streets many years earlier, Mattie literally rescues Ciel from emotional and physical death.

Kiswana Browne is a somewhat naïve community activist who thinks she must give up her middle-class comforts to be "one with the people." Unlike the other women, she *chooses* to live at Brewster Place. Interestingly, though she lives in the community and provides the catalyst for a dramatic change in Cora Lee, Kiswana's relationship with the community seems at times more that of a compassionate anthropologist/social worker than an actual member of the community.

Cora Lee is the unmarried mother of a horde of neglected, unkempt children who run wild in the neighborhood and even eat out of garbage cans. She has been having babies since her early teens; while she enjoys infants (who temporarily replace the dolls she was forced to give up as an adolescent), she is sorely lacking in parenting skills. Kiswana convinces her to bring her children to a neighborhood production of a Shakespeare play. After witnessing her children's positive reactions to the play, Cora Lee begins to take a greater interest in their needs.

The final two characters' stories come packaged together in a section titled "The Two." Lorraine and Theresa comprise a lesbian couple that has "escaped" from middle-class Linden Hills in the hope of living without the sense of persecution they felt there. They find that their new community is equally problematic, and, as it turns out, even dangerous. They become the topic of gossip and innuendo, and finally Lorraine is subjected to a horrifying gang rape and beating that so loosens her faculties that she kills the next person she encounters. As it happens, that person is Ben, the building superintendent and neighborhood wino who had been living with the tortured memory of the daughter he failed. Like many of the women of Brewster Place, Ben's problems have their root in unequal access to economic opportunity. Before he ended up at Brewster Place, he had been a tenant farmer, and the landlord had used the situation to sexually exploit his adolescent daughter. Ironically, Lorraine had reminded Ben of his "lost" daughter, and he had been the only member of the community to offer her comfort and friendship.

Brewster Place, situated in an unnamed northern city, is the literal and figurative dead end for the people who live there. A brick wall separates the community from the rest of the city and even blocks out the sunlight. The wall becomes a symbol for the dead end that impedes social and economic progress. In a false ending to the novel and the real and figurative socioeconomic wall, Mattie Michael dreams that the women band together during a block party to tear down the wall. When Mattie awakens, she looks out her window to see Kiswana taping up a banner on the wall. Readers sometimes miss this reference to the wall because it occurs in the final paragraphs of the section titled "The Block Party." The following section, "Dusk," ends the story and tells of the neighborhood's death.

Toni Morrison and *Beloved* (1987)

Toni Morrison is, among other things, a novelist, scholar, and editor. She was born Chloe Anthony Wofford on February 18, 1931, in Lorain, Ohio, to Ramah Willis and George Wofford. Currently Robert F. Goheen

Professor of the Humanities at Princeton University, she grew up in Ohio in a family of storytellers and musicians. She has said that her parents taught her that racial politics were part of the reality of American life. In 1953, she earned a B.A. from Howard University, and in 1955, she earned an M.A. in English from Cornell University. In her thesis for the M.A., she considered the theme of suicide in the works of William Faulkner and Virginia Woolf. In 1957, she joined the faculty at Howard University. She subsequently met and married Jamaican architect Harold Morrison; they had two sons. Subsequently, Morrison and her husband divorced. She left Howard and returned to her hometown of Lorain. Eighteen months later she moved to Syracuse, New York, to work for a Random House subsidiary. In 1968, she moved to New York City and became a senior editor for Random House. The move proved particularly fortuitous and timely; for almost two decades, she nurtured the careers of a number of contemporary black American writers. The works she edited range in genre from fiction and poetry, to autobiography and "how-to" books. In other manifestations of her career as an editor, she has collected and introduced two volumes of essays on social criticism, and she has reintroduced works by other black writers, including James Baldwin, Toni Cade Bambara, and Huey P. Newton. Morrison came across the story of Margaret Garner while editing *The Black Book*. Garner became the model for Sethe, the protagonist in her Pulitzer Prizewinning *Beloved* (1987). Morrison's other novels include *The Bluest Eye* (1970), *Sula* (1973), *Tar Baby* (1977), *Song of Solomon* (1981), *Jazz* (1992), *Paradise* (1997), and *Love* (2003).

Morrison's outstanding contributions in fiction and criticism often overshadow her powerful presence as an editor. She has collected two very well received volumes of essays on social criticism. *Race-ing Justice, En-Gendering Power: Essays on Anita Hill, Clarence Thomas, and the Construction of Social Reality* (1992) and *Birth of a Nation'Hood: Gaze, Script, and Spectacle in the O. J. Simpson Case* (1997) feature thought-provoking essays by some of America's foremost scholars and social critics. Morrison also reintroduces the work of now deceased authors in *James Baldwin: Collected Essays* (1998), *James Baldwin: Early Novels and Stories* (1998), Toni Cade Bambara's *Deep Sightings and Rescue Missions: Fiction, Essays, and Conversations* (1999), and *To Die for the People: The Writings of Huey P. Newton* (1995). In 1996, she wrote the introduction for a new release of the Mark Twain classic, *The Adventures of Huckleberry Finn*. A trained literary critic, Morrison, in "Unspeakable Things Unspoken: the Afro-American Presence in American Literature" (1988) and *Playing in the Dark:*

Whiteness and the Literary Imagination (1992), issued a call for a reinvestigation of American literature and the ways that canonical texts are structured in relationship to *blackness*.

Beloved fits into the subgenre of African American literature known as the "neofreedom narrative"—the type of neofreedom narrative that is set (at least in part) during slavery and whose fictional plot deals directly with the immediate effects of slavery. Recall that another type of neofreedom narrative, such as Richard Wright's *Native Son* or Ralph Ellison's *Invisible Man*, features a plot that deals with slavery indirectly as the cause or impetus for later social conditions. *Beloved* is set in the free state of Ohio and the slave state of Kentucky; Sethe Suggs, the protagonist, is based on the aforementioned real-life Margaret Garner. Confronted with the reality of an enslaved mother killing her own child, Morrison tried to imagine and represent the scenario by which societal and personal forces could compel an otherwise loving mother to kill her child.

Beloved's narrative unfolds through several narrative voices in flashbacks that take us from freedom to slavery and back again. The narrative meanders forward, slips backward, spirals upward or downward, and then goes forward again. The story is composed of the fragmented recollections of Sethe and the other traumatized survivors of Sweet Home, the Kentucky plantation where Sethe's owner took her to live at the age of thirteen. Individual, personal reminiscences complement one another; readers must become involved in the storytelling process by collecting the partial stories and weaving them into a whole. The present moment of the very intimate story at the center of the novel runs from 1873 to 1875; the Civil War has been over for eight years, and, thus, slavery has been outlawed. Sethe, her eighteen-year-old daughter Denver, and the sad, spiteful spirit of Denver's dead sister live at 124 Bluestone Road near Cincinnati, Ohio. The ghost's presence in the house is evidenced by a glimmering red light. Sethe's sons Howard and Buglar, having tired of living with the anxiety created by the ghost's presence, had left in 1864; Sethe's mother-in-law, Baby Suggs, died not long after. In 1873, no one in the surrounding community comes to visit at 124 Bluestone Road, and Sethe and Denver visit no one.

Emotionally and psychologically traumatized by her past experiences, Sethe has managed physically to survive slavery and the havoc it wreaked on her family; but her continued physical survival has been based on her ability to suppress the memory of past events, including the events that led to the central act of infanticide. Despite her best efforts, however, some aspects of her past manage to seep through cracks in her memory. When Paul D, an old friend from Sweet Home, comes to visit Sethe in 1873, she begins to recall even more. From their interactions, we learn that Sweet Home was anything but sweet for those forced to serve first under the Garners, and then under the cruel slavemaster they called schoolteacher because he was always asking questions and writing things down.

The personification of scientific racism, schoolteacher spent much of his time observing their behavior and listing their attributes under "animal" and "human" subcategories. Sixo was the member of the enslaved community at Sweet Home most easily identified as rebellious. Halle Suggs was sensitive and generous-natured. A year after Sethe arrived at Sweet Home as Baby Suggs's replacement, she had chosen the extraordinary Halle as her future husband. During an attempted mass exodus from Sweet Home slavery, Paul D's brother Paul A was captured and hanged; Sixo was captured, burned, and shot to death. Halle witnessed an atrocious abuse of Sethe and slipped into insanity; Paul D was captured and sold. Sethe and her children (and, presumably, Sixo's woman friend Patsy) were the only ones to make it to freedom.

After Sethe lived free for twenty-eight days, daring for the first time to love her children fully and completely, schoolteacher tracked them all down at Baby Suggs's Bluestone Road residence. In a moment of desperation, Sethe decided that she and her children would be better off dead. She succeeded in killing only the older daughter before she was stopped. After serving time in jail for the child's murder (her real-life counterpart had been tried for theft of her master's property and subsequently "sold South"), she had returned to the house on Bluestone Road to live with her three surviving children and Baby Suggs, and to try to keep the past from consuming her. By the time Paul D arrives in 1873, only Sethe, Denver, and the spiteful ghost remain. Paul D arrives and drives the ghost away, but she returns in the flesh as the twenty-year-old young woman Sethe's daughter would have been had she lived. Based on the only word that Sethe could afford to have carved on the child's tombstone, she believes her name to be B-e-l-o-v-e-d. Denver recognizes her sister almost immediately. After driving Paul D from the house, the ghost proceeds to prey on Sethe's guilt. Beloved, composed of all the desire and deprivation that slavery foments, is literally sucking the life out of Sethe until Denver finally intervenes to save her mother's life. A communal exorcism drives the ghost away, and Paul D and a much debilitated Sethe are poised to resume the love relationship that had been disrupted by the ghost of slavery.

Randall Kenan and *A Visitation of Spirits* (1989)

Randall Kenan was born in Brooklyn, New York, on March 12, 1963. He grew up in a rural area known as Chinquapin, North Carolina, the model for the Tims Creek setting of *A Visitation of Spirits* and others of his stories. He received a B.A. in English from the University of North Carolina at Chapel Hill in 1984. He worked as an editor for Knopf and taught at Sarah Lawrence College, Columbia University, Duke University, The University of North Carolina at Chapel Hill, and the University of Memphis. The youngest of the writers featured in this volume, Kenan published his first novel, *A Visitation of Spirits* (1989), when he was twenty-six years old. He followed with a collection of short stories, *Let the Dead Bury Their Dead* (1992), which won the Lambda Award for best gay men's fiction. In 1994, he published a biography of James Baldwin for Chelsea House Publishers' Lives of Notable Gay Men and Lesbians series. In 1999, he published *Walking on Water: Black American Lives at the Turn of the Twenty-First Century*, which he has referred to as a sort of *The Souls of Black Folk* "redux." Among his awards and honors are the Mary Francis Hobson Medal for Arts and Letters, a Whiting Writer's Award, and the American Academy of Arts and Letters' Prix de Rome.

The protagonist in *A Visitation of Spirits* is sixteen-year-old Horace Cross, who has grown up as a bastard child in a southern black religious dynasty. Horace is already dead when the novel opens; his spirit hovers over the community, however, and much of the story is filtered through his consciousness. The story is primarily about Horace and the way he deals with family and community rejection of his true nature, though Kenan gives us a number of other well-developed characters. Religion permeates the story; Horace's last name is thus highly symbolic. The narration features shifting points of view. The third-person, omniscient narrator gives way to several first-person narrators and even a second-person voice that directly addresses the reader.

The story of ritual and failed transformation comes in segments that are identified by date and time. The novel is divided into five sections: "White Sorcery," "Black Necromancy," "Holy Science," "Old Demonology," and "Old Gods, New Demons." The first segment of "White Sorcery" concerns events that take place on December 8, 1985, at 8:45 A.M., long after Horace's death. The second segment meanders back to April 29, 1984, at 11:30 A.M., the beginning of the last day of Horace's life. "Black Necromancy" begins with Jimmy's confessions during which we learn something of his past and realize that he has managed to suppress his homoerotic tendencies in order to fit in among his family and community. The narrative then picks up with the events of December 8, 1985, forty-five minutes later, and then April 30, 1984, approximately fourteen hours beyond the April 29, 1984, time given in "White Sorcery."

The narrative point of view shifts to reveal the thoughts of several important characters and family members, whose recollections work much like those in Morrison's *Beloved*, to provide fragments of the story that we must participate in piecing together. In this way, moving between the past and present, between religion and magic, between doctrine and faith, Kenan presents the story of what happened to Horace Cross and why it happened. In doing so, he provides the history of the Cross and Greene families, as well as Horace's personal history. Religious dogma permeates the narrative, which takes us through the various generations of the Cross family and its intermarriage with the Greene family. What we get is a history of biblical proportions that provides everything we need to know about how Horace came to destroy himself. Religion, freedom, literacy, the significance of family relationships, and the burden of convention are important issues in the novel.

An avid reader of books on witchcraft, sorcery, and black magic, Horace decides to transform himself into something for which the community makes space: he decides on the red-tailed hawk. At least as a hawk, he would have a place in Tims Creek, a place he cannot have as a gay man. The reader witnesses Horace in the process of transformation—his descent into madness and subsequent suicide. When we first encounter Horace, he is already in the throes of his "transformation." The information spilling through his consciousness during the final moments of his life represent what might be interpreted as "his life flashing before his eyes." He has many visions. Steeped in religious tradition, Horace is caught between the proverbial rock and a hard place in trying to come to terms with his homosexuality. He is as much "in" the community as the community is "in" him, and the community holds no space for the expression of queer identity, Horace's true nature. As he becomes aware of his sexuality, he attempts to discuss it with his cousin Jimmy (James Malachai Greene), a minister. Jimmy, who knew firsthand how it felt to be attracted to other men, effectively tells Horace to "just get over it." Interestingly, a close look at Jimmy's wife Anne reveals that in many ways, she defied gender role expectations. Because she possesses a well-developed social conscience, Anne is not the amoral, centerless figure that Toni Morrison depicts in the title character for *Sula*; she nevertheless exhibits certain behaviors that society typically attributes to maleness.

Horace's story might be called an antifreedom narrative or a journey away from self-discovery. For example, Horace is an avid reader and a very bright student. Following the logic of Frederick Douglass's 1845 *Narrative* and numerous subsequent works, Horace's literacy should assist him in shedding his shackles. Personal freedom for Horace would begin with the end of his own homophobia, for it is homophobia that enslaves him. In his search for answers, Horace reads about magic, sorcery, and necromancy, all of which he will ultimately call upon to assist him in his transformation from human to bird. Thus, the surface story is about Horace's feelings of rejection and alienation, his descent into madness (or sanity—depending on perspective), his suicide, and the community's muted response. The parallel narrative, dated over a year after Horace dies, reveals that Horace's suicide stayed in the minds of certain members of his family, but it had little or no effect on the community's homophobia.

Charles Johnson and *Middle Passage* (1990)

Middle Passage is Charles Johnson's best-known novel, though even Johnson admits that *Oxherding Tale* is a much better effort. Johnson was born on April 23, 1948, in Evanston, Illinois. He earned a B.A. in journalism and an M.A. in philosophy from Southern Illinois University. He studied phenomenology and literary aesthetics in a Ph.D. program at SUNY Stony Brook before taking a position in creative writing at the University of Washington in Seattle. He also worked as a cartoonist and published two books of drawings: *Black Humor* (1970) and *Half-Past Nation-Time* (1972). His literary works include *Faith and the Good Thing* (1974), *Oxherding Tale* (1982), *The Sorcerer's Apprentice, Tales and Conjunctions* (1986), *Being and Race* (1988), *Middle Passage* (1990), and *Dreamer* (1998). *Oxherding Tale* and *Middle Passage* are neofreedom narratives, and *Dreamer* is a novel about Martin Luther King. *Being and Race* is a work of literary criticism.

Middle Passage is among other things a burlesque. Set in 1830, it charts the radical transformation of Rutherford Calhoun, newly freed person, who leaves slavery with the sure knowledge that as a Negro, he was born to lie and steal; to practice deception is his legacy as a formerly enslaved person. He believes he possesses no cultural capital, and so stealing what others own and value brings him material property and the experiences associated with owning material property. Rutherford is already physically free when he comes onstage, though we quickly become aware that he is still bound by the *pre-destination clause* of his former master's narrative, a clause that links Rutherford's destiny to that of Richard Wright's overdetermined thief and doomed murderer, Bigger Thomas from *Native Son* (1940). In his blindness, Rutherford can only see himself as a thief, a deceiver, and an opportunist who seems to engage in human interaction for the sole purpose of self-gratification. The self-reliance that Rutherford learned in his *school* of slavery was that if he wanted food, money, and other resources, he would have to steal them. Clearly, he exhibits a rather pedestrian acceptance of the connection between property and identity throughout most of the narrative. His radical transformation takes place during a *reverse* Middle Passage on the high seas, during which he learns the meaning of self-sacrifice.

When we first encounter Rutherford, he has just arrived in New Orleans, and he waddles gleefully in its many vices. By and by he becomes indebted to Papa Zeringue, a Creole of color who controls a share of the underworld. Rutherford's schoolteacher girlfriend sets the major chain of events into action when she pays off his debt and exacts—through Zeringue—Rutherford's promise of marriage. To escape what he believes to be the hell of marriage, he stows away on a ship bound for Africa. The crew soon discovers him, but Captain Falcon spares his life. As it turns out, the ship is engaged in the outlawed Atlantic slave trade. Even more interesting is the fact that Papa Zeringue owns a share in the ship's cargo. Rutherford becomes aware of this much later. At the African coast, they pick up the load of Africans from a tribe of Allmuseri wizards, and things soon take a turn for the worse. The crew starts murmuring about a mutiny. The Africans start murmuring about a revolt. Scam artist that he is, Rutherford manages to declare loyalty to all three factions onboard: the Africans, the crew, and Captain Falcon. Eventually, the ship—which also contains cultural artifacts looted from around the world—is caught in a turbulent storm, and in the life-and-death struggle to survive, Rutherford learns a valuable lesson about truth, identity, and self-sacrifice.

In constructing Rutherford's story, Johnson invokes and evokes characters and situations from a number of predecessor texts, including Herman Melville's *Moby-Dick* and "Benito Cereno," Dante's *Inferno*, Ralph Ellison's *Invisible Man*, Toni Morrison's *Beloved, The Odyssey*, and others. *Middle Passage* is also rich in the elements of parody, which automatically makes it counterdiscursive. Because of this, and because Rutherford owes *his* existence as a fictional character to the existence of freedom narratives, *Middle Passage,* like Kenan's *A Visitation of Spirits,* has *everything* and *nothing* to do with those freedom narratives. Rutherford's freedom begins with liberated perception, and in this his freedom is not unlike that of Kenan's Horace Cross. Rutherford steals in order to gain the value of experiences that he feels are outside himself and his African heritage. He believes prior to his departure on a reverse Middle Passage that his racial identity renders him culturally and materially bankrupt—that such is his destiny as a "Negro" in the New World. Liberated perception will allow Rutherford to restructure a faulty syllogism that drives his thieving behavior: "Freedom is property. I have property. Therefore, I am Free." Johnson uses Rutherford's exploits to highlight the folly of relying on property as a basis for self-identity. Rutherford's quest, though he is unaware of it when he begins his voyage on *The Republic*, is to free himself from the gridlock of his former master's pronouncement that he is destined for a lynch mob. To change his destiny, he must liberate his mind and acknowledge both his legacy and his responsibility.

Octavia Butler and *Parable of the Sower* (1993)

Octavia Estelle Butler overcame dyslexia as a young child to become one of the most prolific of contemporary black women writers. Born June 22, 1947, in Pasadena, California, Butler was a shy child who liked to daydream. Her father, Laurice Butler, died when she was very young. Butler grew up in a racially mixed neighborhood where she lived with her mother, Octavia M. (Guy) Butler. The budding author developed an interest in science fiction when she was twelve years old. A recipient of one of the prestigious MacArthur Foundation "genius grants," Butler continues to produce outstanding works in the science fiction genre. Her substantial body of work includes "Crossover" (1971), *Patternmaster* (1976), *Mind of My Mind* (1977), *Survivor* (1978), *Kindred* (1979), "Near of Kin" (1979), *Wild Seed* (1980), *Clay's Ark* (1984), *Dawn* (1987), "The Evening and the Morning and the Night" (1987), *Adulthood Rites* (1988), *Imago* (1989), *Parable of the Sower* (1993), *Bloodchild and Other Stories* (1995), *Parable of the Talents* (1998), *Lilith's Brood* (2000). Butler often mixes environmental concerns with themes involving slavery in a variety of manifestations.

In *Parable of the Sower*, she is concerned with global warming and various forms of nouveau slavery. Protagonist Lauren Oya Olamina's journal entries become both the novel's science fiction narrative and the text of Earthseed, Lauren's guide for living in a postapocalyptic world. The future depicted in the narrative is based on projections of current realities, so it does not seem far-fetched. Lauren's journal charts her sojourn from the edge of chaos, into chaos, and finally toward a new beginning. Her story begins inside her walled community in a Los

Angeles suburb where her family is part of an ethnically diverse community. Butler uses thermodynamics—the study of energy—its transformations and its relationship to the properties of matter—as a lens through which to view this community and others described in the text. The narrative spans several years, from 2024 to 2027; Butler projects current production and consumption patterns to suggest that they will culminate in a serious deficit of resources, which, of course, will increase the potential for theft. The earth and most of its inhabitants are fast succumbing to the ravages of an environment that has been stripped of its life-giving capacity by centuries of misuse. Outside the walls and on the streets, people are expected to fear and hate all but their own kind; but inside walled neighborhoods, such as Lauren's, they can ill afford to play the race game.

Thus, Lauren begins her narrative as a middle-class teenager living with her family in a walled and gated community in the Los Angeles suburb of Robledo. Lauren's fearful, walled community has set up an elaborate security system to protect them from thieves; the most aggressive of these are drug addicts, but they also include throngs of homeless people who must steal and scavenge, or starve. Lauren writes early and often of the thieves who manage to get through their security system time and again. Lauren realizes that her childhood community is outmoded, and she tries to encourage change and preparedness, with little success. Nevertheless, once she leaves this community, she does not simply dismiss those past experiences, she uses them as part of her rationale for change.

In strict socioeconomic terms, the gap between the "haves" and the "have-nots" has reached a zenith in *Parable*; the last of the middle-class sit (as Lauren's community does when the story begins) like frightened prey behind walled communities. They live in perpetual anxiety, fearful of crazed drug fiends and other desperate denizens of the street who wait just beyond their locked gates, and who all too often invade their sanctuaries after dark. The only "safe" people are the extremely wealthy, and they live in compounds, typically featuring a big house with smaller servant shacks (dependencies) nearby—not unlike the big house and quarters during slavery. To the homeless and unprotected "outsiders," Lauren's walled community, with its garden and fruit trees, had looked like Paradise. From Lauren's vantage point, her community had been anything but Paradise. Rather, it is like an island surrounded by hungry sharks, hemmed in by seen and unseen forces. She watches and records as "thieves" on the outside grow increasingly aggressive. The feeling is one of impending doom; her community lives in perpetual fear that "the great unwashed" will penetrate its sanctuary, and, eventually, their fear is realized.

Lauren has seen the inevitable and prepared for it as best she can. She escapes and meets up with a couple of people from her old neighborhood; together they join the hordes of homeless sojourners headed North toward a new beginning. Lauren finds herself in the position of having to steal and scavenge in order to survive. Because Lauren is in charge of the narrative, which also becomes the sacred text for her and her followers in their new home, she controls the definition of the term "thief." Along the way, their core group expands to include several others. Lauren becomes the group's leader, and her diary entries become the basis for a new "religion," which she names Earthseed. In it she advances the philosophy that the only lasting truth is Change. Therefore, God is Change. The members of her new community are truly interdependent; their collective situation is akin to that of the survivors aboard the *Republic* in Johnson's *Middle Passage*, where the various factions on the ship become a cooperative—merging into a collective struggle for survival. In order to survive, they must form necessary coalitions across racial and ethnic boundaries; dire economic and social circumstances mandate such cooperatives. The fluidity of water becomes the chaos out of which Rutherford Calhoun emerges transformed in *Middle Passage*; in *Parable*, it is the energy creating capacity of heat and fire that sets Lauren on her journey. Lauren's old community had refused to prepare itself for the inevitable, for change. Lauren is able to emerge (phoenix-like) from this thermodynamic environment because she has prepared herself ahead of time. She has perceived that the old traditions and conceptions of home and family would not sustain them under the extreme circumstances of an overworked environment and late capitalism.

The narrative derives from Lauren's scientific observations of society under the effects of heat and pressure. The principles contained in Earthseed are based on a careful observation and recording of the changes, and thus they point clearly to what they must do for continued survival. Having recorded her observations of the old community in its unwillingness to change, Lauren can apply that knowledge to the new community. Earthseed is itself (purportedly) subject to change—or revision—though there are signs toward the end of the text that Lauren is not eager to revise it. With the emphasis on change, what gets defined as theft is also subject to change, and racial profiling loses its force. Protection becomes even more important than property ownership in *Parable* as society and the environment grow increasingly "lethal." The term *lethal* is a recurring one in Lauren's narration, and it is used to describe various deadly scenarios.

Afrekete (1995)

Afrekete: An Anthology of Black Lesbian Writing (1995) contains short stories, poems, essays, and autobiographical pieces by Audre Lorde, Sapphire, Helen Elaine Lee, Alexis De Veaux, Michelle Parkerson, Carolivia Herron, Jewelle Gomez, Jackie Goldsby, Pat Parker, Michelle Cliff, and several others. The name for the volume comes from the final chapter of Audre Lorde's **biomythography**, *Zami: A New Spelling of My Name* (1984); *Zami* combines poetry, myth, fiction, and life-writing to tell a young woman's journey of self-discovery. Lorde's "Tar Beach" is the opening story for *Afrekete.* Subsequent entries include Sapphire's satirical poem, "American Dream," Jocelyn Maria Taylor's autobiographical "Testimony of a Naked Woman," Carolivia Herron's "The Old Lady," Cynthia Bond's "Ruby," Melanie Hope's "Dare," and Sharee Nash's "Take Care." Audre Lorde's poem about waiting to die of cancer, "Today Is Not the Day," is the last entry in the anthology.

Audre Lorde's "Tar Beach" is from the section of her biomythography in which she comes full circle to herself through the black lover named Kitty, short for Afrekete, a name that carries strong cultural meaning in at least two African societies. In Dahomean mythology, Afrekete is the daughter of Sebouisa, considered the "mother of us all." In the pre-Yoruban tradition, she is the goddess of communication, language, and poetry. Afrekete is also connected with water and natural imagery and reminiscent of the longing Lorde recalls her mother expressing for her homeland of Grenada. In "Tar Beach," Audre and Kitty meet by chance in a bar after not having seen each other for two years. They become *natural* lovers; Audre expresses the feeling that loving Afrekete is like finally coming home to herself. They celebrate the magic of having found each other; they share food, life, dreams, and secrets. Then one day Afrekete, a singer, leaves for a "gig" in Atlanta, and it's all right. The two women have bonded for life, which really means that Audre Lorde has finally come to a full acceptance of the black lesbian self she has previously resisted. She realizes that women had always nurtured and supported her in the same way that Grenadian women nurtured and supported one another while their men were absent. Their relationships were described as "madivine," "friending," "zami," or women giving love and attention to other women, which might or might not include genital sexual relations. Afrekete is the symbolic black woman, and for Audre Lorde, loving Afrekete is loving herself.

Elaine Lee's short story, "Water Call," focuses on the recurring memory of an illegal abortion that almost took the protagonist's life. Ouida's ambivalence about her lesbian identity led to a heterosexual affair and pregnancy. Forced to admit to her partner Zella that she has been unfaithful, she enlists Zella's help in securing an abortion at a time when abortions were illegal. Zella goes to her Aunt Mandy, who runs a boardinghouse for young women. Her aunt is at first relieved at the thought that it is Zella who is in trouble, and therefore heterosexual. Zella quickly enlightens her on that point and leaves with the information she needs. Ouida undergoes the illegal abortion, which is described in disturbing detail. Ouida almost bleeds to death. A panicked Zella, watching her friend and lover cling to consciousness, drives to the home of the family doctor, who refuses to help but gives in to Zella's demand for the name of someone who will. The name turns out to be that of a veterinarian, who provides medication, but will not otherwise treat Ouida. The story ends with Ouida regaining consciousness several days later in the hospital, aware of the lost time and the fact that the experience would haunt her for the rest of her life. The story reveals some of the complexities of lesbian existence, critiques compulsory heterosexuality, and visits the dangers associated with abortion in the time before the Supreme Court decision in *Roe v. Wade*.

Filled with magical realism, Cynthia Bond's short story "Ruby" relates the title character's history of sexual abuse from the age of eight months when the first male relative pushed his penis inside her infant mouth and held her nose to enhance the effect. She cites the betrayal of the female relatives who allowed the abuse to continue through generations. In a flashback we learn that Ruby had returned to her home in rural Texas after leaving her lesbian lover in New York City. She lives a somewhat reclusive life, melded to the land that holds the blood and bodies of her appropriated and murdered children. Proper men from the nearby town come and go, using her various orifices for their temporary sexual release, despite the fact that she is usually covered head to toe with filth. Natural images abound, and at times Ruby is portrayed as part of the landscape—as fallen rain, as a tree, as a stone. Then comes Ephraim, a sensitive mama's boy bearing one of his mother's angel food cakes; Ephraim sees beneath the dirt that literally and figuratively covers Ruby. The story ends as they sit enjoying the cake and each other's company. Ruby's story is both individual and allegorical; it speaks to the history of abuse and exploitation of the black female body and the murder of black children. It also speaks to the possibilities for love and comradeship between black men and women regardless of sexual identity.

Alice Randall and *The Wind Done Gone* (2001)

Alice Randall is a songwriter and screenwriter who lives with her husband, attorney David Ewing, and daughter Caroline Randall Williams, in Nashville, Tennessee. She graduated from Harvard with honors in English and American literature in 1981. *The Wind Done Gone* (2001) is her first novel. Randall's daughter is the great-granddaughter of Arna Bontemps, the Harlem Renaissance poet. Her husband is the great-great-grandson of the first black American to practice law in Tennessee, Prince Albert Ewing. Randall was born in Detroit, Michigan, but grew up in Washington, D.C. She has strong credentials in black history, having researched, lectured, and written on the subject, as well as served on the boards of institutions whose purpose is the preservation of black history. As a screenwriter, she wrote a *movie of the week* for CBS, and has worked on adaptation projects, including one involving Zora Neale Hurston's *Their Eyes Were Watching God.* She is also the only black American woman to have written a number one country song, though she has a number of other songwriting credits. *The Wind Done Gone* has received much attention surrounding its parody of the American classic, *Gone with the Wind* (1936), and the lawsuit filed by author Margaret Mitchell's estate against Randall's publisher, Houghton Mifflin. Randall revealed in an *Oprah Magazine* article that like her protagonist in *Wind*, she too received (in the form of a ten-year cache of letters from her father) vital information that had long been withheld from her. Randall's protagonist, Cynara, received hers primarily through the oral recitation provided by the character named Garlic in the novel. Garlic is called Pork in Mitchell's novel.

Lest *The Wind Done Gone* become known only for its association with the earlier novel, it is important for students to see it in relation to the tradition of African American literature as well. The novel is composed of diary entries of a formerly enslaved mulatta, Cynara, who is also the first-person narrator of most of the story. This immediately evokes Alice Walker's Celie of *The Color Purple*, who spoke letters to God—before she could write—in an effort to better understand the circumstances of her life. Cynara's diary is the "trace" of the absent and absented mulatta offspring of the supposedly "nonexistent" interracial sexual relations of Margaret Mitchell's *Gone with the Wind*; Randall imagines that Cynara's presence was overshadowed and obscured by that of the overwhelming Scarlett O'Hara of Mitchell's novel. Thus, Randall and Cynara join forces to bring Cynara (a representative mulatta figure) into view. Cynara uses her diary and pen to transform herself from invisible woman to Visible Woman. Like Ralph Ellison's unnamed narrator in *Invisible Man*, she is in need of vital information about her past before she can figure out where she's going. Randall, following the revisionist strategies of Gayl Jones and Toni Morrison and others, uses Cynara's recollections to provide details about the *interior lives* of black people during and after slavery.

To parody *Gone with the Wind*, Randall invokes certain characters and situations from Mitchell's novel. Parody is by nature intended to imitate another work in order to suggest its limitations; parody ridicules and burlesques and often renders comic or absurd the most serious aspect of the previous work. Cynara is the daughter of Planter (Gerald O'Hara) and Pallas (Mammy) and the half sister of Other (Scarlett O'Hara). Cynara recalls incidents from her childhood in which Other had always claimed the right to everything, in particular the love and attention of the woman she knew to be her own mother. She, who could not count on being fed regularly, watched as Other plodded up to Mammy, reached into her bosom and pulled out a breast to take her fill. Randall renames Tara "Tata," which she explains means "breast" or "thank-you."

Cynara's reflections about being displaced by Other and finally being banished (disinherited) at puberty by her father and (she initially believes) her mother, reveal her feelings of invisibility. Sold to her father's friends for the sum of one dollar, Cynara ends up bare-breasted on the auction block and later spends time as a cleaning woman in the brothel that R (Rhett Butler) frequents. She becomes his mistress, and on her twenty-eighth birthday (five months after the Emancipation Proclamation is issued), he gives her a pen and diary. She uses the gift to leave behind the information that validates her existence.

The diary reflects that for much of her life, because of the events of her first thirteen years, she was preoccupied with desire for what Other had claimed as her own—particularly Pallas's love and attention. It is after her mother's death that she learns the truth: that Pallas suffered the ultimate sacrifice in giving her up, and she had made R promise to marry her. After Other dies, R and Cynara marry. Finally, she has gained everything that Other had. Here, we begin to see Other as a generic white southern belle and Cynara as any black woman who has ever longed for all the accoutrements of the elusive American Dream. Once Cynara becomes aware of her personal history, assured of her mother's love, she realizes that she has options—that she is Free. She leaves her rich white husband and all the property he has provided for her in order to join the black **Talented Tenth**. She bears a "legitimate heir" for her lover, the black congressman with the last name Conyers, with whom she once had an affair and in whose eyes she saw herself in a positive light. Like Victor Séjour's mulatto (discussed in chapter 2) and numerous mulatto characters of late nineteenth-century black American fiction (discussed in chapter 3), she gladly and proudly joins up with "the race"; with other black Americans, she witnesses the tide turning against them. She is finally free, nevertheless, and no longer living in Other's shadow.

She chooses not to remarry and lives instead in a home of her own near the Potomac. Finally, she has claimed fully her own life; she has become a visible woman, and she has substantially fleshed out the narrow black lives represented in Mitchell's novel. Randall's deft dismantling of many of the myths advanced in *Gone with the Wind* demonstrates resoundingly that the black trickster (a recurring figure in the literature) is alive and well and living in Nashville. Randall's mulatta is a woman of agency who, armed with self-knowledge, makes lasting contributions to black progress. Perhaps in the most provocative move of the entire novel, she writes that Cotton Farm/Tata passed down through generations of African-derived people who were enslaved there. The novel is significant for its ability to invoke characters and themes from a number of texts, including *Incidents in the Life of a Slave Girl* (1861), *Iola Leroy* (1892), *Contending Forces* (1900), *The House Behind the Cedars*, *The Autobiography of an Ex-Coloured Man* (1912), *Invisible Man* (1952), *The Bluest Eye* (1970), *The Color Purple* (1982), *Beloved* (1987), and a host of others. Randall revisits and revises the "proper" mulatta characters of late nineteenth-century novels such as *Iola Leroy* and *Contending Forces*. In telling the story of the neglected black child of slavery, she (like Morrison with *Beloved*) presents the other side of the outraged black mother image that recurs in black women's fiction.

Recurring Themes and Issues

Who could have imagined that in the new millennium, African American authors would still be grappling with issues of identity, disrupted family life, sexual exploitation, miscegenation, property rights, disinheritance, reappropriation, sexual exploitation, illegitimacy, voice, slavery and freedom, and the central role of literacy in articulating the self? By now, you should be able to spot recurring themes and issues without the assistance of this textbook. Identity issues, as always, are central in the literature featured in this chapter. In the postmodern era, they take on added dimension. The impact of the postmodern era is evidenced by the uncertainty and fragmentation that seem to overshadow the lives of many of the characters featured in the stories above, as well as by the lack of closure in the stories.

Some contemporary authors use their works to explore the possibility for positive male-female relationships among the descendants of enslaved persons. Charles Johnson's protagonist must overcome the limitations of his own mind in his quest for healthy relationships. *Beloved* examines, among other things, the difficulty that formerly enslaved persons faced in trying to achieve a healthy sense of self following the trauma of slavery. Though these two texts strongly diverge in some important aspects, both clearly illustrate the significance of love in overcoming desire. A similar scenario is played out in Alice Randall's novel, and certainly unfulfillable desire is at the root of Horace's dilemma in *A Visitation of Spirits*. In these and the other novels discussed above, slavery and freedom take on varying dimensions; slavery is often tied to limited perception, which is often tied to missing or unacknowledged information. Freedom is tied to increased perception and the acquisition of self-knowledge.

The significance of motherhood to self-identity continues to be a central theme in women's fiction. Certainly, it is key to sorting out Sethe's dilemma in *Beloved.* Black feminist scholars, in particular, have identified the figure of the outraged mother as a recurring one in black women's literature, and Sethe is, above all else, an outraged mother (see the Braxton essay listed in the chapter bibliography). Related issues and themes include the sexual and reproductive exploitation that figured prominently as a part of the system of chattel slavery. We learn, for example, that Halle was the only one of Baby Suggs's eight or nine children that she was allowed to keep. Another character, Ella, had been forced as an adolescent to serve as an object for the perversions of a father-and-son team; so bad was her treatment that she uses the experience as a yardstick by which to measure all other atrocities. Sethe's own mother had been forced to mate with a variety of men for the purpose of enriching the slaveowner's supply of free labor. Paul D witnesses the lynching of a black woman who is accused of theft for trying to gather ducks she believes to be her lost children. Because the system made no provision for either, enslaved women who were allowed to keep their children in close proximity faced the problem of providing proper childcare and forming maternal bonds with them. In *Beloved*, Sethe had almost no contact with her own mother. The myriad issues surrounding motherhood that Morrison addresses in *Beloved* are addressed to varying degrees in some of the best-known freedom narratives, including Frederick Douglass's *Narrative of the Life of Frederick Douglass* (1845), Harriet Jacobs's *Incidents in the Life of a Slave Girl* (1861), and Booker T. Washington's *Up from Slavery* (1901). Alice Randall suggests in *The Wind Done Gone* (2001) that the mother/child bond suffered even in cases where both served in the big house. Additionally, manhood and masculinity are recurring issues in several of the novels discussed in this chapter.

The concept of double-consciousness is as apparent in Alice Randall's novel as it is in James Weldon Johnson's *The Autobiography of an Ex-Coloured Man*. Randall Kenan's doomed protagonist in *A Visitation of Spirits*, like Johnson's ex-coloured man, understands the judgment being visited upon him. Kenan's protagonist is so intricately tied to his homophobic community that he can only stand in harsh judgment of his own homosexuality. He can no more separate himself from the judgment of the community than he can (in reality) turn himself into a bird. Kenan's implicit and explicit critique of the pillars of certain conventions and traditions connects it to the freedom narratives of Frederick Douglass, Harriet Jacobs, and others. Ishmael Reed and Octavia Butler offer alternatives to the Bible in the Osiris stories and Earthseed, respectively. Doubleconsciousness also plays a role in Lorraine and Theresa's decision to move to Brewster Place in Gloria Naylor's novel.

When black women writers such as Alice Walker and Gloria Naylor write about abusive relationships in black families, they are accused of being in collusion with "the enemy," of inciting the so-called gender debate. Trey Ellis uses *Platitudes* to *thematize* one aspect of the so-called gender debate of recent decades, which involves the proliferation of black women's texts published in the 1970s and 1980s. Ellis writes also of a "new black aesthetic" featuring "cultural mulattos." Hip-hop poet Paul Beatty *thematizes* the cultural mulatto in the hilariously funny *The White Boy Shuffle*, a novel that revisits and revises Johnson's *The Autobiography of an Ex-Coloured Man*. In his fiction and nonfiction, Charles Johnson calls for a celebration of the cultural mongrel. In *Parable of the Sower*, Butler depicts the genesis of a naturally multicultural community.

In the past few years, a new generation of authors and scholars has begun to stress the importance of charting new and ever more positive directions in the field. Sound familiar? The more conscientious of these pay homage to their forefathers and foremothers, while serving notice that there is no one African American experience. The study of African American literature has become increasingly diasporic in focus, and rightly so. Recall from chapter 2 that Victor Séjour, a Louisiana Creole of color, wrote the earliest extant work of African American fiction, "The Mulatto," which was actually published in France. William Wells Brown's *Clotel* was first published in Britain. The first major autobiographical work, *The Interesting Narrative of Olaudah Equiano*, was also published in Britain. (At the time, Equiano considered himself a British citizen, though he had previously lived in the United States.) Thus, the license for the recent anthology by hip-hop generation's Kevin Powell, *Step into a World,* has been in place for centuries. African American literature as a field of study now expands far beyond the confines of the United States. The dimension and texture of the works produced in this field now command the attention of the best critical and theoretical minds in literary studies.

Bibliography

Andrews, William L., and Trudier Harris, eds. *The Oxford Companion to African American Literature*. New York: Oxford UP, 1997.

Auger, Philip. *Native Sons in No Man's Land: Rewriting Afro-American Manhood in the Novels of Baldwin, Walker, Wideman, and Gaines*. New York: Garland, 2000.

Banks, Erma Davis, and Keith Byerman. *Alice Walker: An Annotated Bibliography 1968–1986*. New York: Garland, 1989.

Barksdale, Richard, and Keneth Kinnamon, eds. *Black Writers of America: A Comprehensive Anthology*. Upper Saddle River, N.J.: Prentice Hall, 1972.

Bell, Bernard. *The Afro-American Novel and Its Tradition*. Amherst: U of Massachusetts P, 1987.

Boyer, Jay. *Ishmael Reed*. Boise State University Western Writers Series. Boise: Boise State UP, 1993.

Braxton, Joanne. "Ancestral Presence: The Outraged Mother Figure in Contemporary Afra-American Writing." *Wild Women in the Whirlwind*. Eds. Braxton and Andrée Nicola McLaughlin. New Brunswick: Rutgers, 1990. 299–315.

Braxton, Joanne M., and Andree Nicola McLaughlin, eds. *Wild Women in the Whirlwind: Afra-American Culture and the Contemporary Literary Renaissance*. New Brunswick, Rutgers UP, 1990.

Brown, William Wells. *Clotel, or The President's Daughter*. 1853. Bedford Cultural Edition. Ed. Robert S. Levine. New York: Bedford/St. Martin's, 2000.

Butler, Octavia. *Adulthood Rites*. 1988. New York: Warner Books, 1997.

—. *Bloodchild and Other Stories*. New York: Four Walls Eight Windows, 1995.
—. *Clay's Ark*. 1984. New York: Warner Books, 1996.
—. *Dawn: Xenogenesis*. 1987. New York: Popular Library, 1988.
—. *Imago*. New York: Warner Books, 1989.
—. *Kindred*. 1979. Boston: Beacon, 1988.
—. *Lilith's Brood*. 1989. New York: Warner Books, 2000.
—. *Mind of My Mind*. 1977. New York: Warner Books, 1994.
—. *Parable of the Sower*. 1993. New York: Warner Books, 2000.
—. *Parable of the Talents*. New York: Seven Stories Press, 1998.
—. *Patternmaster*. Garden City, N.Y.: Doubleday, 1976.
—. *Survivor*. Garden City, N.Y.: Doubleday, 1978.
—. *Wild Seed*. 1980. New York: Warner Books, 2001.
Butler-Evans, Elliott. *Race, Gender, and Desire: Narrative Strategies in the Fiction of Toni Cade Bambara, Toni Morrison, and Alice Walker*. Philadelphia: Temple UP, 1989.
Byerman, Keith E. *Fingering the Jagged Grain: Tradition and Form in Recent Black Fiction*. Athens: U of Georgia P, 1985.
Byrd, Rudolph, ed. *I Call Myself an Artist: Writings by and about Charles Johnson*. Bloomington: Indiana UP, 1999.
Christian, Barbara. *Alice Walker's The Color Purple and Other Works: A Critical Commentary*. New York: Simon & Schuster, 1987.
—. *Black Feminist Criticism*. New York: Pergamon, 1985.
Davies, Carole Boyce. *Black Women, Writing and Identity: Migrations of the Subject*. New York: Routledge, 1994.
Decker, Jeffrey Louis, ed. *The Black Aesthetic Movement*. Detroit: Gale Research Company, 1991.
Dick, Bruce, and Amritjit Singh, eds. *Conversations with Ishmael Reed*. Jackson: UP of Mississippi, 1995.
Dick, Bruce Allen, and Pavel Zemliansky, eds. *The Critical Response to Ishmael Reed*. Westport, Conn.: Greenwood P, 1999.
Diedrich, Maria, Henry Louis Gates, Jr., and Carl Pedersen, eds. *Black Imagination and the Middle Passage*. New York: Oxford, 1999.
Dieke, Ikenna, ed. *Critical Essays on Alice Walker*. Westport, Conn.: Greenwood P, 1999.
Dubey, Madhu. African American Women Novelists and the Nationalist Aesthetic. Bloomington: Indiana UP, 1994.
Ellison, Ralph. *Invisible Man*. 1952. Introd. Ralph Ellison. 1981. New York: Random House, 1995.
Equiano, Olaudah. *The Interesting Narrative of the Life of Olaudah Equiano, or Gustavus Vassa, the African, Written by Himself*. 1789.

The Interesting Narrative and Other Writings. Ed. Vincent Carretta. New York: Penguin, 1996.

Ervin, Hazel Arnett. *African American Literary Criticism, 1773–2000*. New York: Twayne, 1999. Evans, Mari. *Black Women Writers 1950–1980*. New York: Anchor/Doubleday, 1983.

Fabre, Geneviève and Robert O'Meally, eds. *History and Memory in African-American Culture*. New York: Oxford UP, 1994.

Felton, Sharon, and Michelle C. Loris. *The Critical Response to Gloria Naylor*. Westport, Conn.: Greenwood P, 1997.

Fowler, Virginia. *Gloria Naylor: In Search of Sanctuary*. New York: Twayne, 1996.

Fox, Robert Elliot. *Conscientious Sorcerers: The Black Postmodernist Fiction of LeRoi Jones/Amiri Baraka, Ishmael Reed and Samuel R. Delany*. New York: Greenwood P, 1987.

Gaines, Ernest J. *The Autobiography of Miss Jane Pittman*. New York: Dial, 1971.

—. *Bloodline*. 1968. New York: Vintage, 1997.

—. *Catherine Carmier*. 1964. New York: Vintage, 1993.

—. *Conversations with Ernest Gaines*. Ed. John Lowe. Jackson: UP of Mississippi, 1995.

—. *A Gathering of Old Men*. New York: Knopf, 1983.

—. *In My Father's House*. 1978. New York: Norton, 1983.

—. *A Lesson before Dying*. New York: Knopf, 1993.

Gates, Jr., Henry Louis. *Figures in Black: Words, Signs, and the "Racial Self."* New York and Oxford: Oxford UP, 1987.

—. *The Signifying Monkey*. New York: Oxford, 1985.

—. "Writing 'Race' and the Difference it Makes." *"Race," Writing, and Difference*. U Chicago P, 1985. 1–20.

Gates, Jr., Henry Louis, ed. *Black Literature and Literary Theory*. 1984. New York: Routledge, 1990.

Gates, Jr., Henry Louis, and Kwame Anthony Appiah, ed. *Alice Walker: Critical Perspectives Past and Present.* Amistad Literary Series. New York: Amistad, 1993.

—. *Gloria Naylor: Critical Perspectives Past and Present*. New York: Amistad, 1993.

—. *Toni Morrison: Critical Perspectives Past and Present*. New York: Amistad, 1993.

Gilroy, Paul. "Living Memory: A Meeting with Toni Morrison." *Small Acts: Thoughts on the Politics of Black Cultures*. London: Serpent's Tail, 1993. 175–82.

Goudie, S. X. "Leavin' a Mark on the Wor(l)d: Marksman and Marked Men in *Middle Passage.*" *African American Review*, 29:1 (1995): 109–12.

Govan, Sandra Y. "Connections, Links, and Extended Networks: Patterns in Octavia Butler's Science Fiction." *African American literature Forum* 18 (Fall 1984): 82–7.

—. "Homage to Tradition: Octavia Butler Renovates the Historical Novel." *MELUS*, 13:1–2 (Spring-Summer 1986): 79–96.

Harris, Trudier. *Fiction and Folklore: The Novels of Toni Morrison.* Knoxville: U of Tennessee P, 1991.

—. *The Power of the Porch: The Storyteller's Craft in Zora Neale Hurston, Gloria Naylor, and Randall Kenan.* Athens: U of Georgia P, 1996.

—. *Saints, Sinners, and Saviors: Strong Black Women in African American Literature.* New York: Palgrave/St. Martin's, 2001.

Heinze, Denise. *The Dilemma of Double Consciousness: Toni Morrison's Novels.* Athens: University of Georgia P, 1993.

Henderson, Mae G. "Toni Morrison's *Beloved*: Re-membering the Body as Historical Text." *Comparative American Identities: Race, Sex, and Nationality in the Modern Text.* Ed. Hortense Spillers. London: Routledge, 1991. 62–86.

Hernton, Calvin C. *The Sexual Mountain and Black Women Writers: Adventures in Sex, Literature and Real Life.* New York: Anchor P, 1987.

Hill, Patricia Liggins, gen. ed. *Call & Response: The Riverside Anthology of the African American Literary Tradition.* Boston: Houghton Mifflin, 1998.

Holloway, Karla F. C. *Moorings and Metaphors: Figures of Culture and Gender in Black Women's Literature.* New Brunswick: Rutgers UP, 1992.

Holloway, Karla F. C., and Stephanie A. Demetrakopoulas. *New Dimensions of Spirituality: A Biracial and Bicultural Reading of the Novels of Toni Morrison.* Westport, Conn.: Greenwood, 1987.

hooks, bell. *Yearning: Race, Gender, and Cultural Politics.* Boston: South End P, 1990.

Howard, Lillie P., ed. *Alice Walker and Zora Neale Hurston: The Common Bond.* Westport, Conn.: Greenwood, 1993.

Hull, Akasha Gloria. *Soul Talk: The New Spirituality of African American Women.* Rochester, Vt.: Inner Traditions, 2001.

Jacobs, Harriet. *Incidents in the Life of a Slave Girl, Written by Herself.* 1861. Ed. Jean Fagan Yellin. Cambridge: Harvard UP, 1987.

James, Joy, and T. Denean Sharpley-Whiting. *The Black Feminist Reader*. Malden, Mass.: Blackwell, 2000.

Jarrett, Joyce M., Doreatha Drummond Mbalia, and Margaret Giles Lee. *Heritage: African American Readings for Writing*. Upper Saddle River, N.J.: Prentice Hall, 1997.

Johnson, Charles R. *Being and Race*. Bloomington and Indianapolis: Indiana UP, 1988.

—. *Black Humor*. Chicago: Johnson Publishing Company, 1970.

—. *Dreamer*. 1998. New York: Scribner, 1999.

—. *Faith and the Good Thing*. 1974. New York: Scribner, 2001.

—. *Middle Passage*. 1991. New York: Simon & Schuster, 1998.

—. *Oxherding Tale*. 1982. New York: Plume, 1994.

—. "Philosophy and Black Fiction." *Obsidian* 6:1–2 (1980): 55–61.

—. *The Sorcerer's Apprentice*. 1986. New York: Plume, 1994.

—. *Soulcatcher and Other Stories*. San Diego: Harcourt, 2001.

Johnson, James Weldon. *The Autobiography of an Ex-Coloured Man*. 1912. Introd. Henry Louis Gates, Jr. New York: Vintage/Random House, 1989.

Johnson, Yvonne. *The Voices of African American Women: The Use of Narrative and Authorial Voice in the Works of Harriet Jacobs, Zora Neale Hurston, and Alice Walker*. New York: Peter Lang, 1998.

Jones, Gayl. *Corregidora*. 1975. Boston: Beacon, 1986.

—. *Eva's Man*. 1976. Boston: Beacon, 1987.

—. *The Healing*. Boston: Beacon, 1998.

—. *Mosquito*. Boston: Beacon, 1999.

Joyce, Joyce A. *Warriors, Conjurers, and Priests: Defining African-Centered Literary Criticism*. Chicago: Third World P, 1994.

Kelley, Margot Anne. *Gloria Naylor's Early Novels*. Gainesville: UP of Florida, 1999.

Kenan, Randall. "An Interview with Octavia E. Butler." *Callaloo* 14:2 (Spring 1991): 495–504.

—. *Let the Dead Bury Their Dead and Other Stories*. San Diego: Harcourt Brace Jovanovich, 1992.

—. *Walking on Water: Black American Lives at the Turn of the Twenty-First Century*. New York: Knopf, 1999.

—. *A Visitation of Spirits*. 1989. New York: Vintage, 2000.

Killens, John Oliver, and Jerry W. Ward, Jr., eds. *Black Southern Voices: An Anthology of Fiction, Poetry, Drama, Nonfiction, and Critical Essays*. New York: Penguin/Meridian, 1992.

Kubitschek, Missy Dehn. *Toni Morrison*. Westport: Greenwood, 1998.

Lauret, Maria. *Alice Walker*. New York: St. Martin's, 2000.

Lee, Helen Elaine. *The Serpent's Gift*. New York: Maxwell Macmillan International, 1994.

—. *Water Marked*. New York: Simon & Schuster, 1999.

Lidell, Janice Lee, and Yakini Belinda Kemp, eds. *Arms Akimbo: Africana Women in Contemporary Literature*. Gainesville: UP of Florida, 1999.

Lorde, Audre. *The Cancer Journals*. Argyle, N.Y.: Spinsters Ink, 1980.

—. *I Am Your Sister: Black Women Organizing across Sexualities*. New York: Kitchen Table Women of Color P, 1985.

—. *Sister Outsider: Essays and Speeches*. Trumansburg, N.Y.: Crossing P, 1984.

Martin, Reginald. *Ishmael Reed and the New Black Aesthetic Critics*. New York: St. Martin's, 1988.

McDowell, Deborah. *The Changing Same: Black Women's Literature, Criticism, and Theory*. Bloomington: Indiana UP, 1995.

McGee, Patrick. *Ishmael Reed and the Ends of Race*. New York: St. Martin's, 1997.

Mitchell, Angelyn, ed. *Within the Circle*. Durham: Duke UP, 1994.

Morrison, Toni. *Beloved*. New York: Knopf, 1987.

—. *The Bluest Eye*. New York: Knopf, 2000, 1970.

—. *Jazz*. New York: Knopf, 1992.

—. *Paradise*. New York: Knopf, 1998.

—. *Playing in the Dark: Whiteness and the Literary Imagination*. Cambridge: Harvard UP, 1992.

—. *Song of Solomon*. New York: Knopf, 1977.

—. *Sula*. New York: Knopf, 1974.

—. *Tar Baby*. New York: Knopf, 1981.

Mostern, Kenneth. *Autobiography and Black Identity Politics: Racialization in Twentieth-Century America*. New York: Cambridge UP, 1999.

Napier, Winston. *African American Literary Theory: A Reader*. New York: New York UP, 2000.

Naylor, Gloria. *Bailey's Café*. New York: Harcourt Brace Jovanovich, 1992.

—. *Mama Day*. New York: Random House, 1988.

—. *The Men of Brewster Place*. New York: Hyperion, 1998.

—. *The Women of Brewster Place*. New York: Penguin, 1980.

Powell, Kevin, ed. *Step into a World: A Global Anthology of the New Black Literature*. New York: John Wiley & Sons, Inc., 2000.

Pratt, Louis H., and Darnell D. Pratt. *Alice Malsenior Walker: An Annotated Bibliography*, 1968–1986. Westport, Conn.: Meckler, 1988.

Quashie, Everod, Joyce Lausch, and Keith D. Miller. *New Bones: Contemporary Black Writers in America*. Upper Saddle River, N.J.: Prentice Hall, 2000.

Randall, Alice. *The Wind Done Gone*. Boston: Houghton-Mifflin, 2001.

Reed, Ishmael. *Airing Dirty Laundry*. Reading, Mass.: Addison-Wesley, 1993.

—. *Flight to Canada*. New York: Random House, 1976.

—. *The Last Days of Louisiana Red*. 1974. New York: Atheneum, 1989.

—. *Mumbo Jumbo*. 1972. New York: Simon & Schuster, 1996.

—. *Reckless Eyeballing*. New York: St. Martin's, 1986.

—. *The Reed Reader*. New York: Basic Books, 2000.

—. *Wrightin' is Fightin': Thirty-Seven Years of Boxing on Paper*. New York: Atheneum, 1988.

—. *Yellow Back Radio Broke-Down*. 1969. Normal, Ill: Dalkey Archive P, 2000.

Ruff, Shawn Stewart, ed. *Go the Way Your Blood Beats: An Anthology of Lesbian and Gay Fiction by African-American Writers*. New York: Henry Holt, 1996.

Rushdy, Ashraf H. A. *Neo-Slave Narratives: Studies in the Social Logic of a Literary Form*. New York: Oxford UP, 1999.

Smith, Valerie, ed. *African American Writers*. New York: Scribners, 2001.

—. *Not Just Race, Not Just Gender: Black Feminist Readings*. New York: Routledge, 1998.

Somerville, Siobhan B. *Queering the Color Line: Race and the Invention of Homosexuality in American Culture*. Durham: Duke UP, 2000.

Stave, Shirley, ed. *Gloria Naylor: Strategy and Technique, Magic and Myth*. Newark: U of Delaware P, 2001.

Tate, Claudia. "Alice Walker." *African American Women Writers at Work*. New York: Continuum, 1983.

Walker, Alice. *Anything You Love Can Be Saved: A Writer's Activism*. New York: Random House, 1997.

—. *By the Light of My Father's Smile*. New York: Random House, 1998.

—. *The Color Purple*. New York: Harcourt Brace & Company, 1982.

—. *The Complete Short Stories*. London: The Women's Press, 1994.

—. *Everyday Use*. Ed. Barbara T. Christian. New Brunswick, N.J.: Rutgers UP, 1994.

—. *In Love and Trouble; Stories of Black Women*. New York: Harcourt Brace Jovanovich, 1973.

—. *In Search of Our Mothers' Gardens*. New York: Harcourt Brace & Company, 1983.

—. *Meridian*. New York: Harcourt Brace Jovanovich, 1976.

—. *Possessing the Secret of Joy*. New York: Harcourt Brace Jovanovich, 1992.

—. *The Same River Twice*. New York: Scribner, 1996.

—. *The Temple of My Familiar*. New York: Harcourt Brace Jovanovich, 1989.

—. *The Third Life of Grange Copeland*. 1970. New York: Simon & Schuster/Pocket Books, 1988.

—. *You Can't Keep a Good Woman Down*. New York: Harcourt Brace Jovanovich, 1981.

Walker, Alice, ed. *I Love Myself When I Am Laughing...and Then Again When I Am Looking Mean and Impressive: A Zora Neale Hurston Reader*. New York: The Feminist Press, 1979.

Wall, Cheryl, ed. *Changing Our Own Words: Essays on Criticism, Theory, and Writing by Black Women*. New Brunswick: Rutgers UP, 1989.

Whitt, Margaret Earley. *Understanding Gloria Naylor*. Columbia: U of South Carolina P, 1999.

Wilson, Charles E., ed. *Gloria Naylor: A Critical Companion*. Westport, Conn.: Greenwood, 2001.

Periodicals

American Black Book Writers Association (*ABBWA*) Journal, Marina del Rey, California.

African American Review, Department of English, Indiana State University, Terre Haute, Indiana. (continues *African American literature Forum*, which continued *Negro American Literature Forum*).

Black Books Bulletin, Institute of Positive Education, Chicago, Illinois.

Black Orpheus. Ministry of Education, Ibadan, Nigeria.

Black World. Johnson Publishing Company, Chicago, Illinois.

Callaloo. University of Texas-Austin.

College Language Association Journal. Department of English, Morehouse College, Atlanta, Georgia.

Directory of African American Poets and Writers. Black Angels Press, Palo Alto, California.

The Langston Hughes Review, Afro-American Studies Program, Brown University, Providence, Rhode Island.

The Literary Griot. Indiana, Pennsylvania.

Mosaic, Bronx, New York.

Obsidian III. Department of English, North Carolina State University, Raleigh, North Carolina.

Other Countries: Black Gay Voices. New York, New York.

Proud Black Images. Ohio State University, Columbus, Ohio.

QBR, The Black Book Review, New York, New York.

Quilt. Berkeley, California.

San Francisco Black Writers Literary Quarterly, San Francisco, California.

Shooting Star Review. Pittsburgh, Pennsylvania.

Studies in African American literature. Greenwood, Florida.

Umbra: Blackworks from the Black Galaxy. New York, New York.

Suggested Topics for Writing Critical Essays

1. Explore the use of trauma and memory in *Beloved* and Elaine Lee's "Water Call."
2. Alternatively, explore the use of memory or cultural memory in two novels or stories featured in this chapter.
3. Explore the subject of religion and philosophy in *Mumbo Jumbo* and *Middle Passage*.
4. Compare and contrast the treatment of slavery in *Beloved* and *Middle Passage*.
5. Examine the ways in which Toni Morrison's *Beloved* revisits and revises Harriet Jacobs's *Incidents in the Life of a Slave Girl* (chapter 1) and Frances Harper's *Iola Leroy* (chapter 3).
6. Examine the ways in which *Middle Passage* revisits and revises the story of Bigger Thomas in Richard Wright's *Native Son* (chapter 1).
7. Compare the journeys to liberated perception in any two novels and stories featured in this chapter. As an alternative, use a novel or story from this chapter in comparison with one from any of the previous chapters.
8. Compare the representation of the natural environment in *Parable of the Sower* and Hurston's *Their Eyes Were Watching God* (chapter 4).

9. Explore complementary themes in *Beloved* and *The Wind Done Gone* relating to the outraged mother and the neglected black child. How is "mother's breast milk" used as a dominant symbol in each?
10. Conduct a comparative analysis of the relationship between the lesbian characters ("The Two") and their "community" in Naylor's *The Women of Brewster Place* and the gay protagonist and his "community" in Kenan's *A Visitation of Spirits*. Be sure to note how "freedom" and "slavery" are defined in each text.

Questions to Guide Your Reading

Mumbo Jumbo

1. What is Jes Grew? When does it occur, and why is it always changing?
2. What is the Book of Thoth? What is the Wallflower Order? Who is Papa LaBas? How old is he, and what does he do for a living?
3. What is Papa LaBas's quest? Does he achieve it? Does he have assistants? Who are his enemies? Is he disappointed that he does not find the sacred text of Jes Grew? What happens to the text?
4. Why is *Mumbo Jumbo* considered a detective story? What are art detention centers?
5. What is the setting (time and place) for this novel?
6. What is the *gist* of the long oral lecture on black history that Papa LaBas gives toward the end of *Mumbo Jumbo*? Does it explain Jes Grew?
7. What is neohoodooism? What is necromancy?
8. According to *Mumbo Jumbo* and Papa LaBas, how did the Bible become a sacred text?
9. Why is *Mumbo Jumbo* considered parody? What is Reed parodying?

The Color Purple

1. *The Color Purple* is an epistolary novel because its narrative is composed of letters. To whom are the letters directed at the beginning of the novel? Who writes them? What about later in the novel—who is writing to whom?
2. In what ways does Celie's treatment by her stepfather compare to the treatment of enslaved women? What happens to Celie's children?
3. Is it significant that Celie and Nettie's room is located away from the main house? Is this a neofreedom narrative?

4. Note the relationship among the women in the novel. How would you characterize the friendship that develops between Shug and Celie? Is the friendship helpful to Celie? Is it helpful to Shug? Explain.
5. Who besides Celie undergoes a transformation during the course of the story? How do we know this?
6. Under what circumstances does Celie leave Albert, and when does she return to the community? Is the happy ending problematic?
7. What roles do money and property (or the lack thereof) play in this tale?
8. What is the chief metaphor or trope for Celie's story?
9. Does Nettie's language change when she writes from Africa?
10. What role does literacy play in this narrative, and what other narratives can you connect to it in that regard?

The Women of Brewster Place

1. Where and what is Brewster Place? How do the women of this novel come to be in Brewster Place? Are they upwardly mobile? What types emerge? Of the major women characters, which is most pivotal?
2. What makes this text a novel as opposed to a collection of short stories? What links the women and their individual stories?
3. Is Naylor making a statement about sisterhood? What happens to sisterhood when two of the sisters are lesbians?
4. Do you agree with Naylor's decision to combine Lorraine's and Theresa's stories, or do you think each woman deserves her own story?
5. Have you read *The Men of Brewster Place*? How does this novel compare in terms of structure and narration? How do the men's stories compare to the women's stories in terms of content? What is the significance of "class" in each novel?
6. The first and last segments of *The Women of Brewster Place* are titled "Dawn" and "Dusk," respectively. What is the significance of these titles? What do they suggest about the structure of the narrative?
7. Who narrates these women's stories and what is her/his posture toward the women? Is the narrator judgmental? hostile? sympathetic? jealous? Describe some of the peripheral characters in the novel—such as Sophie, the busybody.

8. How are men portrayed in the stories? Do you feel the need to know more about what "makes them tick"? How do the male characters respond to the lesbian characters?
9. What is the purpose of the block party? Is it successful? What happens to the wall at the end and why? Is this an imagined moment of real sisterhood? Explain. What happens to Brewster Place?

Beloved

1. This is a text about coming to terms with a traumatic past. Why do you suppose Morrison has decided to diverge from a linear structure for her narrative?
2. Why is the story related to us in seemingly fragmented form? What is "rememory"?
3. Who is Beloved? When does this character enter the story? Why is the character present?
4. How many characters yearn for Halle's presence? Why? Why is Halle only present in memory?
5. The central character, Sethe, is forcibly milked like a cow at one point. This event speaks both to the way that enslaved persons were viewed, and it also sets the stage for the signal event of the text. Can you elaborate on the meaning of this episode? What has it to do with Sethe's decision to kill her children?
6. What is the present moment of this story? When are the events that form the narrative being recalled?
7. The conflict between Sixo and schoolteacher over a piece of "stolen" meat (190) provides a basic model of "power" and "resistance." Schoolteacher represents "power." He expects Sixo to confess to a crime—theft. Sixo refuses to accept schoolteacher's label—thief. Read the passage. Why is it that each man can take the same event and offer a completely different narrative about it? Why is Sixo "present" in memory only? What kind of "slave" was he?
8. How do we know that motherhood is a very important aspect of Sethe's self-identity?
9. Schoolteacher serves as the embodiment of Scientific Racism. Can you point to passages that demonstrate this?
10. Which character best represents the site for "spiritual resistance," posing an alternative to slaveholder religious practices and beliefs? Which character serves as the best around-the-clock representative of physical resistance?

11. What kind of people are the Garners? How do Mr. Garner's brand of slavery and schoolteacher's brand of slavery differ?
12. What is Paul D's reaction when he learns the truth about Beloved and Sethe?
13. Why must schoolteacher destroy Sixo? What is the basic difference between Sixo and Paul D? How does Paul D define "manhood"?

A Visitation of Spirits

1. Some sections of this story are marked by dates. One series of dates in 1984 leads to Horace's suicide. What happens in the sections dated 1985? What does this tell you about community reaction to Horace's suicide? What are the other section markers?
2. Who is Horace Thomas Cross and what is his relationship to James Malachai Greene?
3. What is the significance of Horace killing himself in front of James/Jimmy—the minister?
4. How does Jimmy deal with his homoerotic desire?
5. This story features shifting points of view. Can you identify the places where these shifts take place? As you read this novel, note the juxtaposition of contrasting words (black/white) passages, and/or ideas (normal/queer).
6. How do the people in Horace's community define "normal" and "queer"?
7. Mark passages that illustrate how important community and family approval are to Horace. What is the "straw that breaks the camel's back" for Horace? After what event does he begin to retreat from life?
8. Kenan has inserted small mini-dramas into the story. Are they related? Explain. What purpose do they serve?
9. What kind of bird does Horace settle on for his transformation and why? Are you familiar with the flying Africans myth? What, finally, is freedom to Horace? Underline the word "freedom" whenever you encounter it in the text.
10. What role does religion play in the story and in Horace's life? Is the name "Cross" significant?

Middle Passage

1. The protagonist's name is Rutherford Calhoun. The name invokes Rutherford B. Hayes, a U.S. president during a period of

special significance in black American history, and John C. Calhoun, famous as a prominent proponent of colonization ("resettling" African Americans in Africa). Why do you suppose the author chose to invoke these two men?

2. How does Rutherford describe himself, and why? Whose pronouncement about his destiny is he living out?
3. How is Rutherford different from his brother Jackson? Describe the basic attributes of each brother. Does one brother seem more realistic than the other? Explain.
4. What is the Middle Passage? Why do you suppose the author sends his protagonist on a reverse Middle Passage? How does the protagonist change as a result of his experiences on the *Republic*?
5. Johnson invokes a number of predecessor texts with this story. Can you identify any of them?
6. Is there such a thing as a good thief? Explain. Is Rutherford still a thief and a liar at the end of his voyage?
7. Describe the Allmuseri. Describe Captain Falcon. What is the basic difference between Allmuseri philosophy and Falcon's philosophy?

Parable of the Sower

1. Who is narrating this story? In what format? What period does the narrative cover?
2. What point of view is represented?
3. What is Earthseed? What is its central tenet? How is God defined in Earthseed? Pay close attention to the epigraphs used throughout Lauren's narrative.
4. Describe the Olamina family and their Robledo, California, neighborhood before it is destroyed. Describe Lauren Olamina's relationship to her father. Is there conflict or tension? At what point do her beliefs diverge from those of her father? What is empath syndrome?
5. When and how does Lauren become homeless? How has she prepared for the inevitable? Why is she better prepared than others in her community? What does Lauren say about freedom, in particular personal freedoms? In what forms does slavery exist in the story?
6. Before she becomes homeless, Lauren often writes about thieves who try to break into their community. Later, she becomes a

thief herself. This scenario suggests that the term *thief* is unstable and changes with Lauren's circumstances. How is this possible?

7. Who comprises the new Earthseed community? Where is the community located? How did its members come to be a community?
8. Why is society in such a chaotic state? What evidence of slavery does Lauren provide in her narrative? What does she say about the results of global warming? Where is the science in this work of science fiction?

Stories from Afrekete

1. What is the symbolic nature of the name Afrekete in "Tar Beach"? What images are associated with Kitty? What point of view is used for the narration?
2. What is the difference in meaning between the word zami and the word lesbian in "Tar Beach"? Of what importance have women been in the narrator's life?
3. Analyze passages in which nature and natural images dominate in "Tar Beach." What is happening during those passages?
4. How does Elaine Lee use memory in "Water Call"? Whose memory does she use?
5. Who is recalling the events of the story?
6. Who are the other named characters in the story?
7. What does Ouida's condition reveal about her attitude toward her sexuality? How does Zella respond? Which is the more sympathetic character?
8. Compare the use of natural images in "Ruby" with those in "Tar Beach." Are there major differences? Explain.
9. What is the nature of Ruby's malaise? Why do you suppose the author chose to use that particular point of view to tell the story?
10. Does the angel food cake baked by Ephraim's mother carry symbolic weight?

The Wind Done Gone

1. What time period does the narrative encompass? What is the point of view? Whose story is this?
2. How important is the "Notes on the Text" page to your understanding of the novel? How important is the "Postscript" to your understanding of the novel? Why do you suppose Randall included these two pages?

3. This novel is a parody of Margaret Mitchell's classic novel, *Gone with the Wind* (1936). If you are familiar with that novel, can you identify what themes and issues from it are referenced in Randall's novel? How does Randall change the characters and situations from the earlier novel?
4. How did Other and Cynara become half sisters? How did Lady come to be married to Planter?
5. Profile each of the following characters: R, or Debt Chauffeur; Lady; Mealy Mouth; Dreamy Gentleman; Garlic; Mrs. Garlic; Miss Priss; Other; Beauty; Planter; Pallas.
6. What black historical figures do you recognize in the story?
7. Why do you suppose Cynara chose not to marry the black congressman?
8. What happened to the proceeds from Cotton Farm/Tata? How is freedom defined in the novel? When does Cynara realize that she is free?

APPENDIX
Sample Student Essays

On Slavery and Religion
by Noel M. Tieszen

Religion appears over and over again in the contexts of antebellum freedom narratives and post-Civil War writings of formerly enslaved individuals. Though many African Americans who lived during the eras of slavery and Reconstruction practiced Christianity to some degree, the freedom narratives of Frederick Douglass (*Narrative of the Life of Frederick Douglass, an American Slave, Written by Himself,* 1845), Harriet Jacobs (*Incidents in the Life of a Slave Girl, Written by Herself,* 1861), and Jacobs's brother John S. Jacobs (*A True Tale of Slavery,* 1861) castigate southern slaveholding Christians for their religious hypocrisy. However, writing at the turn of the twentieth century, Booker T. Washington (in *Up from Slavery,* 1901) expresses respect for former slaveholders and their religious practices, even as he condemns many black religious leaders. The chasm dividing Washington's perspective from those of the other three Christian writers is extensive.

Of the writers I discuss in this essay, Frederick Douglass seems to go the most out of his way to clarify his seemingly conflicting views on the matter of Christianity. Throughout the eleven chapters of his narrative, he complains that religious slaveholders are the worst kind because they use Christianity to excuse their evil behavior toward slaves. He writes,

> I assert most unhesitatingly, that the religion of the south is a mere covering for the most horrid crimes,— a justifier of the most appalling barbarity,— a sanctifier of the most hateful frauds,— and a dark shelter under which the darkest, foulest, grossest, and most infernal deeds of slaveholders find the strongest protection. (53)

This strong condemnation of southern Christianity could be misconstrued to signify lack of religious faith on Douglass's part. However, Douglass evidences in other ways that he does believe in the Christian God. He writes of holding Sabbath schools to "learn to read the will of God" (55), of his belief in "a special interposition of divine Providence" (28) in his life, and of heartfelt prayers to "the Almighty" (46). Still, because his charges against the church are so great, Douglass apparently feels compelled to add an appendix to his story in order to persuade his readership that he is indeed a God-fearing man. He states his position most clearly in the opening paragraph of the appendix:

> What I have said respecting and against religion, I mean strictly to apply to the *slaveholding religion* of this land, and with no possible reference to Christianity proper; for, between the Christianity of this land, and the Christianity of Christ, I recognize the widest possible difference—so wide, that to receive the one as good, pure, and holy, is of necessity to reject the other as bad, corrupt, and wicked . . . I love the pure, peaceable, and impartial Christianity of Christ: I therefore hate the corrupt, slaveholding, women-whipping, cradle-plundering, partial and hypocritical Christianity of this land. Indeed, I can see no reason, but the most deceitful one, for calling the religion of this land Christianity. (75)

This strong statement leaves no room to question Douglass's divergent attitudes toward slaveholders' religion and his personal belief and faith in the Christian God.

But Douglass doesn't stop at drawing distinctions between his faith and that of the slaveholders. He goes on to write of "devils dressed in angels' robes, and hell presenting the semblance of paradise" (76). In these metaphors, Douglass draws on the old cliché of wolves who are trusted because they look like sheep. The implication is that Douglass blames slavery for posing as a Christian institution and thereby mischievously corrupting American Christianity and American Christians.

Harriet Jacobs, in contrast, needs no preachy appendix to prove her faith. The deeply personal style of her narrative provides ample opportunity for natural demonstrations of her personal commitment to Christian piety. At every good turn, she gives thanks and praise to God; at every trial, she prays for strength to sustain her. Even as she begs for leniency in the reader's judgment of her sins and the sins of fellow slaves, she holds fast to her trust that her god sees all and will judge accordingly.

However, Jacobs also indicts the slaveholders' interpretation of Christianity as a corrupting force in southern society. The story about Mr. Litch, the money-hungry slaveholder who asks to be buried with his money as he enters into hell (46–47), is just one example of Jacobs's assurance that earthly wrongs will be righted in the afterlife. Throughout her narrative Jacobs bemoans the fact that "few slaveholders seem to be aware of the widespread moral ruin occasioned by this wicked system. Their talk is of blighted cotton crops—not of the blight on their children's souls" (52). It is clear to Jacobs that the institution of slavery has detrimental effects not only on slaves, but also on slaveholders, their families, and their associates, as they become blind to their hypocrisy and as they twist the Christian scriptures to justify their sins.

Harriet Jacobs's brother, John S. Jacobs, presents a much shorter narrative, *A True Tale of Slavery*. Even in his twenty pages, Jacobs finds room to emphasize the moral hypocrisy of slaveholders who call themselves Christians. He writes, "None but political tyrants would ever establish slavery, and none but religious hypocrites would ever support it" (227). Jacobs also asserts that "everything droops that feels [slavery's] sting" (227), implying that everyone and everything involved in any aspect of slavery experiences negative effects. Slaves experience obvious physical, emotional, mental, and spiritual oppression; slaveholders (and other supporters of the institution) cannot help but be corrupted because the very state of owning another human being requires moral hypocrisy that only leads to greater and greater contortions of religious and moral sophistry for justification.

However, in his final paragraph, John S. Jacobs removes any doubt as to his own faith in the Christian God. He writes, "In conclusion, let me say that the experience of the past, the present feelings, and above all this, the promise of God, assure me that the oppressor's rod shall be broken" (228). In this way, Jacobs grounds his final thought in his faith that the Christian God's sense of justice will bring resolution to the injustices of slavery in good time.

Although the Jacobs siblings and Douglass present their religious perspectives in differing ways, the distinctions between them almost disappear when compared with the chasm separating their perspectives from that of Booker T. Washington. Far short of condemning Christian slaveholders for their hypocrisy, Washington comes close to excusing them. He goes so far as to posit that formerly enslaved Africans are in many ways better off because of their experiences in slavery, particularly with regard to religion and morality. He writes that

> . . .the ten million Negroes inhabiting this country, who themselves or whose ancestors went through the school of American slavery, are in a stronger and more hopeful condition, materially, intellectually, morally, and religiously, than is true of an equal number of black people in any other portion of the globe. This is so to such an extent that Negroes in this country, who themselves or whose forefathers went through the school of slavery, are constantly returning to Africa as missionaries to enlighten those who remained in the fatherland. (13–14)

In particularly direct contrast to Douglass, who describes slavery as an institution that corrupts the truth and morality of Christianity, Washington argues that "Providence so often uses men and institutions to accomplish a purpose" (14), implying that slavery was God's means to provide certain Africans with the opportunity to rise above the intellectual and moral station of the brethren they left behind.

Washington's personal commitment to Christianity is unquestionable throughout his narrative. He continually expresses Christian ideals, and he strives to make Tuskegee Institute a place founded on Christian thought and morality. However, what is perhaps most interesting about Washington is that, while he fails to condemn white Christians for hypocrisy, he goes out of his way to speak out against black Christian leaders. He castigates black ministers broadly and publicly, decrying their supposed ignorance, unworthiness, and immorality (41). It is astounding to contrast Washington's attitude toward black ministers with his perspective on Christian slaveholders, who claimed ownership over beings made in God's image.

While Douglass and the Jacobses argue against the Christian tradition as practiced by slaveholders and their counterparts, Washington praises it and expresses gratitude for the moral and religious lessons learned through African Americans' experiences in slavery in America. Whereas Douglass and the Jacobses blame white Christians for their roles in slavery and the resulting corruption of Christianity, Washington actually states that "the black man got nearly as much out of slavery as the white man did" (14). Rather than discussing the moral and religious corruption inherent in slaveholding, he cites the loss of work ethic and homemaking skills as the major source of harm to slaveholders.

Douglass and the Jacobses find a great deal of common ground in their analyses of slavery's effect on religion. Compared to them, Washington's perspective on the relationship between slavery and religion appears to be relatively anomalous. Though all four autobiographers share personal Christianity and the experience of slavery in America, their perspectives on the relationship between Christianity and slavery differ in profoundly fundamental ways.

Bibliography

Douglass, Frederick. *Narrative of the Life of Frederick Douglass, an American Slave, Written by Himself.* 1845. Ed. William L. Andrews and William McFeely, Norton Critical Edition. New York: W. W. Norton, 1997.

Jacobs, Harriet. *Incidents in the Life of a Slave Girl* and *A True Tale of Slavery*. 1861. Ed. Jean Fagan Yellin. Cambridge: Harvard University P, 2000.

Washington, Booker T. *Up from Slavery*. 1901. Ed. William L. Andrews, Norton Critical Edition. New York: W. W. Norton, 1996.

Douglass and Washington
by M. Triffitt

It is interesting to see the way two men, both ex-slaves, portrayed their time spent in bondage and their subsequent time after. Given the fact that Frederick Douglass's and Booker T. Washington's stories are slanted by their involvement in their telling, it is hard to see their stories as unbiased articulations of historical fact. Instead, they can be seen as two different reflections upon one of the darkest chapters in our nation's history. While they share many commonalities, what makes these stories so different is their historical context. Douglass's story was published almost twenty years before the Civil War, while Washington's was not published until almost forty years after the end of slavery in the United States. It is this difference in time and, more importantly, the changing attitudes of these eras that give each of these stories its own unique portrayal of slavery.

Douglass's autobiography begins the way many freedom narratives do, with the author retelling the location, time, and circumstances of his birth. Douglass wastes no time mentioning the fact that slaves seldom, if ever, knew the dates of their birth. The master, in hopes of keeping the slave "ignorant" and manageable, suppressed this information. Inquiring about such information was seen as ". . . evidence of a restless spirit" (Douglass, 12). The idea here was to keep the slave from interpreting his/her birth as a memorable or special occasion. Few slaveholders, if any, actually recorded the exact birthdate of their slaves because they were seen as merely possessions or, like livestock, not worthy of such concern. It is interesting to think of the humanizing effect being able to trace one's roots back to the very beginning of life has on the individual. In the master's eyes this was something to be avoided.

In his story Douglass immediately appeals to the nurturing instinct of the reader by describing the conditions of his family life and the custom of separating the slave child from his parents at an early age in hopes of destroying any familial unity that could potentially become dangerous to the master. It was the opinion of the slaveholders that the only loyalty a slave should show was that toward his master and his property, not to another slave. A simple proclamation or the fear of punishment was not enough to override the love of a mother for her child, and Douglass shows this through the retelling of his own experiences with his mother. Passages describing her secret visits to see him and her death help to illustrate the loyalty, caring, and risks taken in the name of the family.

Here was something not unique to slaveholders or, more importantly, not subject to their absolute control. Given the 1845 (pre-Civil War) publication of his story Douglass wants to show that slaves were not simply the master's property; they were people with hopes and dreams for themselves and their children.

Almost every page in Douglass's narrative reports on the abuse, degradation, and contempt slaves suffered at the hands of the master. He weaves his own story of hardship with the poignant stories of others in order to paint a disturbing portrait of our society at the time. One story that illustrated how little concern was given to the lives of slaves was the beating death of his wife's cousin simply for falling asleep and allowing her mistress's baby to cry during the night. It appears, though, that he held the system of slavery itself beneath any contempt he felt for whites themselves. Given the absolute power dynamic in the master/slave relationship, he attempted to show that even those Southerners supposedly without prejudice could be turned and corrupted by the powers vested in the slaveholder. He told the story of Sophia Auld, who had never owned a slave before, initially treating him like an equal only later to become as ruthless as any person born into the role of master. It seems as if he felt that whites were not fully to blame for the conditions of the time, but rather that these corruptions of morality were the result of the institution of slavery itself.

One of the most telling stories in Douglass's narrative was that of his altercation with Mr. Covey. As a "nigger-breaker" Covey's job was to break the spirit of those slaves he was given charge of and to make them subservient and manageable. Given his indomitable spirit, Douglass refuses to yield to his new master and, during his stay with Covey, suffers repeated whippings. This changed one afternoon when Douglass stood up to Covey's cruelty and fought back. After getting the better of Covey, a white man dedicated to the destruction of the black man's soul, Douglass states, "my long-crushed spirit rose, cowardice departed, bold defiance took its place; and I now resolved that, however long I might remain a slave in form, the day had passed forever when I could be a slave in fact" (50). Here Douglass advocates uprising against the tyranny of slavery and striking back at those individuals that mistreat the individual. His internal liberation during the fight changes his worldview for the lifetime following it. Douglass's methods, however, would not be looked upon favorably by an individual like Booker T. Washington.

Where Douglass's story concentrates on the horrors of slavery as an institution that should end, Washington's story deals more with the "picking up of the pieces" left in slavery's wake. Washington, like

Douglass, blames the whole of our society for slavery rather than just laying the blame on the South. While he does not condone slavery, he is careful not to go into the specifics of its brutality for fear of alienating certain segments of his audience. Washington's story is reminiscent of Horatio Alger's *Ragged Dick* in which a young, underprivileged boy, through honesty and hard work, is able to build himself up into a respected member of society. Washington's statement that "there are few instances, either in slavery or freedom, in which a member of my race has been known to betray a specific trust" (12) leaves the reader with a quizzical look and the impression that Washington was trying to be everything to everyone. It should be obvious to the reader that such generalizations are not accurate. However, Washington spends much of his story preaching only the positive aspects of *everything*.

His theory that honesty and diligence are the keys to success for the ex-slave is important to his doctrine, and by portraying others and himself in this way he attempts to make African Americans more "palatable" to his white readers. It is almost as if he is saying "See, we're not the lazy thieves you think we are." He even goes so far as to say that those who "went through the school of American slavery, are in a stronger and more hopeful condition, materially, intellectually, morally, and religiously, than is true of an equal number of black people in any other portion of the globe" (13). With this infuriating statement Washington again attempts to curry the favor of white intellectuals, businessmen, and clergy by not blaming them for slavery but instead almost thanking them for all the opportunities America allows. That Washington is engaged in a serious game of minstrelsy is obvious. He has a mask for everyone.

It is apparent that those writers, such as Harriet Jacobs and Frederick Douglass, whose works were written in the pre-Civil War era, were trying to paint as bleak a picture as possible of the South in the hopes that their stories of pain and suffering would help to open people's eyes to the horrible treatment and conditions endured by the slaves in this country. To say that there is mistreatment of a people is one thing, but to present a visual of a woman living in a crawl space for almost seven years, as Jacobs did, gives the reader some sense of the desperate measures taken to ensure even basic survival.

The purpose of their stories was to get people agitated, to evoke some feeling. By questioning and criticizing the practices and mores of the nation, they sought to enrage activists and gain sympathy for the plight of their people. Douglass daringly brings into the open the way "Christians" of the time ignored their own teachings, hid behind the basic tenants of their religion, and treated their fellow men like beasts. He uses shame as a weapon of change and wields it masterfully throughout his story. By gaining support in the North, antebellum narrators hoped to alienate the South, help in causing economic pressure on the South, and eventually to assist in ending slavery.

However, at the turn of the twentieth century, Washington saw little reason to rub salt in the wounds of a defeated South, and instead chose to focus on the hard work, perseverance, and integration of the ex-slaves into American society. Washington knew that by criticizing the South, or southern whites in particular, he would be alienating himself and, more importantly, many of the black people he was trying to help. Whites controlled the majority of the money needed for the building of Tuskegee Institute, and without their support his dream would have remained just that. Although some of his language and approaches were questionable, and make for a hearty debate, it is hard not to commend him for the altruistic sacrifice of his own image for that of the greater good.

Given the pre-Civil War release of his autobiography, Douglass's main concern was the abolition of slavery in America. Through the graphic representation of his own story, he hoped to appeal to those African Americans in the North, who might have been free or in bondage. It appears that to Douglass "freedom" was those decisions made outside of the control of anyone but himself. When Washington's story was published almost sixty years later, black people were "free" but still subject to persecution at the hands of whites. He saw that to be free was not enough. Newly emancipated persons needed skills that would make them self-reliant, productive members of society, able to reap the benefits of their labor for perhaps the first time in their lives. His tale could be likened to that of America's voluntary immigrants who sacrifice and toil so that their children might have it better than they did. That truly is the American Dream.

While reading these stories, one cannot help but see a partial parallel to two leaders in our own recent history. Douglass appears much like Malcolm X in his attempt to take what he felt was his "by any means necessary." When he strikes back against Covey, he claims an internal freedom and strength that would never have been given to him. Washington, however, seems more like a Martin Luther King, Jr., of his time. By establishing ties with the white community, through reaching out for support both financially and spiritually, he attempted to integrate the two races in a nonviolent fashion.

It is hard to fault either man for his viewpoints because they were both working toward what they saw as the betterment of their race. By criticizing the South, religious hypocrisy, and our society as a whole, Douglass put himself in great danger in the name of his people. Washington, too, had to suffer because of his desire to establish the black man in a society that was not open to him. Unable to see past his language and approach, there are critics even today who still speak harshly of his unwillingness to speak out against the whites of his time. What makes both Douglass and Washington so integral to our understanding of slavery and its demise, and subsequent racial attitudes, is their ability to sacrifice themselves for the greater good. Regardless of skin color, these men can serve as an inspiration to anyone wanting to change a desperate situation. Although there are still slaves in this world, hopefully for all our sakes, there are Douglasses and Washingtons, as well.

Bibliography

Douglass, Frederick. *Narrative of the Life of Frederick Douglass, An American Slave, Written by Himself.* 1845. Ed. William L. Andrews and William McFeely. Norton Critical Edition. New York: W. W. Norton, 1997.

Jacobs, Harriet. *Incidents in the Life of a Slave Girl.* 1861. Ed. Jean Fagan Yellin. Cambridge: Harvard U P, 2000.

Keckley, Elizabeth. *Behind the Scenes.* 1868. Introd. James Olney. New York: Oxford UP, 1988.

Washington, Booker T. *Up from Slavery.* 1901. Ed. William L. Andrews. Norton Critical Edition. New York: W. W. Norton, 1996.

The Ties That Bind? The Problem of Community in Gloria Naylor's *The Women of Brewster Place* and Randall Kenan's *A Visitation of Spirits*
by Tammy Ames

What is "community"? How are we to conceive of it to gain an understanding of it? What does it imply? *Webster's Ninth New Collegiate Dictionary* first defines community as "a unified body of individuals," and then lists some of the myriad ways by which people may be brought together: by state or commonwealth; by geographic location; by political interests; by economic interests, by common history; by professional interests; and so on (267). It stands to reason that there are, by this definition and our own common sense, degrees to which a person is a member of any one community depending on the strength of that particular common bond, and as most people belong to many communities at the same time, there naturally are some that are more important to an individual than others. These are primary, everyday communities such as family, friends, and neighbors. Community, in that sense of caring relationships, is as necessary to human beings as breathing. However, what happens when people are denied one or all of their primary communities? What happens when family, friends, and neighbors turn their backs on an individual, when love, support, and camaraderie are withheld? What does this say about community then? Gloria Naylor's *The Women of Brewster Place* and Randall Kenan's *A Visitation of Spirits* boldly explore these issues and more in their disturbing depictions of the plights of gay characters living in communities hostile to homosexuality. Each novel unflinchingly offers a hard, sometimes brutal perspective on the nature of "community" when accepted behavioral norms are crossed, and each offers its own not unproblematic take on the possibilities for freedom within those contexts.

In *The Women of Brewster Place*, Naylor's characterizations of Lorraine and Theresa offer the reader two opposing perspectives. Lorraine, on the one hand, believes in the universality of humanity, particularly in the common bonds among persons of African descent, and she desires to live her life as any other person might, as a part of her neighborhood, her community. Lorraine reflects that she "want[s] to be liked by the people around her," and wonders why she should "feel different from the people she live[s] around." She further maintains that, "black people were all in the same boat . . . and if they didn't row together, they would sink together" (142). In contrast, Theresa takes a much more separatist and militant perspective. This viewpoint permeates her thoughts as she contemplates what she desires in a partner: "She wanted someone who could stand toe to toe with her and be willing to slug it out at times. If they practiced that way with each other, then they could turn back to back and beat the hell out of the world for trying to invade their territory" (136).

Here Theresa testifies to her belief that to be a lesbian was to, of necessity, be a fighter, to be prepared for the attacks from the dominant heterosexual culture when they came. She feels no special kinship to her neighbors because they too are black; she does not attempt to make friends on the block. Instead, Theresa's philosophy focuses on being cognizant of the power relationships between the dominant culture and homosexuals, on what it means to be marginalized, to be outcast, ostracized. She has no intention of opening herself up to be hurt or victimized just because she is a lesbian. She knows who she is and she knows the consequences of being who she is. Theresa expresses her attitude to Lorraine: ". . . as long as they own the whole damn world, it's them and us, Sister—them and us. And that spells different" (166). Homosexuality, in Lorraine's view, is a difference transcending all others.

To further delineate the ideological differences between Lorraine and Theresa, Naylor places Theresa within a gay community outside of Brewster Place. She and her gay friends frequent an unnamed club located outside of the neighborhood. Lorraine, the reader is told, does not like these friends of Theresa's and makes reference to them as "weirdos" whom she hates. She calls them "coarse" and "bitter" and doesn't like the fact that they make fun of others unlike themselves. Lorraine denies that she is even like them, bridling under the assumption that, just because she is gay, she is similar to them and a part of their group (142). Furthermore, Lorraine wishes Theresa would "make the best of things [at Brewster Place] and get involved in [that] community," instead of reading all the time and keeping to herself (141–142). Lorraine's view is the opposite. She believes that "they weren't ever going to be accepted by these people, and there was no point in trying" (163). Where Lorraine is searching for acceptance, Theresa is damned if she will look, and that makes Lorraine's rejection by the neighborhood (by and large) at the tenants meeting in Kiswana's apartment, solely on the grounds of being gay, all the more tragically ironic.

Once Lorraine has been rejected by the Brewster Place community, for all intents and purposes a social outcast within their midst, the reader learns that, upon discovering that she was a lesbian, Lorraine's father had rejected her totally. (No mention is made of Lorraine's mother, so it's not unlikely that she is dead or that she abandoned Lorraine at some point when Lorraine was a child.) After being thrown out of her father's home with only the clothing on her back, Lorraine works hard to put herself through college. Later on, Lorraine is fired from a teaching position in Detroit because she is a lesbian. To the reader, it now appeared that Theresa is all the family, all the community that Lorraine has, and that her only other friend is the janitor Ben, whose own personal pain requires that he spend much of his life drunk in his basement apartment. It is during this period of intense isolation that Lorraine begins a transformative process. Theresa makes note of it on page 155 as she ponders that there's something different about Lorraine, that she is indeed "changing" and that it has something to do with the drunkard Ben. At this point in the story, the stage is skillfully set for Naylor to offer an answer to the question of what happens to individuals cut off from their community.

The end of Lorraine and Theresa's story in *The Women of Brewster Place* happens very quickly, but it is at the end that Naylor provides the reader with the greatest payoff. First, Lorraine tells Theresa:

> . . . [I] just want[ ] to be a human being—a lousy human being who's somebody's daughter or somebody's friend or even somebody's enemy. But they make me feel like a freak out there, and you try to make me feel like one in here . . . the only place I've found some peace . . . is in that damp ugly basement, where I'm not different. (165)

These statements make it clear that Lorraine finds no sanctuary even in her own apartment with Theresa because their relationship is influenced by larger social pressures. The only time she is free from the limits of the socially constructed label "lesbian," the only place she is able just to be a human being, is in Ben's basement apartment. Freedom in this passage is defined as freedom from persecution in her home and in her community, freedom from the narrow-minded bigotry, the hostility, and the fear projected on her by her neighbors, and freedom from her own fear of rejection, from the worry about what her neighbors are thinking.

Next, Lorraine insists that she must attend a party hosted by Theresa's gay friends by herself or else "there'll be nothing left in [her] to love [Theresa]" (167). One may read this as Lorraine's effort to halt the self-transformation that began in earnest with her isolation from Theresa and the Brewster Place community. This was Lorraine's desperate attempt to assert her will and return to some part of humanity, to try to connect with other human beings out in the world. Furthermore, because the party was being given by a group of other gay individuals, chances are that they would have accepted her if she could have accepted them. However, Naylor did not allow that. Instead, she had Lorraine raped on her return home from the party, her body abused to the point that she became deranged. When the group of young hoodlum rapists was finished with her, Lorraine was like a mindless animal crawling through the alley, never, as the text vaguely alludes, to regain her sensibilities again: transformation complete. Even more ambivalently, directly following the rape Naylor has Lorraine bludgeon Ben to death with a brick. Naylor's message appears to be that individuals isolated and cut off from society eventually lose their humanity. Far from finding freedom, Lorraine moves from enslavement by social identity as a lesbian to the enslavement of insanity and complete dehumanization, and a dehumanized individual is capable of anything, even murder. Lorraine's instinctive, animalistic killing of Ben, who, in the end, seems to be her only friend, serves as an ironic bit of sacrificial justice. Ben pays for the sins of the community that harbored the gang of young hoodlum rapists, while treating the two lesbians as outcasts.

The themes of freedom and transformation found in *The Women of Brewster Place* are also present in Randall Kenan's *A Visitation of Spirits*. Specifically, the novel's gay protagonist Horace seeks to transform himself in order to escape the soul-crushing tyranny of his community—family, church, and town—which brooks no deviation from its rigid guidelines, its taboos and absolutisms on the topics of self, sin, and acceptable (heterosexual) social identity. Unlike Lorraine and Theresa, Horace has no experience in the wider world, and so literacy becomes his primary research tool in his quest for freedom from his particular community. Although initially only a quietly subversive means of discovering knowledge, of encountering different modes of thought, ways of being and systems of belief in the world, Horace's use of literacy becomes a desperate avenue of escape. He reflects on the library and his love of books:

> The library. Here was the world he had come to love, his mission field, his church away from church. *The real world* [emphasis added]. Here he had been introduced to words, sentences, and books. Books. He relished books, books, on religion, history, science . . . . Books that revealed Hinduism and Islam, Judaism and Buddhism. (88)

He adds that "At home there were no answers, only questions, only faith, hope, and believing. Here, amid the books and tools of modern information, there were answers, concrete and inviolate" (88). For Horace, the real world could be apprehended in books, and in contrast to the world at home, his world was founded on unanswered questions, on taking on faith the "truths" fed to him by his family and his church. These "truths" failed to offer Horace any relief, any succor or understanding as he in turn sought to understand his evolving self. Instead, they offered condemnation. Horace goes on to wonder "if even then [in the fourth grade] he had dreamed of transforming himself, through knowledge" (89).

Later, as the older Horace becomes more and more isolated and desperate to escape the enslavement of his situation, he turns to reading voraciously, first on a range of subjects from the classics to comic books, and then with singular focus on the occult. Horace researches the "facts," the written "evidence" of magic, and deeply engrosses himself in the task of "perfecting the perfect spell" of transformation (18). At the same time he lets go of other reading, of other engagements of his self in scholastic pursuits, he detaches from his old life in preparation for the new, for freedom. Horace's freedom quest, ironically, causes his performance in school to slip drastically, the opposite effect desired by his grandfather's dictates and by his family's, but not surprising considering the extreme nature of his social isolation.

Horace evolves to embrace the occult as a means of escape, and then, when that fails, when his spell fails, the reader is taken on a journey of alleged demonic possession leading to the ultimate evolution, the ultimate transformation, the ultimate step to freedom, from life to death. In this story literacy leads to freedom and literacy leads to death, a new twist on the old "freedom narrative" convention. One may argue that Randall Kenan's answer to the question of what happens to an individual cut off from his community is indeed death, suicide. However, that is only after the social death of being ostracized, of being outcast. Social scientists would certainly agree that for a human being living in extreme isolation, suicide is within the range of possibilities. Unlike Naylor's character Lorraine, who becomes completely dehumanized but lives on in an animalistic, broken state, Horace's suicide releases him from the entrapment of society altogether, a much more liberating end.

Horace's relationship to his community is also different from Lorraine and Theresa's relationships to their community in several noteworthy ways. First, Horace is much younger than Lorraine and Theresa; he's a minor, a teenager. Horace is unable legally to set out on his own and explore other areas of the world, other communities outside of Tims Creek. He is also unable to determine his own friendships *within* Tims Creek, as evidenced by his grandfather's decree on page 185: "...those friends of yours. This group. No more. You understand me? You're to leave them alone and they're to leave you alone." In their small, rural, deeply religious southern town, Horace's grandfather's word to him is law. In contrast, Lorraine and Theresa are adults living in a northern, urban environment where religion is present but not with the particularly southern revivalist depth to blood and bone. Additionally, Lorraine and Theresa embody two different approaches to living as a gay person in the world: Lorraine expresses a philosophy to work within the system, within the community, whereas Theresa articulates and follows a separatist view. Lorraine and Theresa struggle with their different takes on how to get along in the world, but at least they have each other to some degree. At least Theresa has a community outside of the mainstream, outside of Brewster Place to support her, a group of gay friends whom she meets at a club in another part of the city. Horace, in contrast, has absolutely no gay role models, no one who will tell him that it's okay to be gay. Finally, because Horace's family and community hold so fervently to their religious beliefs, Horace is forced to struggle with the community's message of his condemnation, the Old Testament fire and brimstone that must, by community definition, await all homosexuals. Lorraine and Theresa, unlike Horace, don't have to deal with the internalization of that particularly strong religious belief system.

In their novels Gloria Naylor and Randall Kenan offer a view of "community" that is far from ideal. Each highlights the oppression of individuals when community becomes, in effect, anti-community, a means of persecution. In particular, Naylor and Kenan focus on the persecution of gay individuals in black communities, a kind of marginalization in the ranks of the traditionally marginalized. While Kenan plants the seeds of possible transcendence of oppression through Horace's death in the mind of the reader, Naylor allows the reader only the two possibilities of a dehumanized victim/killer in Lorraine, and a total separatist in Theresa, one who is divorced completely from reality, and one who is divorced completely from the mainstream in every material way outside of the workplace. In this limited scope there is a common bleakness, a dark commentary on what happens when society is used to stamp out differences rather than allow for them when fear and loathing are funneled, directed to attack that which is not understood, that which is different. Instead of embracing an ideology of "this and that," the communities of Brewster Place and Tims Creek adhere to a divisive credo of "this, *not* that." While the nuances of the two novels are different, clearly individual, their illumination of intolerance is obviously the same.

Bibliography

Kenan, Randall. *A Visitation of Spirits*. New York: Doubleday, 1989.

Naylor, Gloria. *The Women of Brewster Place*. New York: Penguin Books, 1983.

Assignment: Write a two-page response to the following question: Is Alfrado, the protagonist in Harriet Wilson's *Our Nig,* enslaved or free? Is *Our Nig* a freedom narrative or a novel?

Our Nig: Fiction, History, or Both?
by David Fernandez

The answer to this question is not so clear. On the one hand, Alfrado is a free woman; this is based solely on technicality, however. I mean that because her story takes place in the North, it is at the outset more difficult to think of her as enslaved, though we know that slavery had previously existed in the North. When I think of slavery, I think of plantation slavery, of people being routinely marketed and sold. This is not the case with Alfrado. However, aside from the trivial technicality, she is, based on what I have learned about slavery, treated as a slave. This fact makes the phrase "free woman" in the title completely devoid of meaning.

This technicality, though completely unimportant and meaningless to Alfrado and other African Americans in her position, is, however, crucial in terms of the story's purpose, which leads me back to one of the study guide questions that asks us to consider whether this is indeed a freedom narrative or a novel. In this case I would have to assert that this story is a novel. Take, for example, the elaborate title of this novel: *Our Nig; or, Sketches from the Life of a Free Black in a Two Story White House, North.* The title makes it obvious that this story has a purpose and that purpose is to juxtapose the definitions of "free" and "slave." Included in the title page, the author presents yet another extension to the title that reads, "Showing That Slavery's Shadows Fall Even There." In other words, the fact that there is a clear intention placed before the reader on the title page shows that this is more than just a narrative or an autobiographical account. What this intent stands for is, in fact, an attempt at a calculated specific message on the part of the author.

Although there is no clear evidence within the story itself to prove that it is not a freedom narrative, another way to distinguish it as a novel is by closely scrutinizing the voice of the narrator. The typical autobiography, which includes the freedom narrative, would be written in the first person. This story is written primarily in the third person, in which case you would need to ask why anyone would write an autobiographical narrative without shaping it in memoir form unless he or she were trying to convey specific lesson to the reader.

As for the content of the appendix, in conjunction with assertions made earlier, it works much like the back cover of the modern-day novel in that it validates the author's message and lends credibility to the author herself. The only difference between the critical appraisal of a contemporary novel—the short "blurbs" on the back cover—and the "just-plain-okaying" of this one by the letters attached to the novel is that with the contemporary novel, criticism has become a mainstay marketing tool. This, as opposed to the sincere wish to spread a valid message to the masses in support of a directive, meant to mobilize American citizens to a much needed social reformation. The message is obvious and as pertinent today as it was in Wilson's time: The fight against slavery and oppression isn't over, lest we forget that social equality has not yet been reached. While I am convinced that Wilson's novel is somewhat autobiographical, and the attached documents paradoxically serve as authentication for a story represented as fiction, the fact that we are reading the story as part of a course in the Black American Novel suggests strongly that the story is more fiction than fact. Nevertheless, I do believe that Alfrado's position in the Bellmont household is that of a slave and that Wilson means to represent it that way.

Assignment: Write a two-page response paper on the subject of motherhood in Harriet Wilson's *Our Nig*.

Motherhood Equals No Mercy
by Latia King

I have decided on this title because when one thinks of motherhood, one usually thinks of love and compassion. This is not the case with *Our Nig*. We are introduced to Mag Smith right from the start, and we learn that she is lonely and walks with sad eyes and a heavy heart due to her situation. We also learn that her first child, who is a girl, dies after living for only a few weeks. Surprisingly though, this is not the reason for Mag's sadness. She is thankful to God for summoning her daughter at such an early age so that "no one can taunt her with my ruin" (290).

We do not find out that Mag is a white woman until two pages later when Jim is thinking about the contrast between his dark skin and her fair face. Two pages after that comes the information that Jim, "proud of his treasure,—a white wife,—tried hard to fulfill his promises; and furnished her with a more comfortable dwelling, diet, and apparel" (294). Jim and Mag are blessed with two children, one of whom is called Frado. Unexpectedly, Jim dies and Mag marries Seth, who had been Jim's business partner. Mag and Seth try to provide for their family, but, at long last, give up and decide that they can not afford to keep both children. They decide that Frado will stay with the Bellmonts, a fact unaware to the Bellmonts at the time they leave the child at their home. Along with Frado, they realize that Seth and Mag are not coming back for the child. All this happens to Frado at the tender age of six.

Frado is no clueless infant. She knows that she has been abandoned, and hence the title of my paper—"Motherhood Equals No Mercy." I feel that it is possible that Mag cares for her daughter, but that there is no genuine love involved. How can you love your child and still refer to her as a black devil and later abandon her? To make matters worse, Mag leaves her daughter with a woman whom she herself characterized as a she-devil! Obviously, the child's safety is not Mag's top priority. The next time we see merciless mothering is in the interactions between Mrs. Bellmont and Frado. Mrs. Bellmont exhibits a strong dislike for Frado. She makes Frado's life a living hell, if you can even call what Frado is doing living. Frado is to feed the hens, drive the cows to pasture, wash the dishes, get firewood, and eat her food "standing by the kitchen table" and "not be over ten minutes about it" (302). As Frado grows older, more chores are added on.

We have been blessed to only be able to imagine what someone like Frado must have felt under such circumstances. Her biological mother abandons her, and the woman who might fill the role of mother to her turns out to be her abuser—someone who relishes torturing Frado day and night. At the hands of Mrs. Bellmont, Frado suffers cruel beatings, with a piece of wood placed between her teeth, or a cloth shoved in her mouth to stifle her screams. Generally, Frado suffers isolation, pain, tears, hatred, and the feeling of not being loved and valued. Nevertheless, Frado loves and cares for her dog, Fido, and she also provides care for James when he is dying. Frado receives more treatment akin to nurturing from the Bellmont sons, James and Jack, than she does from Mrs. Bellmont. Jane and Aunt Abby also do what they could to look out for Frado, but they lack any real power in the household. Frado suffered all manner of mental and physical torment during the twelve years she serves as the indentured servant for the Bellmonts. Wilson tells us that it is finally faith that keeps Frado going when all else fails, the faith she finds in the Christianity that Abby encourages.

Assignment: Write a two-page response paper that addresses the ambiguous ending of Nella Larsen's *Passing*.

The Passing of Clare Kendry?
By Kaitlin Kelsey

At the end of *Passing*, Clare Kendry falls, jumps, or is pushed to her death. This final scene brings together all the major conflicts that arise within the novel. All the main characters appear in a scene together, filling the atmosphere with tension. The author leaves the matter of responsibility for Clare's death ambiguous in order to allow Irene to remain a sympathetic character and thus compel the reader to view the situation from all sides. If Larsen simply informed the reader that Irene pushed Clare, the information would invoke feelings of rage and resentment toward Irene. One could not but conclude that Irene is a selfish woman ruled by her jealousy. If we do not know exactly how Clare dies, we are able to approach the situation more critically. The reader can understand Irene's jealousy and at the same time express empathy about Clare's unhappy married life. Like the issue of closeted sexual identity in the novel, evidence exists for all three interpretations about how Clare dies.

Despite the fact that she is a black woman passing for white in a marriage to a white bigot, Clare might have panicked when her husband discovers her among the black people whose company she so craves. John Bellew enters the scene as if he were an animal. His voice is described as a "roar," a "snarl," and a "moan," while Clare's response is, in contrast, a "silver chill." John is filled with passion and rage after being faced with the irony of his wife being intimately associated with members of a race that he hates. Clare, on the other hand, is perfectly composed. She is seemingly unaware of her situation. Clare has married John in order to make the final transition into the white world, abandoning her African American background. This transition is a matter of money and pleasure, not one based in love. John's real feelings about his wife never become completely clear; his character serves as a device for emphasizing the story's irony. Clare seems ruled by her own desires and impulses and ignorant of the feelings of others. She uses her charm and beauty to obtain whatever she desires from those around her. It seems plausible that Clare commits suicide when she is confronted with all of the actions that have led her to her present life filled with lies.

Although it seems that Irene has a role in Clare's death, we can never be completely sure. When Clare is reintroduced into Irene's life, everything changes and Irene is forced to reexamine herself. She feels a passionate connection to Clare, which may be sexual but also resembles a sisterhood, or family bond. Irene is unable to say "no" to Clare. She is entranced by Clare's elegance and charisma. Unlike Irene, Clare is free to act however she pleases. She has relinquished responsibility for her daughter, her husband, and her race. Clare acts with careless neglect for her own safety and well-being, or that of those she loves. Although Irene understands that Clare is often immoral and cruel, she also envies the notion of freedom that Clare represents. By the end of the story, Irene expresses frustration at the havoc Clare has caused in her life. Clare has replaced Irene's domestic security (all she truly has) with worry and paranoia.

By leaving room for interpretation about the cause of Clare's death, Larsen allows us to identify with both Clare and Irene, rather than hate or pity either one. Clare is beautiful, captivating, and spontaneous, while Irene is moral and thoughtful, all worthy qualities. The reader is able to admire these traits and put themselves in the place of the characters. Larsen does not provide the reader with a villain or a scapegoat, but instead emphasizes the importance of Clare's or Irene's struggles.

All this falls apart, however, if we consider our discussions about the unreliable narrator, for though the story seems to be told by a semi-omniscient narrator, everything we learn about anything and anyone is filtered through Irene Redfield's conniving, somewhat paranoid consciousness. Even more than that, however, one wonders how much Nella Larsen has been manipulating her readers. Does Clare's presence unsettle Irene because Irene finds her sexually attractive, because she believes her husband finds her sexually attractive, or because Irene finds Clare's boldness in passing attractive? Ultimately, the novel leaves us with a lot more unanswered questions than whether Clare jumped, was pushed, or fell to her death.

GLOSSARY

Abolitionist – in the United States, a member of the movement calling for the abolishment of slavery during the decades leading up to the the Civil War.

Amanuensis – in African American autobiography, a person who captures and represents in print the oral recitation of another person's life story.

Antebellum – pertaining to the historical period immediately preceding the United States Civil War.

Antislavery movement – in the United States, a movement whose proponents opposed the enslavement of human beings, especially from the time of the Declaration of Independence (1776) to the Emancipation Proclamation (1863).

Archetype – a literary term that refers primarily to characters, but which may also refer to images, themes, or plots, that recur throughout literary history. Some archetypes include the "villain" and the "abandoned child."

Authenticating documents – in African American autobiographical narratives, particularly antebellum slave narratives, the documents attached to the narrative that attest to the narrator's authenticity and/or veracity. Such documents may include letters, prefaces, appendixes, and so forth.

Autobiography – generally speaking, the story of a person's life as written by herself or himself. In African American literature, the first-person freedom narratives that describe the horrors of slavery and the accompanying quest for freedom form a major part of the foundation for African American literature, particularly the autobiographical tradition.

Biomythography – a term coined by Audre Lorde to define the narrative of her life in *Zami: A New Spelling of My Name* (1982) as a way of acknowledging the reality that in the process of crafting a narrative out of biographical facts, one also engages in mythmaking.

Blues/Blues aesthetic – The blues is a folk-derived art form expressed through music. In relationship to African American literature, to enact a blues aesthetic means to invoke the blues mood or ethos that captures at once the suffering and (usually) the will to endure that derives from the African American experience of slavery and racial discrimination. The blues aesthetic is also enacted via the use of certain formal features of the typical blues stanza.

Double-consciousness – refers to the tensions inherent in the African American's quest to assert an identity vis-à-vis a society dominated by European Americans. See W. E. B. Du Bois's "Of Our Spiritual Strivings" in the classic, *The Souls of Black Folk* (1903).

Freedom narratives – in African American literature, refers to real life stories of the experience of slavery and the quest for freedom.

Fugitive slave law – a law set in place to assist in the recapture of persons who had escaped from slavery. The United States enacted several such laws between 1793 and 1850.

Identity – the way one sees and expresses herself or himself, the "I," vis-à-vis social interactions and contexts. See, **double-consciousness.**

Jim Crow – generally refers to the system of legal segregation (or apartheid) that functioned in the southern United States from around the turn of the twentieth century through the mid-twentieth century Civil Rights Movement. The term derives from a white blackface performer, Thomas D. Rice, who copied the dance routine of an enslaved man owned by a Mr. Crow, and recast it as "jumping Jim Crow." The term was later applied to segregated public facilities and subsequently (after the landmark Supreme Court decision in *Plessy v. Ferguson* of 1896) came to describe the aforementioned system of segregation.

Manhood – in African American literature, refers to the recurring quest among African American male characters (or African Americans as a nation) to recover the sense of self-determination, power, and autonomy lost in the African subject's New World experience, particularly the experience of slavery and racial discrimination.

Maroons – a term used to describe groups of formerly enslaved persons (officially fugitives) in Caribbean colonies. Having taken their freedom, such groups developed their own communities and often staged raids on nearby plantations, further disrupting the operations of slavery. In the United States, such persons were referred to as *outlyers*.

Masking – the term refers to a survival strategy employed by African Americans in the presence of whites, or generally speaking, in a racist society. It consists of covering up one's true identity or intentions for the sake of survival and/or for the sake of making progress amid unfavorable odds.

Melodrama – a literary convention popular in the nineteenth century featuring the overdramatized scenario often accompanied by the heavy-handed use of coincidence.

Middle Passage – refers to the approximately two-month period during which Africans were taken across the Atlantic Ocean to become slaves in the New World, and during which they either died en route or withstood the horrors of the journey in the ship's hold to become African Americans.

Nadir – refers, generally, to the lowest point on a continuum. Historian Rayford Logan used the term in *The Betrayal of the Negro* (1967) to characterize the social situation of African Americans during the roughly twenty-five-year period between 1890 and 1915.

Neofreedom narrative (also neoslave narrative) – refers to fictional narratives that articulate a quest for freedom and are either set during slavery or deal with the effects of slavery. Examples include Toni Morrison's *Beloved* (1987) and Charles Johnson's *Middle Passage* (1990).

Neohoodooism – refers to a process or aesthetic for producing and analyzing African American literature that is grounded in African and African-derived religious and spiritual traditions. See specifically the works of black male writers such as Ishmael Reed and Arthur Flowers.

Neoslave narrative (see neofreedom narrative)

Oration – refers generally to oral recitation, in contemporary parlance—the spoken word. In African American literature, this takes on added significance because of the combined effect of cutting Africans off from their African languages and forbidding them to attain literacy in American English during slavery. With voice so important to asserting identity, African American authors place great emphasis on the speaking subject.

Parody – refers to a work that invokes a previous work in order to point to its inadequacies. Alice Randall's *The Wind Done Gone* (2001) enjoys a parodic relationship to Margaret Mitchell's *Gone with the Wind* (1936) by pointing to, for example, the previous novel's problematic representations of African American characters.

Plantation tradition – refers overwhelmingly to the romanticized visions of plantation life that white southerners created after the Civil War. The fiction featured an idealized setting in which the genteel and chivalrous white plantation master ruled magnanimously over white southern belles and the totally dependent, childlike black people who served them both.

Pseudonymous narrator – in African American literature, the first-person narrator of an autobiographical narrative, such as Linda Brent in Harriet Jacobs's *Incidents in the Life of a Slave Girl* (1861), whose story is also that of the author.

Reconstruction – refers to the period between the end of the United States Civil War and 1877 whose name represents a primary aim of rebuilding the devastated American South. The Reconstruction Act of 1867 also articulated a goal of helping newly freed African Americans make the transition to freedom.

School of slavery – refers to the idea advanced in some freedom narratives written after the Civil War that slavery was a school that prepared formerly enslaved persons to deal with the realities of life in America.

Sharecropping – a practice by which poor families traded their labor for a share of the profits from the year's agricultural production. The downside of the arrangement was that families often ended up in a deficit situation at the end of the year.

Slave narrative – a written, often autobiographical, account of the experience of slavery and the quest for freedom.

Subjectivity – the quality associated with asserting the "I," claiming the status of subject, and asserting self-identity.

Talented Tenth – a term used in the late nineteenth and early twentieth centuries to refer to the 10 percent of African Americans purportedly best suited to lead the race toward progress in American life. Though the term is often attributed to W. E. B. Du Bois, Frances Ellen Watkins Harper used it earlier.

Transcendentalism – a consciousness-raising project that gained force as a movement in New England (specifically the Boston area) in the 1830s, and spread to other centers such as Cincinnati, Ohio, Providence, Rhode Island, New York City, and St. Louis, Missouri. Transcendentalists (including Ralph Waldo Emerson and Henry David Thoreau) valued spiritual experience over religion's institutionalized structures. Many transcendentalists were also abolitionists.

Trickster – in African American literature, a figure signifying cultural survival. A crafty figure, who is also adept at disguise, the trickster is known for its ability to transgress boundaries, which makes it an excellent vehicle for depicting resistance to all manner of oppression. Popular tricksters in African American literature include John of "John and the Old Master" tales, Brer Rabbit, and the signifying monkey.

True womanhood – refers to a prevailing nineteenth-century ideology under which "true women" relegated their activities to the domestic sphere and were submissive, chaste, and pious.